Daytrips QUÉBEC

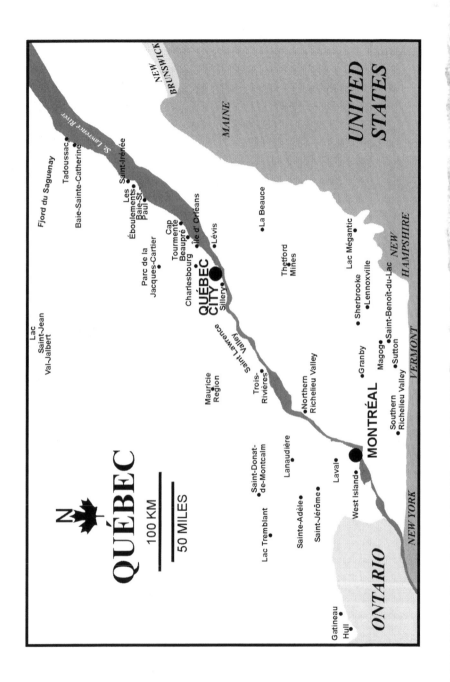

Daytrips
QUÉBEC

48 *one day adventures in and around Québec City, Montréal and throughout the province*

KAREN DESROSIERS

HASTINGS HOUSE/DAYTRIPS
Publishers
Winter Park, Florida

Dedication:

For my son Devlin — the best travel companion I could have wished for.

Acknowledgements:

There are many people that I would like to thank who made it possible for me to complete this book and who kept me going when exhaustion threatened to stop me.

Devlin, my boy, for being such a good sport, eating five-course meals of gourmet French cuisine, spending almost every weekend on the road, and keeping silent while we passed through the border time-and-again.

Sharon and Issac Valdez and Amber Fogg for helping me to take care of Devlin and caring for him when I just couldn't haul him off to Canada yet again or desperately needed quiet time to write.

Laurel Earnshaw, Deborah Regan, Sue Wereska, Charlene Pollano, Barbara Benham, and Martha Walsh — the amazing women of the Southern New Hampshire Women's Writing Group — without whom I would never have come this far. I am a writer because of you all!

Richard and Donna Desrosiers, my beloved parents, for giving me unending support (even when you were afraid I was being crazy) and for passing on the travel bug.

And Susan Lager, for helping me to believe and sharing so completely in my excitement.

ISBN: 0-8038-2054-2
or 978-0-8038-2054-8
Printed in the United States of America, Canada, Panama, United Kingdom, Netherlands, Spain, Poland, or Australia by Booksurge Global, using on-demand technology.

All photos by the author.
Peter Leers, Publisher.

Contents

Introduction

Canada is a travel destination that many people tend to overlook. It is, after all, in North America, so how much different can it be from the United States? A world of difference! Despite proximity to its southern neighbor, and intertwining histories, Québec Province is much more like Europe — without the seven-hour plane trip.

Québec Province has had a tumultuous history, with many nations fighting for rights to the rich land. The region was originally inhabited by Amerindian nations, known as the First Nations. Among them were the Huron, Iroquois, Abenaki, and Inuit tribes. The culture, traditions, and influences of these nations can still be found throughout the province.

French explorer Jacques Cartier sailed to the New World in the 15th century, in search of gold and a route to India. Samuel de Champlain followed him in 1608, establishing a colony, founding Québec City, and signaling the birth of New France. An active fur trade was quickly established and settlers and Jesuits soon followed. By 1663 there were nearly 3,000 inhabitants, and King Louis XIV proclaimed New France a royal colony.

During the 18th century, the British and French fought for control of the region in a number of bloody battles that ended with the British Conquest. During this time, some of the French influence and contribution to the development of Québec was lost. With the influx of anglophone immigrants, the British, Irish, and Scottish all left their mark.

Today, Québec Province maintains a predominately French atmosphere, with the language, cuisine, and many architectural elements reflecting the region's beginnings. However, the influences of the other nations and cultures can also be found.

Around its industrial strongholds and developed cities Québec has preserved vast natural resources and wild landscapes. Enormous parks are found throughout, providing home to abundant wildlife as well as recreational facilities for visitors and residents. The people of Québec are quite proud of their land, as is evident in the sheer size and beauty of the undeveloped portions.

The people of Québec are also fiercely proud of their heritage and culture. Many towns and villages have been preserved, almost as they were hundreds of years earlier when the first settlers arrived.

Québec Province is divided into a number of tourist regions, most of which extend around the cities of Montréal and Québec, and are quite manageable as daytrips. The excursions in this book are organized first around Québec City as a home base, and then around Montréal.

The city of Québec and its surroundings are fascinating for their historical importance and Old World charm. Not far from the city, to the north and northeast, a bounty of natural treasures awaits in the Jacques Cartier Park, Saguenay Fjord, Saint Lawrence River, and rugged Charlevoix Coast.

Montréal is the cosmopolitan heart of modern-day Québec. Still steeped in history, the city and its surroundings offer a fascinating mix of heritage and contemporary culture. More natural wonders await near Montréal, along with picturesque villages and outdoor activities in the Eastern Townships, Laurentians, Appalachians, and Hull.

Wherever you choose to visit throughout the province you will find warm welcoming people, excellent food, and European culture.

Weather is an important consideration when traveling to Québec. The winter months can be harsh and long, with a tremendous amount of snowfall. The people of Québec take full advantage of the winter and celebrate it with numerous festivals. The Winter Carnival in Québec City is world-renowned and not to be missed. Winter sports, such as downhill and cross-country skiing, snowshoeing, and snowmobiling are popular throughout the province. However, many of the tourist attractions may be closed or have shorter hours during the winter. Some roads, particularly those leading to the northern regions of the province, may be closed during bad weather.

Spring and early summer are good times to visit, particularly if you are interested in any of the numerous waterfalls highlighted in this guide, which are especially spectacular during the spring thaw.

The more you visit the lively cities, quaint villages, and rugged natural landscapes of Québec, the more it will call you back. Nations fought for this rich and diverse land for hundreds of years — it is easy to understand why.

Please remember that places have a way of changing without warning and that sometimes errors happen. We would like all of the information presented to be 100% accurate, but things change. If you are interested in a particular site, you should really call ahead to confirm their hours and admission fees.

Happy Daytripping !

Section I

DAYTRIP STRATEGIES

The word "Daytrip" may not have made it into dictionaries yet, but for experienced independent travelers it represents the easiest, most natural, and often the least expensive approach to exploring many of the world's most interesting areas. This strategy, in which you base yourself in a city and probe the surrounding region on a series of one-day excursions, is effective in Québec, where the tourist regions radiate around the central cities.

ADVANTAGES:

1. Freedom from a fixed itinerary. You can go wherever you feel like going whenever the mood strikes you.

2. Freedom from the burden of luggage. Your bags remain in your hotel while you run around with only a guidebook and a camera.

3. Freedom from the worry of reservation foul-ups. You don't have the anxiety each day about whether that night's lodging is okay.

4. The flexibility of making last-minute changes to allow for unexpected weather, serendipitous discoveries, changing interests, new-found passions, and so on.

5. The flexibility to take breaks from sightseeing whenever you feel tired or bored, without upsetting a planned itinerary. Why not sleep late in your base city for a change?

6. The opportunity to sample different travel experiences without committing more than a day to them.

7. The opportunity to become a "temporary resident" of your base city. By staying there for a while you can get to know it in depth, becoming familiar with the local restaurants, shops, theaters, night life, and other attractions - enjoying them as a native would.

8. The convenience of not having to pack and unpack your bags each day. Your clothes can hang in a closet where they belong, or even be sent out for cleaning.

9. The convenience (and security) of having a fixed address in your base city, where friends, relatives, and business associates can reach you in an emergency.

10. The economy of staying at one hotel on a discounted longer-term basis, especially in conjunction with package plans. You can make advance reservations for your base city without sacrificing any flexibility at all.

And, of course, for those who actually live in Québec Province, or near the borders, daytrips are the key to discovering one of Canada's oldest and most diverse regions — one day at a time.

CHOOSING A BASE CITY

QUÉBEC CITY:

The capital of the province and the only walled city in North America, Québec City is full of European culture and charm. The city is perched high atop rugged Cap Diamant, overlooking the Saint Lawrence River. With narrow cobblestone streets, historic stone buildings, and impressive fortification walls the city is an inviting and mysterious place. Friendly people, incredible food, and a wealth of tradition welcome visitors who will fall instantly in love with it.

GETTING TO QUÉBEC CITY:

By Air: Though small, the **Jean-Lesage Airport** is able to accommodate international flights. It is located about 16 km (10 miles) from the city on Rue Principale, Sainte-Foy, and is easily reached by taxi or airport shuttle. **T**: (418) 640-2700 for airport information. The **airport shuttle** runs between the airport and several city hotels for $9 one-way. **T**: (418) 872-5525 for schedule and information.

By Rail: VIA Rail Canada connects cities across Canada. **Amtrak** has a number of rail services from U.S. cities to Canada. **T**: 1-800-561-3949 for information, schedules, and prices.

By Car: Québec City is easily accessible by road from across the province, other parts of Canada, and the northeast United States. **Routes 73**, **20**, and **40** all lead to the city. Commuter traffic can get heavy on weekdays 7–9 and 4–6.

Driving distances to Québec City are: from Boston, 653 km (408 miles); from New York, 904 km (565 miles); Philadelphia, 1,011 km (632 miles); Montréal, 251 km (157 miles).

ACCOMMODATIONS IN AND AROUND QUÉBEC CITY:

There is a wide range of accommodations available in and around Québec City but they can fill up, particularly during the summer months and winter carnival. Advance reservations are recommended.

Within the walled city, the **Fairmont Château Frontenac** is perhaps the most spectacular place to stay. The imposing castle-like hotel is rich in Old-World charm and classic elegance.

Other hotels lie just outside the walled city, affording easy access to Old Québec, with parking and better room availability. The **Radisson Gouverneurs Québec**, **Château Laurier**, and **Hilton Québec** are all excellent choices.

Going a little farther from the city center is usually a bit cheaper. There are a number of choices available in Sainte-Foy and the outskirts of Québec City.

MONTRÉAL:

The largest city in Québec is also the most cosmopolitan. Modern skyscrapers sit side-by-side with centuries-old landmarks. World-class art museums, archaeological treasures, vast parks, and historical sites offer a feast of activities for everyone. The city is beautiful, with character, history, and personality at every turn.

GETTING TO MONTRÉAL:

By Air: There are two international airports within easy access to Montréal. **Pierre Elliott Trudeau (Dorval) International Airport** is located on the West Island, about 20 km (12.5 miles) from the city. **T**: (514) 394-7377 for schedule and information. **Mirabel Airport** is 50 minutes north of Montréal in Mirabel. **T**: (514) 394-7377 for airport information. **Buses** run between the airports and the city. **T**: (514) 931-9002 for schedule, cost, and information.

By Rail: VIA Rail Canada connects cities across Canada. **Amtrak** has a number of rail services from U.S. cities to Canada. **T**: 1-800-561-3949 for information, schedules, and prices.

By Car: Montréal is easily accessible by road from across the province, other parts of Canada, and the northeast United States. **Routes 10, 20, 15,** and **40** all lead to the city. Traffic around the city is often heavy at any time of day — plan on extra time if you are on a schedule.

Driving distances to Montréal are: from Boston, 496 km (310 miles); from New York, 611 km (382 miles); Philadelphia, 750 km (469 miles); Québec City, 251 km (157 miles).

ACCOMMODATIONS IN AND AROUND MONTRÉAL:

Each neighborhood has its own personality — and there are many neighborhoods to choose from. While there are numerous choices of accommodations throughout the city, some will fill quickly in the summer. Advanced reservations are recommended.

The Latin Quarter is a fun place to stay, with a busy nightlife, a number of festivals, and plenty of restaurants. **Hôtel de Paris** and **Hôtel des Gouverneurs Place Dupuis** are both fine choices.

Old Montréal is one of the busiest, and most interesting, parts of the city, filled with history and culture. The downtown area has a good selection of hotels, including a Marriott, Fairmont, and Holiday Inn. The **Ritz-Carlton** is spectacular.

OTHER BASES:

There are clusters of daytrip destinations around Montréal and Québec City that explore some of the most beautiful and diverse regions of the country. Overnighting in other cities or towns provides the opportunity to explore the countryside in depth and enjoy a quiet stay away from the bustle of the city. Overnight trips also allow you to combine multiple trips to better experience the region.

CHOOSING DESTINATIONS

With 48 trips to choose from, and several attractions for each trip, deciding which are the most enjoyable for you and yours might be challenging. You could, of course, read through the whole book and mark the most appealing spots, but there's an easier way to at least start. Just turn to the index and scan it, looking out for the special-interest categories set in **BOLD FACE** type. These will immediately lead you to choices under such headings as Museums, Historic Sites, Outdoor Activities, and the like.

The elements of one trip can often be combined with another to create a custom itinerary, using the book maps as a rough guide and a good road map for the final routing.

Some of the trips, listed in the index as **SCENIC DRIVES** are just that. They are primarily designed for the pure pleasure of driving, with just enough attractions along the way to keep things lively. These are especially enjoyable if you're blessed with a car that's fun to drive.

GETTING AROUND

The driving directions for each trip assume you are leaving from either Québec City or Montréal. If you are doing an overnight or staying (or live) elsewhere in the province you will have to modify the routes a little.

The route **maps** scattered throughout the book show you approximately where the sites are and which main roads lead to them. In many cases though, you'll still need a suitable, up-to-date roadmap. The free maps distributed by the tourist information offices are often quite good, and they also usually have road maps for sale.

The majority of the daytrips in this book are designed to be done by **car**, affording the greatest freedom. Public transportation throughout the province does not provide adequate flexibility for exploring the nooks-and-crannies. If you arrived by plane or train, you will need to rent a car. Other alternatives have been suggested throughout the book, where available, such as riverboats and ferries.

Within the cities, most tours are designed for walking. Public transportation has been listed as an alternative, or in case of bad weather.

RULES OF THE ROAD:

Québec Province uses the metric system, so all of the signs posting mileage and speed are in kilometers (km) — not miles. The speed limit on the highways is a maximum of 100 kph (60 minimum). Before you get carried away, remember that it's 100 kilometers per hour, which is only a little over 60 mph.

The possession of a radar detector, connected or not, is illegal. If you are caught with one, police officers may confiscate it and fine you up to $1,000.

Turning right on red is strictly prohibited in most parts of the province, unless otherwise marked by a green arrow.

Seatbelts are required for the driver and all passengers in the car.

Québec has an agreement of reciprocity with the states of New York and Maine. Residents of these jurisdictions found guilty of a motor vehicle offense in Québec will have it entered into their record, just as if the offense had been committed in their home state.

FOOD AND DRINK

Several choice restaurants that make sense for daytrippers are listed for each destination in this book. Most of these are open for lunch, are on or near the suggested tour route, and provide some atmosphere. Many feature French cuisine, as well as Quebecois and Canadian specialties not generally found elsewhere. Their approximate price range is shown as:

$	Inexpensive
$$	Reasonable
$$$	Luxurious and expensive
X:	Days closed

Prices listed in the text are in Canadian dollars (CDN).

Many of the excursions lend themselves very nicely to picnicking. What would be more perfect than stopping at one of the many French delis and packing a gourmet picnic? Or try the grocery stores, which have excellent selections of prepared, gourmet, and French foods.

Canadians love children, so family dining is very common. Even some of the most elegant, gourmet restaurants offer a children's menu, although it may just be a smaller version of the adult menu.

PRACTICALITIES

WEATHER:

Québec Province is unique for its seasonal extremes in climate. Temperatures can range from -25°C (-13°F) in the winter to 30°C (86°F) in the summer. The region seems to change significantly from summer to winter, not only in appearance, but also in the activities and attitude.

Summer in Québec can be extremely hot — perfect for taking advantage of the countless rivers and lakes in the province. Flowers are in bloom and many restaurants open their outdoor terraces. The province comes alive with festivals and concerts.

Québec is perhaps more commonly known for its winters, which can be quite harsh and snow-filled. Winter starts early, especially in the regions north of Québec City, and runs late. Snow is common from mid-November through March. It's no wonder the province has an abundance of winter sports activities available from downhill and cross-country skiing to snowmobiling and dogsledding.

Spring and autumn are generally short, each lasting up to two months (April to May and September to October). Spring arrives with mud and slush, but awakens quickly to the blossoming flowers and fresh leaves. Fall erupts rapidly into a feast of color, from bright red to golden yellow. Temperatures drop quickly, especially at night, bringing crispness to the air.

OPENING TIMES, FEES, AND FACILITIES:

When planning a daytrip, be sure to note carefully the **opening times** of the various sites — these can sometimes be rather quirky. Anything unusual that you should know before starting, such as "don't make this trip on a Monday," is summarized in the "Practicalities" section of each trip.

Admission fees listed in the text are, naturally, subject to change — and they rarely go down. Prices listed in the text are in Canadian dollars (CDN). For the most part, admissions are quite reasonable considering the cost of maintaining the sites. Places with free entry, especially those not operated by governments, are usually staffed with unpaid volunteers and may have a donation box to help keep the wolves from the door. Please put something in it.

Any special **facilities** that a site may offer are listed in the *italicized* information for that site, along with the address and phone number. **Telephone numbers** are indicated with a **T:**, and Internet addresses by a **W:**.

HOLIDAYS:

The following is a list of public holidays in Québec, when most post offices, banks, and government offices are closed.

January 1st and 2nd	New Year's Day

Easter Monday	
3rd Monday in May	Fête de Dollard and Victoria Day
June 24th	Saint-Jean-Baptiste Day, Québec's national holiday
July 1st	Canada Day
1st Monday in September	Labor Day
2nd Monday in October	Thanksgiving
November 11th	Remembrance Day (only banks and federal offices are closed)
December 25th and 26th	Christmas

SAFETY:

Québec Province has far less violence than the United States, so the cities of Montréal and Québec are quite safe. In fact the people of Québec boast an extreme "no violence" philosophy. Visitors who use the same commonsense approaches to safety that they use at home will feel more than secure in Québec.

Should there be any emergency, **911** has been instituted throughout the province.

HANDICAPPED TRAVELERS:

Accessibility varies throughout the province; however, most public buildings, hotels, restaurants, churches, and museums are handicapped accessible.

A guide called ***Accessible Québec*** is available through Keroul, an organization that provides information for disabled visitors. The guide lists hotels, restaurants, and attractions, organized by tourist region, that are accessible for disabled travelers. **T**: (514) 252-3104 or **W**: keroul.qc.ca

GROUP TRAVELERS:

If you are planning a group outing, always call ahead. Most sites require advanced reservations and offer special discounts for groups, often at a substantial saving over the regular admission fee. Some sites have specific hours set aside or will open specially to accommodate groups; some have tours, demonstrations, lectures, and so on available only to groups; and some have facilities for rental to groups.

LANGUAGE:

The official language of Québec Province is **French**. There are also some idiosyncrasies in Canadian French that are not found in classic French. The farther north you venture into the region, the more predominate the French language will be. Although you may occasionally encounter people, signs, or menus that do not speak any English, it is generally very easy to get by without any French.

English is the second language of the province and is spoken quite fluently, commonly, and willingly. Unlike the experience many tourists have in France, the people of Québec are quite pleased to communicate in either French or English.

A **glossary** of common menu items, phrases, and terms can be found in the appendix.

MONEY:

The monetary unit in Québec is the Canadian dollar. Coins are issued in 1, 5, 10, and 25 cent, and 1 and 2 dollar coins. Bills are issued in 5, 10, 20, 50, 100, 500, and 1,000 dollar denominations. The 1-dollar coin is lovingly referred to as a "loonie" in honor of the loon bird portrayed on it.

ATM machines are widely available throughout the province and make access to funds easy and reliable.

At the time of printing, the following exchange rate was in effect:

$1 US = 1.25$ CDN

1$ CDN = $0.80 US

Note that exchange rates tend to fluctuate frequently.

TIPPING:

It is a common misconception that people do not tip in Canada. In Québec it is practice to tip in restaurants (for table service), bars, and nightclubs 10–15% of the before-tax bill. Hotel porters should be tipped $1 per bag. Taxi drivers and hairdressers are tipped at the customer's discretion, usually about 10%.

TAXES:

Prices quoted within the text do not include any tax. In general, prices listed on menus, items, and bills do not include any tax. The tax is added at the time of sale. The Federal Goods and Services Tax (TPS) is 7% and the Provincial Sales Tax (TVQ) is 7.5%. The cumulative tax (14.5%) must be paid on most items, as well as hotel and restaurant bills. Food, except for ready-made meals, is not taxed.

A **refund** of the Federal Goods and Services Tax is available for all non-residents, on most goods and accommodations. Be sure to keep your receipts — original receipts are required for refunds. Items purchased for use outside of Canada for $50 or more, and accommodations, are eligible. Restaurant receipts are not. You must have a total amount of $200 or more before taxes. Receipts for goods must be authorized at the customs agent prior to leaving the country. Forms can be found in most hotels and at Tourist Information Offices. Return the form and original receipts from outside Canada.

SUGGESTED TOURS

Two different methods of organizing daytrips are used in this book, depending on local circumstances. Some are based on **structured itineraries** such as

European flare and American history — visitors fall instantly in love with this world-class city. Ancient buildings and narrow cobbled streets, protected by high fortification walls, make Québec a unique destination. The city itself has been ranked an UNESCO World Heritage Site.

Québec City is famous for its Winter Carnival, with its mascot red-capped snowman — nicknamed Bonhomme Carnival. For ten days each February, the streets of Québec become a winter wonderland celebration. Festivities include an impressive parade, ice sculptures, an ice palace, and canoe races on the Saint Lawrence River.

Québec City's Château Frontenac

QUÉBEC CITY   19

Trip 1
Québec City

Old Québec

The heart of the city of Québec, and its administrative center, is known as Old Québec. Completely enclosed in fortification walls, the narrow streets and ancient buildings are alive with history and culture. Perched high on the hill of Cap Diamant (Cape Diamond), overlooking the Saint Lawrence River, Old Québec is also referred to as the Upper City.

After the initial settling of the city by Samuel de Champlain in 1620, with the construction of Fort Saint-Louis, the imposing rock of the cape was proclaimed inhospitable. It wasn't until a group of wealthy merchants began looking to expand the colony that the upper town started to develop. Then Governor Montmagny devised a plan to build a large fortified city atop the cape. Houses appeared near the end of the 17th century in the area of Place d'Armes and along Rue Saint-Louis.

Much of the land on the cape belonged to the Ursuline, Augustine, and Jesuit religious orders, all of whom refused to divide up their land, thus slowing the city's growth. At the end of the 18th century the buildings and city still reflected the heavy religious presence. However, during the 19th century elegant new residential neighborhoods grew, culminating with the development of the Grande Allée in 1880.

Today, Old Québec still retains all of its culture, charm, history, and flavor. Visitors will be struck by the European feel of this original North American city.

GETTING THERE:

Start the tour at **Place d'Armes**.

By Car, consider parking in the Old Port, off Boulevard Champlain or Rue Dalhousie and take the **funiculaire** from Petit Champlain up to Place d'Armes. Or, park by Battlefields Park, off Avenue Wilfrid-Laurier, and walk up Grande Allée, through the Saint Louis Gate, and up Rue Saint-Louis to Place d'Armes.

By Bus, take Bus number **3** or **11** to reach the Place d'Armes. The fare is $1.75 for tickets purchased at a tobacco stand, or $2.25 (exact change only) on the bus. A daily pass is $5.10.

PRACTICALITIES:

There is a lot to do in Old Québec, including just strolling leisurely and drinking in the atmosphere. You may want to consider allotting two days to fully explore and appreciate the city.

The **Québec Tourist Office**, 12 Rue Sainte-Anne, is open late June to Labor Day daily 8:30–7:30; Labor Day to late June daily 9–5. **Audio-guided walking tours** are available there for Old Québec, as well as other areas of the city. **T**:(418) 990-8687. Cost is $10 per person, $15 for two.

Parking is somewhat of a problem inside the walls of Old Québec.

Québec is world renowned for its **Winter Carnival**, which takes place for ten days every February. The streets are filled with activities, parades, ice sculptures, and contests.

FOOD AND DRINK:

La Maison Serge Bruyère (1200 Rue Saint-Jean) Three inviting restaurants in one location, to meet all tastes: Livernois is a comfortable bistro featuring steak; Saint-Patrick Irish Pub is a friendly pub with live music, great beer, and hearty food; La Grande Table boasts excellent French food in a sophisticated atmosphere. **T**:(418) 694-0618. $$ through $$$+

Aux Anciens Canadiens (34 Rue Saint-Louis) Located in Québec's oldest house, with antique furnishings, and featuring traditional Québec cuisine. **T**: (418) 692-1627. $$$+

Saint Alexandre Pub (1087 Rue Saint-Jean) Authentic British pub with more than 200 types of beer from around the world, and hearty pub food. **T**: (418) 694-0015. $$

SUGGESTED TOUR:

Circled numbers correspond to numbers on the map.

Place d'Armes ①, at the intersections of Rue du Fort with Rue Saint-Louis and Rue Sainte-Anne, was originally used by the military for drill exercises in 1620. When the citadel was built in the early 20th century, the square was no longer needed by the military and it became a park. The Gothic sculpture and fountain in the center of the park, **Monument de la Foi**, was built in 1916 to commemorate the third centennial of the arrival of the Récollet Missionaries.

Château Frontenac ② is by far Québec's most prominent and recognizable landmark. The hotel is named after Louis de Baude, Count de Frontenac, who was governor of New France for nineteen non-consecutive years.

American architect Bruce Price designed the massive horseshoe-shaped building in the château style, inspired by Scottish manors and Loire Valley castles, and popular in the city at that time. He topped the brick walls, adorned with cut stone, with steeply sloping copper roofs. The hotel was an instant success when it opened in 1893, with the completion of the Riverview Wing. Other wings were added later. From 1930–34 the massive tower was added, making the hotel the imposing structure that it is today.

Two historic conferences were held at the château in 1943 and 1944, attended by Franklin Roosevelt and Winston Churchill.

The Count du Frontenac's coat-of-arms can be seen at the entrance for Rue Saint-Louis. Above the arch that overlooks the courtyard is a stone engraved with the Maltese Cross, dated 1647, which originally adorned Governor Montmagny's Château Saint-Louis.

The ground floor of the hotel boasts many beautiful boutiques and galleries, as well as several restaurants and cafés.

Guided tours of the château are available, departing every hour, May to mid-Oct. daily 10–6; mid-Oct. to Apr. Sat.–Sun. 1-5. **T**: *(418) 691-2166. Tours $7 for adults, $3.75 for children 6-16.*

In front of the Château, admire views of the Saint Lawrence River and the Château Frontenac from the **Dufferin Terrace**. On the opposite shores of the Saint Lawrence, Lévis is sprawled across the steep slope rising up from the river.

Walk up Rue Saint-Louis, past Château Frontenac. The Old Courthouse, **Ancien Palais de Justice** ③, 12 Rue Saint-Louis, is now home to the Ministry of Finance. The building, erected in 1887, was designed in the style of a 16th-century Loire Valley château. Decorated with fleurs-de-lis and the coats-of-arms of Jacques Cartier and Samuel de Champlain, the building has a very formal and French appearance.

Continue walking up **Rue Saint-Louis** ④. Note the large stone **Maison Maillou**, 17 Rue Saint Louis, with turquoise trim. Built in 1736 as a single-story residence, the building was enlarged several times. In the 19th century the house was used by the British army.

Next door is the notable **Maison Kent**, 25 Rue Saint-Louis, dating from the 18th century. It is said that the Duke of Kent, Queen Victoria's father, lived here between 1792 and 1794. The large white house, with bright blue trim, is now the office of the Consulate General of France.

The **Maison Jacquet**, 34 Rue Saint-Louis, is the oldest preserved house in Québec. Built in 1674, the single story house with bright white walls and a steep red roof has been expanded several times to the side and rear. The author Philippe Aubert de Gaspé lived here from 1815 to 1824.

Turn right on **Rue de Jardins**, beside Maison Jacquet. Note the sculpture at the intersection of Rue de Jardins and Rue Donnacona. "Monument des Femmes" is a memorial to nuns who dedicated their lives to education. Turn left onto **Rue Donnacona**.

MUSÉE des URSULINES ⑤, 12 Rue Donnacona, **T**: (418) 694-0694. *Open May–Sept. Tues.–Sat. 10–noon and 1–5, Sun. 1–5; Oct.–Apr. Tues.–Sun. 1–4:30. Admission $4 for adults, $2.50 for children 12–16, children under 12 are free.*

This museum exhibits the occupations and talents of the Ursuline Nuns. Documents, works of art, and other items trace the history of this community from the Ursulines' arrival in Québec in 1639 to the British Conquest in 1759.

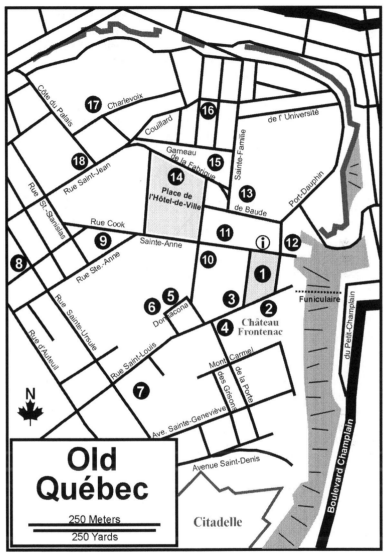

Old
Québec

250 Meters

250 Yards

Exhibitions introduce visitors to the culture and climate of the period, re-create the living quarters of the order's founder Madame de la Peltrie, and display handicrafts. A display of beautiful gilding and embroideries illustrate why the nuns had become well known for these talents.

Across from the museum, take a look at the **Chapelle des Ursulines**. The chapel, dating back to 1902, features a primitive interior preserved from a chapel dating back to 1723. The beloved founder, Marie de l'Incarnation and General

Montcalm are entombed in the chapel. T:*(418) 694-0413. Open May–Oct. Tues.–Sat. 10–11:30 and 1:30–4:30, Sun. 1:30–4:30. Admission is free.*

Nearby is the **Monastère des Ursulines** ⑥. The Ursuline Sisters community was founded in 1535 by Sainte-Angèle Merici, in Brescia, Italy. After becoming established in France, the order dedicated itself to teaching.

Founded by Marie de l'Incarnation and Madame de la Peltrie in 1639, the convent provided the first institute of learning for girls in New France. Although the main construction was started in 1641, the complex suffered severe damage with several fires, and has undergone construction into the 20th century. The massive gray complex also boasts gardens and an orchard.

The convent still serves as a school for girls, and is the longest operating girls' school in North America.

Turn left and walk up Rue de Parloir. At the end, turn right, continuing on Rue Saint-Louis.

Take a peek in the **Musée d'Art Inuit Brousseau**, 39 Rue Saint-Louis, dedicated exclusively to Inuit art and culture from across the Canadian Arctic. The personal exhibit includes more than 450 sculptures from Canadian Arctic Inuit artists. Artwork effectively illustrates the history, lifestyle, myths, and legends of these mysterious people. Temporary exhibits are usually themed, including Nanuk art and a look at Polar Bears in native art. T:*(418) 694-1828. Open year-round daily 9:30-5:30. Admission $6 for adults, $4 for students, children 12 and under are free.*

Across from 58 Rue Saint-Louis, on the corner of Rue Corps-de-Garde, notice the **cannonball** still stuck in the trunk of a tree. At 72 Rue Saint-Louis, a **plaque** dedicated to American General Richard Montgomery can be found.

Maison Sewell, 87 Rue Saint-Louis, dates back to 1803 and was the Post Office department from 1859 to 1865.

Turn left onto Rue Sainte-Ursule and take a look at the neo-Gothic **Notre-Dame du Sacré-Coeur** ⑦, 71 Rue Sainte-Ursule, built in 1910. The interior boasts magnificent stained-glass windows and walls covered with marble plaques in recognition of favors that have been granted to the faithful. T: *(418) 692-3787. Open year-round daily 7-8. Admission is free.*

Across the street is the **Chalmers-Wesley United Church**, 78 Rue Sainte-Ursule. This church, built in 1852, also features beautiful stained-glass windows, as well as superb woodwork, and a century-old organ. The church is currently home to two congregations, the Chalmers-Wesley United Church and Église Unie Saint-Pierre. Organ concerts are held on Sunday nights, and the church hosts a painting exhibit in the summer. T: *(418) 692-0431. Open July–Aug. daily 10–5. Admission is free.*

Walk back along Rue Sainte-Ursule, crossing over Rue Saint-Louis. Turn left at Rue Dauphine to the **Chapelle des Jésuites** ⑧, 20 Rue Dauphine, which was built in 1817. The chapel, dedicated to Canadian Martyrs, houses many artistic objects of the faith, including statues dating back to 1750. T: *(418)*

694-9616. Open year-round Mon.–Fri. 11:30–1:30. Admission is free.

Leaving the chapel, turn left on Rue Dauphine and continue across Rue Saint-Stanislas, to Rue Cook.

Take a peek at **Saint-Andrew's Presbyterian Church** ⑨, 106 Rue Sainte-Anne. In 1759, the first Presbyterians arrived in Québec with Scottish troops belonging to Wolfe's army. Inside are beautiful stained-glass windows and a Casavant organ. **T**: *(418) 694-1347. Open July and Aug. Mon.–Fri. 10–4:30. Admission is free.*

Continue walking up Rue Sainte-Anne and note the **Édifice Price**, 65 Rue Sainte-Anne. Built in 1929, this is the only skyscraper built inside the walls of Old Québec. The Art-Deco-style building has an interesting lobby, with bronze bas-reliefs depicting the history of the Price Pulp and Paper Company.

HOLY TRINITY ANGLICAN CATHEDRAL ⑩, on the corner of Rue Sainte-Anne and Rue des Jardins, **T**:(418) 692-2193. *Open May–June daily 9–6; July–Aug. daily 9–8; Sept.–Oct. daily 10–4. Admission is free.*

Dating from 1804, this is the oldest Anglican cathedral outside of the British Isles. The cathedral is a replica of St. Martin-in-the-Fields in London and houses a fine collection of treasures received from King George III. The cathedral also boasts a set of bells, an impressive organ, and extraordinary stained-glass windows.

Stroll along **Rue Sainte-Anne**, a charming, cobblestoned pedestrian street with boutiques, bistros and restaurants. During summers, since 1978, the street has welcomed portrait and caricature artists.

Running between Rue Sainte-Anne and Rue de Buade, don't miss **Rue du Trésor**, a small alley crowded with local artists displaying their work. It was on this street, during the French Regime, that the settlers would come to pay their taxes.

MUSÉE de CIRE QUÉBEC ⑪, 22 Rue Sainte-Anne, **T**: (418) 692-2289. *Open May–Oct. daily 9–9; Nov.–Apr. 10–5. Admission $3 for adults, $2 for students, children are free.*

The only wax museum in Québec Province is housed in one of the oldest buildings in the city, built in 1632. Exquisitely created, life-size wax figures represent key individuals throughout Québec's history, as well as contemporary celebrities.

MUSÉE du FORT ⑫, 10 Rue Sainte-Anne, **T**: (418) 692-2175. *Open Feb.–Mar. Thurs.–Sun. 12–4; Apr.–June and mid-Sept. to Oct. daily 10–5; July to mid-Sept. daily 10–7. Admission $6.50 for adults, $4 for children.*

A 400-square-foot model reproduction of Québec City as it was in 1759, and a multimedia show reenact the six sieges of Québec, including the famous battle on the Plains of Abraham, inviting visitors to relive the tumultuous history.

Leaving Musée du Fort, turn right onto Rue du Fort and then left onto Rue de Buade. Stop into **Au Royaume du Père Noël**, 43 Rue de Buade, 2nd Floor, for a snowy look at Québec City of yesteryear and all things Christmas. The large permanent model Christmas village is delightful, with more than 275 porcelain houses, 1,500 figurines, and 5,000 trees. **T**: *(418) 692-3022. Open late June to Labor Day daily 9–9, by appointment the rest of the year. Admission $2.25 per person.*

The **Québec Expérience**, accessible at 43 Rue de Buade or 8 Rue du Trésor, is a great multi-media experience that leads visitors on a 30-minute trip into Québec's past and present with holographic characters, mobile screens, and three-dimensional characters. **T**:*(418) 694-4000,* **W***: quebecexperience.com. Shows run mid-May to mid-Oct. daily every 90 minutes from 10:45–9:15; mid-Oct. to mid-May last show at 4:45. Admission $7.50 for adults, $5 for children, children under 6 are free.*

NOTRE-DAME de QUÉBEC CATHEDRAL ⑬, 20 Rue de Buade, **T**: (418) 692-2533, **W**: patrimoine-religieux.com. *Open year-round daily 7:30–4:30, except during sound-and-light show. Guided tours May–Oct. Mon.–Fri. 9–2:30, Sat. 9–4:30, Sun. 12:30–4:30; Nov.–Apr. by reservation. Admission is free.*

Originally built in 1647, the cathedral was devastated by fire three times. Each time, it was rebuilt from its original walls and plans. On the right side aisle, facing the altar, note the old **sanctuary lamp**. The lamp was a gift to Bishop Laval from King Louis XIV and is one of the few items that survived from the cathedral's early days, miraculously escaping the fires.

The **main altar** is a miniature replica of the altar in Saint Peter's Basilica in Rome. It was sculpted from wood in 1797 and covered with gold leaf.

François-de-Laval, the first Bishop of Québec, arrived at the cathedral in 1659 and was a central figure in its history. The **funeral chapel**, inaugurated in May 1993, holds his tomb, while the **Centre d'Animation François de Laval**, located nearby, depicts his life. *Open year-round daily; Nov.-May closed on Sunday. Admission is free.*

Don't miss the **Act of Faith Sound-and-Light Show**, which presents a unique look at the architecture and history of the cathedral through a dazzling sound-and-light show. **T**:*(418) 694-4000,* **W***: quebecexperience.com. Shows run May to mid-Oct. every hour from 1–9; mid-Oct. to Apr. Call for an appointment. Admission $7.50 for adults, $5 for children, children 5 and under are free.*

Across the street from the cathedral is Québec's **Hôtel de Ville** ⑭, 43 Côte de la Fabrique, built in 1895 on the site of the former Collège de Jésuits. The Place de l'Hôtel-de-Ville park is a great place to rest and people-watch. A memorial to Canada's first cardinal, Cardinal Taschereau, rests here.

Located in the basement is **Centre d'Interprétation de la Vie Urbaine de la Ville de Québec**, which has twelve listening stations that enable visitors to hear reenactments of the development of the city, from 1608 to present day. There is also a large-scale model of the city. An exhibit of sculptures by local artists illustrates the history of public art from 1960 to the present. **T**: *(418) 691-4606*, **W**: *ville.quebec.qc.ca or* **W**: *museocapitale.qc.ca. Open late June through Aug. daily 10–5; Sept.–June Tues.–Sun. 10–5. Admission $3 for adults, $2 for students, children 12 and under are free.*

Cross back to the Notre-Dame de Québec Cathedral and turn left.

MUSÉE de l'AMÉRIQUE-FRANÇAISE ⑮, 2 Côte de la Fabrique, **T**: (418) 692-2843, **W**: *mcq.org. Open late June to Labor Day daily 9:30–5; Sept. to late June Tues.–Sun. 10–5. Admission $5 for adults, $2 for children 12–16, children under 12 are free.*

This pleasant museum interprets the history of the French in North America and the founding of Québec through a number of diverse displays. A small exhibit introduces visitors to Louis Hébert and his family — the first settlers of Québec City, whose homestead was on the same spot where the museum and the Séminaire de Québec now stand. Stroll through the beautiful and peaceful chapel that is now used for piano concerts. In a second pavilion, witness the development of New France in three-dimensional color with a fascinating three-story museum featuring wax statues, artifacts and a video presentation. A small collection of genealogical records is also available at the top level of the second building.

Leave the second building of the museum and stroll up into the courtyard of the **Le Petit Séminaire**. The unadorned starched white walls and the vast open courtyard are striking. Walk back past the building where you exited the museum and turn left on Rue de l'Université and turn right on Rue Sainte-Famille. Turn left on Rue Couillard.

MUSÉE BON-PASTEUR ⑯, 14 Rue Couillard, **T**: (418) 694-0243. *Open year-round Tues.–Sun. 1–5. Admission $2 for adults, children are free.*

Get a glimpse into the past 150 years of social history of Québec, and experience the social and cultural works of the Sisters of the Good Shepherd.

Turn right, continuing on Rue Couillard. Turn right on Rue Hamel and then left on Rue Charlevoix.

HÔTEL DIEU HOSPITAL and MUSÉE des AUGUSTINES ⑰, 32 Rue Charlevoix, **T**: (418) 692-2492. *Open year-round Tues.–Sat. 9:30–12 and 1:30–5, Sun. 1:30–5. Admission free, donations accepted.*

Augustine Sisters of the Convent of Dieppe, Normandy, established the first hospital in North America north of Mexico in 1639. The Hôtel Dieu Hospital has been providing medical services to the people of Québec since 1644. Today, the hospital is also at the forefront of medical research.

Beside the hospital is the convent, built in 1757 during the French Regime. The long corridors and worn staircases still echo the history of the place. The church was built between 1800 and 1803. Note the sculptures made from 1829-32 by French Canadian artist Thomas Baillargé. In the vaulted cellars, architectural remnants dating back to 1695 can be found in the old monastery walls and the convent's original foundation.

A history-and-art museum relates the story of the sisters who formed this, the first women-run missionary. Displays include antique furniture, medical instruments from 17th century and today, everyday items, art, and embroidery.

The old Saint Patrick's Church, built in 1832 for the Irish community, is now a medical research facility for the hospital.

The Center Catherine-de-Saint-Augustin is dedicated to Marie-Catherine-de-Saint-Augustine, who was one of the pioneers of faith in New France and who helped to found the church in Canada. Her remains are kept at the site. Extraordinary stained-glass windows illustrate her life. *Open Tues.–Sat. 10–12 and 2–5, Sun. 2–5. Admission free, donations accepted.*

Leaving the museum, go right, continuing on Rue Charlevoix. Turn left on Côte du Palais and then right on Rue Saint-Jean. End your tour with strolling and window shopping on **Rue Saint-Jean** ⑲. Admire the high-end boutiques and stop for a glass of wine or local beer at one of the sidewalk cafés.

Porte Saint-Louis in Old Québec

OLD QUÉBEC 28

Petit Champlain and Old Port

Narrow cobblestone roads, fieldstone buildings, small squares, and courtyards tucked away — all just waiting to be discovered. As you enter the Petit Champlain area, the oldest business district in North America, you'll feel as though you have stepped directly from North America to Europe. Many delights await around every corner in this tightly settled neighborhood just outside the fortification walls of Québec.

Owing to the neighborhood's location at the foot of Cap Diamant, in the shadow of Old Québec, this part of the city is also referred to as the Lower Town. It was here, in Place Royale, that Samuel de Champlain first settled Québec City, signaling the birth of New France. In the mid-18th century, during the British Conquest, most of the city was destroyed. It took more than twenty years to rebuild. With the expansion of the city to the top of Cap Diamant, the Petit-Champlain area suffered greatly, falling into disrepair and abandon. Restoration of the area began in the mid-19th century; much of it being claimed by artists who set up studios and galleries along the picturesque streets.

East of Petit Champlain, along the Saint Lawrence River, the Old Port of Québec was the hub of shipbuilding and trade. After the Conquest, the British expanded the city by filling in marshlands and building wharves along the Saint Lawrence and Saint Charles rivers. Today, the Old Port is still thriving with commercial and tourist traffic, activities, and a large open-air amphitheater, the Agora.

GETTING THERE:

One option is to start your tour at **Place d'Armes**. Take the **Funiculaire** — a steep elevator-like cable car — from the **Terrasse Dufferin**, beside Château Frontenac, to **Rue du Petit-Champlain**. *Operates June to mid-Oct. daily 8– midnight; mid-Oct. through May daily 7:30–11:30. Fare is $1.50 each way.*

There is also a steep staircase that descends from **Terrasse Dufferin** to **Côte de la Montagne**. Continue walking down hill, through **Porte Prescott**, and take the **Casse-Cou** stairway on the right, to **Rue du Petit-Champlain**.

By Car, consider parking by Battlefields Park, off Avenue Wilfrid-Laurier, and walk up Grande Allée, through the Saint Louis Gate, and up Rue Saint-Louis to Place d'Armes.

By Bus, take Bus number **3** or **11** to reach the Place d'Armes. The fare is $1.75 for tickets purchased at a tobacco stand, or $2.25 (exact change only) on the bus. A daily pass is $5.10.

Another option is to start the tour in **Petit-Champlain** and skip the funiculaire.

By Car, consider parking at the Old Port, off Boulevard Champlain or Rue Dalhousie, and walk to **Rue Petit-Champlain** via Boulevard Champlain or Rue Dalhousie and Rue du Marché-Champlain.

By Bus, take Bus number **1** to reach the Petit Champlain. The fare is $1.75 for tickets purchased at a tobacco stand, or $2.25 (exact change only) on the bus. A daily pass is $5.10.

PRACTICALITIES:

The **Tourist Information Center** is located at Place de Paris, 215 Rue du Marché-Finlay. Open May to late Sept. daily 10-6; Oct. to early May by appointment. **T**: (418) 643-6631.

Audio-guided walking tours are available at the tourist information office for the Plains of Abraham Park, as well as other areas of the city. **T**: (418) 990-8687. *Cost is $10 per person, $15 for two.*

FOOD AND DRINK:

Le Café du Monde Bistro (57 Rue Dalhousie) This local favorite offers "good food, good times, Parisian style," featuring an extensive selection of wines and a lively atmosphere. **T**: (418) 692-4455. $$

Poisson d'Avril Restaurant (115 Quai Saint-André) A seafood restaurant, on the Old Port, with a charming nautical decor — a favorite with the locals. **T**: (418) 692-1010. $$$

Le Délice du Roy (33 Rue Saint-Pierre, in Place Royale) Traditional, regional, and local dishes with québécois-brewed beer. **T**: (418) 694-9161. $$ and $$$

Lapin Sauté (52 Rue du Petit-Champlain) Picturesque bistro serving hearty Québec country cuisine, including rabbit specialties, rosemary chicken, and traditional meat pies. **T**: (418) 692-5325. $$$

SUGGESTED TOUR:

Circled numbers correspond to numbers on the map.

The lower station of the **funiculaire** ① is located in the **Maison Louis-Jolliet**, 16 Rue du Petit-Champlain. This two-story stone house, built in 1683, was the home of Louis Jolliet who, along with Father Jacques Marquette, discovered the Mississippi River in 1673. The funicular began operation in

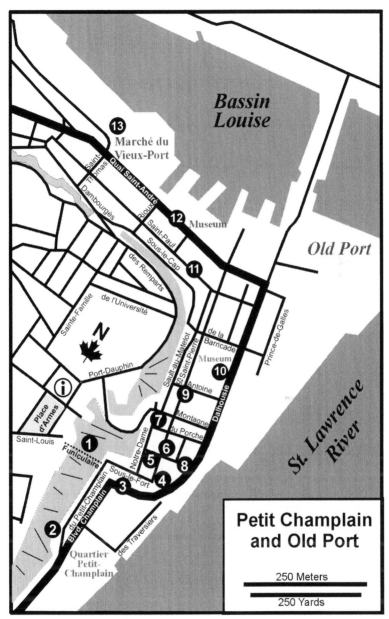

Petit Champlain and Old Port

250 Meters

250 Yards

November 1879, but the open-air cars were only in use during nice weather. It was rebuilt in 1997 with updated technology and enclosed cars. T:*(418) 692-1132*, W: *funiculaire-quebec.com*

Rue du Petit-Champlain ②, first laid down in the 1680s, is a cobblestone pedestrian street that runs along the base of the cliff. Some of the old wooden buildings along this street were home to laborers and craftspeople until the 19th century. Irish immigrants, arriving and working in the Old Port, settled in the neighborhood. Today, the street is alive with shoppers and strollers who come to enjoy the many shops, galleries, and cafés. If you're lucky you may be able to catch an artist at work in one of the studio galleries.

Check out the **5 Nations Indian Art Gallery**, 25½ Rue Petit-Champlain, which has an amazing collection of Indian artworks. Note the Iroquois contemporary sculptures, rooted in spirituality and history.

Meander along Rue du Petit-Champlain and drink in the charm and beauty. At the end, turn left and walk up **Boulevard Champlain**. Bear right onto **Rue du Marché-Champlain** and walk to the corner for a spectacular view of the **Château Frontenac** towering over the Petit Champlain from the top of the cliff.

Walk back up Rue du Marché-Champlain to **Maison Chevalier** ③, 50 Rue du Marché-Champlain. This was once the site of a natural port, discovered in 1603 by Samuel de Champlain. Three historical buildings, connected into a single horseshoe-shaped entity, preserve the feel of family life from the early days of Québec. Period furniture and décor enable visitors to clearly imagine the life style of local sailors, crafts people, and wealthy families. **T***:(418) 643-2158,* **W***: mcq.org. Open May–June Tues.–Sun. 10–5; July–Aug. daily 10–5; Sept.– Oct. Tues.–Sun. 10–5; Nov.–Apr. Sat.–Sun. 10–5. Admission is free.*

Turn left on **Rue Notre-Dame** and then right onto **Rue Sous-le-Fort**.

BATTERIE ROYALE ④, at the end of Rue Sous-le-Fort, **T**:(418) 643-6631. *Open year round daily. Admission is free.*

Situated outside the rampart walls of the city, the lower city needed some means of defense. At the request of King Louis XIV of France, the four-sided earthen rampart was built in 1691. The battery was destroyed during the British Conquest and was not rebuilt. The British chose to erect warehouses and a wharf on the site instead, and the battery was eventually buried and lost. In 1972, archaeologists working in the area unearthed the ruined rampart. The battery was rebuilt and replicas of 18th-century cannons were positioned where the originals once stood. Programs are held at the battery during the summer months to demonstrate how the cannons would have been used during the French Regime.

Walk back up **Rue Sous-le-Fort** and turn right onto **Rue Notre-Dame.**

ÉGLISE NOTRE-DAME-des-VICTOIRES ⑤, Place Royale, **T**:(418) 692-1650. *Open May to mid-Oct. Mon.–Sat. 9–5:30, Sun. 1–5:30; mid-Oct. through Apr. Mon.–Sat. 9–4, Sun. 1–4. Admission is free.*

In 1608, Samuel de Champlain came to New France to establish a fur trading post. He built a wooden fort on this site, named Habitation and consisting of two buildings and a garden, which functioned as fort, trading post, and residence. A larger fort was later built on the site in 1624.

Erected from 1668 to 1723, the church was used as an auxiliary chapel of Québec's main cathedral, serving the community of the lower city. It was destroyed during the British Conquest, but was soon rebuilt. The name, Our Lady of the Victories, was given to the church to commemorate two successful occasions that Québec City was able to withstand the British armies.

The interior boasts art that tells of the community's history. Frescos in the choir depict the two British advances that the city was able to withstand. A model ship hanging high above the nave represents the 17th-century *Brézé*, which carried French troops into Québec's port.

Nearby is **Place Royale** ⑥, a beautiful cobblestone square that was also once the site of Champlain's Habitation. As the town developed around the fort, and more permanent structures were built, a market was set up in the square. The area around the square was the heart of Québec's economic activity until the mid-19th century.

The bronze statue of King Louis XIV that rests in the middle of the square was given to the city in 1928 by the French government. It is a copy of Bernini's 1665 marble sculpture housed at Versailles. Out of fear of offending the city's anglophone population, the statue was not erected in the square until 1948.

The **Centre d'Interprétation de Place-Royale**, 27 Rue Notre-Dame, has a multimedia presentation, exhibits, and activities introducing visitors to more than 400 years of Québec history. Artifacts help illustrate the local and international trading that took place when the city was founded. In the vaults, a hands-on discovery space enables visitors to experience family life in Québec more than 200 years ago. **T***:(418) 646-3167,* **W***: mcq.org. Open Sept.–June Tues.–Sun. 10–5; July–Aug. daily 9:30–5. Admission $3 for adults, $1 for children 12–16, children under 12 are free.*

Continue walking up Rue Notre-Dame. Stop in at the **"Living Heritage Workshop,"** 42 Rue Notre-Dame, where artisans and craftspeople carry on traditional practices of art, music, and dance. **T***:(418) 643-2158. Open May–Aug. daily 10–5; Sept. to mid-Oct. Wed.–Sun. 10–5. Admission is free.*

It's just steps to **Parc La Cetière** ⑦, at the corner of Rue Notre-Dame and Côte de la Montagne. Admire the stunning mural of Québec's community and culture that covers the side of the three-story building beside the park. The mural illustrates 400 years of the city's history in splendid color and detail. It is difficult to pull yourself away from the lively scene that holds many interesting discoveries.

Opposite the mural are the remains of several foundations from buildings dating back to 1685. The structures, originally destroyed during the British conquest, were rebuilt, only to be destroyed again by several fires in 1948 and 1957. After the fires, the site was covered and forgotten until being unearthed by archaeologists in 1972. Note the size of the separate dwellings represented, the chimney base in one and the remains of an interior wall in another.

Walk down **Rue du Porche** across from Parc La Cetière. Note **Parc de l'Unesco** on the right. Children can get a break playing games related to history and the maritime. Continue on Rue du Porche, cross **Rue Saint-Pierre** and turn right on **Rue de l'Union.**

As more markets developed around the city, outgrowing Place Royal, **Place de Paris** ⑧ was formed. Taking full advantage of its proximity to the Saint Lawrence River, the original Finlay Market prospered on this site from 1817 until the early 1950's.

The contemporary **sculpture** in the square, entitled *Dialogue with History*, was a gift from the City of Paris. Positioned in line with the statue of King Louis XIV in Place Royale, the statue is intended to represent a dialogue between the present-day community and the monarchy of the past.

The former **Thibodeau Warehouse** stands along one edge of the square, with the Tourist Information Center located on its ground floor. Inside, there is a map of New France in 1688 and a display of artifacts recovered from the archaeological digs beneath the square. A slide show and guided tours are available to give visitors more details about the area.

Walk out of the square along Rue du Marché-Finlay and turn left onto **Rue Dalhousie**. Turn left onto **Côte de la Montagne** and then right onto **Rue Saint-Pierre**.

During the 19th century **Rue Saint-Pierre** ⑨ was the backbone of Québec's financial district. Banks and various commercial centers began to build their headquarters along this road. Note the **National Bank**, 71 Rue Saint-Pierre, built in 1862.

Turn right on **Rue Saint-Antoine** and then left onto **Rue Dalhousie**.

MUSÉE de la CIVILISATION ⑩, 85 Rue Dalhousie, **T**: (418) 643-2158, **W**: mcq.org. *Open late June to Labor Day daily 9:30–6:30; Sept. to late June Tues.–Sun. 10–5. Admission $7 for adults, $2 for children 12–16, children under 12 are free.*

The architect Moshe Safdie, who also designed the Habitat complex in Montréal, designed this building, which fills the entire block between Rue Saint-Pierre and Rue Dalhousie, Rue Saint-Antoine and Rue Saint-Jacques. The complex consists of two angular limestone buildings, a lot of glass, and a copper roof pierced by stylized dormers. Between the two limestone buildings is a massive staircase leading to a terrace that overlooks the **Maison Estèbe**. This small stone house, built in 1752, was saved and built into the design of the museum as another reminder of the bond between past and present. The large entryway holds an impressive statue, ***La Débâcle***, which represents ice breaking in spring.

The mission of the museum is to encourage visitors to examine his/her own traditions and values by exhibiting life and culture in an open and objective way. The museum's collection of more than 50,000 items, displayed in ten rooms, includes art, textiles, costumes, everyday objects, furniture, and Aboriginal artifacts.

Discovery spaces are set up, with changing themes, providing hands-on exhibits for the whole family. Learn about such topics as the human body, the circus, and space.

Leaving the museum, turn left onto **Rue Dalhousie** and left again onto **Rue Saint-Jacques**. Turn right and continue walking up **Rue Saint-Pierre**. Note the **Imperial Bank of Canada**, 113–115 Rue Saint-Jacques, dating from 1913. The **Dominion Building**, 126 Rue Saint-Jacques, was Québec's first skyscraper.

Turn left onto **Rue Saint-Paul** ⑪, built in 1816 on top of the wharves that ran along the Saint Charles River. In 1906, every building at this end of the street was demolished, except the **Renaud Warehouse**, number 82, in order to widen the street. The buildings on the south side of the street, dating from 1850, today house antique shops and galleries.

Turn right onto **Rue des Navigateurs**, and left onto **Rue Saint-André**.

CENTRE d'INTERPRÉTATION du VIEUX-PORT-de-QUÉBEC ⑫, 100 Rue Saint-André, **T**:(418) 648-3300, **W**: parkscanada.qc.ca/vieuxport. *Open May-Oct. daily 10–5; Sept.–Oct. daily noon–4; Nov.–Apr. by appointment only. Admission $3 for adults, $2 for children 6–16, children under 6 are free.*

The museum offers an interesting look at the important role the timber and shipping industries have played in Québec's port. A diorama re-creates the thriving port and wharves along the Saint Charles River during the 19th century. Other exhibits take a look at the businesses of logging and shipbuilding, and explore the culture and life-style of the people involved in these industries. A glassed-in terrace on the top floor provides a sweeping look at today's port and the lower city.

Walking farther along Rue Saint-André, you will find the **Marché du Vieux-Port** ⑬, 160 Rue du Quai Saint-André. This impressive market was reconstructed based on the original Marché Saint-André, built in 1841. Today the market maintains the traditional atmosphere. Local and regional produce is displayed and sold amongst restaurants and shops. **T**:*(418) 692-2517.*

Return back to the Funiculaire via Rue Saint-Paul, Rue Saint-Pierre, and Rue Sous-le-Fort or walk up **Rue Rioux** and **Côte Dambourgès** to **Rue des Ramparts** and Old Québec.

Trip 3
Québec City

Grande Allée

The Grande Allée was once the most fashionable street in Québec, and is commonly thought of as the local "Champs Élysées." Dating back to the French Administration of the city, the road was originally the main route connecting Québec with the Amerindian mission in Sillery.

Once a rough country road, bordered by large agricultural properties owned by a few wealthy families and clergy, Grande Allée was transformed at the end of the 18th century when the British began developing the area as a popular resort location. As Old Québec expanded during the early 19th century, bourgeois manors and elegant homes were built along the street. The residential thoroughfare, which also connects many of Québec's ministries, gradually became one of the city's main arteries.

This beautiful tree-lined street has a lot of noteworthy architecture. As you meander along the busy sidewalks, note the varied designs of the Victorian homes. You can still feel the unique history of the area and sense the 19th-century elite who once strolled the neighborhood.

GETTING THERE:

The tour of Grande Allée begins at the **Parliament Building**.

By Car, consider parking on **Rue Louis Alexandre-Taschereau**, off Boulevard René-Levesque, or park near Battlefields Park on **Avenue Wilfrid-Laurier**. Walk to the Parliament Building along either Boulevard René-Levesque or Grande Allée to **Avenue Honoré-Mercier**.

By Bus, take Bus number **3**, **7**, **11**, or **25** to reach the Parliament Building. The fare is $1.75 for tickets purchased at a tobacco stand, or $2.25 (exact change only) on the bus.

PRACTICALITIES:

The **Tourist Information Center** is located at 835 Avenue Wilifrid-Laurier, in the Discovery Pavilion of the Plains of Abraham. **T**: (418) 649-2608. Open late June through Sept. daily 8:30-7:30; Oct. to late June Mon.-Sat. 9–5, Sun. 10–4.

Audio-guided walking tours are available at the tourist information office for the Parliament Building and Parliament Hill, as well as other areas of the city. **T**: (418) 990-8687. *Cost $10 per person, $15 for two.*

FOOD AND DRINK:

Le Parlementaire (in the Parliament Building) Excellent regional Québec cuisine in one of the most historic buildings in the city. Open Tues.–Fri. 8–2:30. **T**: (418) 643-6640. $$

Cosmos Café (575 Grande Allée East) Casual food, including hamburgers and salads, comfortable atmosphere with a futuristic décor. **T**:(418) 640-0606. $$

Voo Doo Grill (575 Grande Allée East) An exotic atmosphere of African art and drums, and fabulous grilled dishes with an international flare. Live music every night. Downstairs is the Maurice Nightclub and a cigar lounge. **T**: (418) 647-2000. $$$

Paris Brest (590 Grande Allée East) Gourmet French cuisine in an exquisitely elegant setting. **T**: (418) 529-2243. $$$+

SUGGESTED TOUR:

Circled numbers correspond to numbers on the map.

ASSEMBLÉE NATIONALE du QUÉBEC ①, on the corner of Rue Honoré-Mercier and Grande Allée East, **T**:(418) 643-7239 or 1-866-337-8837, **W**: assnat.qc.ca. *Open for guided tours, year-round Mon.–Fri. 9–4:30; July–Aug. also on Sat.–Sun. 10–4:30. Tours available in French, English, and Spanish. Admission is free.*

This striking Parliament Building was erected in the Second Empire style between 1877 and 1886. A close look at the façade reveals in 22 bronze statues the people and events that formed the great city. Under the province's coat of arms, the words "Je me souviens" is carved in the stone, meaning "I remember" to ensure that the people of Québec always remember and incorporate the many changes and phases the city has endured in its history. The central tower is dedicated to Jacques Cartier, who discovered Canada. A fountain at the foot of the central tower has a sculpture called "Nigog Fisherman." Above it is another sculpture depicting an aboriginal family in honor of the original inhabitants of the area.

Guided tours take visitors through a number of working rooms, including the **National Assembly Chamber**, where Parliament meets to debate. The chamber is filled with magnificent works of art and decorative items.

Several windows in the building sport spectacular Art-Nouveau stained glass. Note also, the magnificent arch that adorns the entrance to the restaurant.

Leaving the Parliament Building, follow the **footpath** marked with interpretive panels. At the end of the path, on your left, is **Édifice Pamphile-Le May**, built from 1910–16. This is home to the Parliament Library. Facing it note the **Totem Memorial to the Centennial of British Columbia's Entrance into the Confederation**, which was given to Québec in 1971. On the opposite side of the

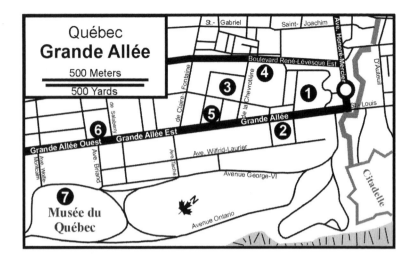

footpath is the monument "**Geodesy for the Future**" which is dedicated to Canadian surveyors.

At the end of the footpath turn left onto Promenade des Premiers-Ministres. Turn right onto Rue Saint-Augustine and then right on Grande Allée.

Place George V ② is a quiet, green park used as a training area and parade grounds for the military's equestrian regiments. The park has several monuments and cannons.

As you stroll along Grande Allée, note the row of English-style neoclassical townhouses, dating back to 1847, known as **Terrasse Stadacona**, 640–664 Grande-Allée East, sharing a common façade. The once-residential buildings now sport numerous restaurants, cafés, and nightclubs, many with terraces for outdoor dining and people watching.

On the opposite side of the street is a group of Second Empire-style buildings dating back to 1882, 661–695 Grande Allée West, reflecting the influences that the Parliament Building and wealthy business people had on the street.

Continue along Grande Allée and turn right on Rue de la Chevrotière.

BON-PASTEUR CHAPEL ③, 1080 Rue de la Chevrotière, **T**: (418) 641-1069. *Open for guided tours July–Aug. Tues.–Sat. 1:30–4:30; Sept.–June upon request. Admission is free.*

Under the administration of the Good Shepherd Sisters of Québec, dedicated to the education of abandoned and delinquent girls, this chapel is striking for its height and length, and comparatively narrow width. Inside is an outstanding collection of religious art, and three noteworthy altars. The chapel also boasts an authentic Baroque-style tabernacle dating back to 1730. Concerts are held in the chapel from October to June. A special artists' mass is held every Sunday at 11.

L'OBSERVATOIRE de la CAPITALE ④, 1037 Rue de la Chevrotière, on the 31st floor, **T**:(418) 644-9841 or 1-888-497-4322, **W**: observatoirecapitale.org. *Open June and Sept. daily 10–7; July–Aug. daily 10–5; Oct.–May Tue.–Sun. 10–5. Admission $5 for adults, $4 for children over 12, children 12 and under are free.*

At 750 feet above sea level, this observation point gives visitors a breathtaking panoramic view of the Québec City area. Guided tours are available to point out all the interesting sites and help visitors to better understand the capital area.

The observatory is located in the **Édifice Marie-Guyart**, built from 1967–72. The building is named after Marie Guyart de l'Incarnation who co-founded the convent for Ursuline Sisters and the first school for girls in North America. Near the entrance note the **sculpture** titled "1+1=1," by Charles Daudelin in 1996.

Walk back along Rue de la Chevrotière and turn right on Grande Allée.

Église Saint-Coeur de Marie ⑤, 530 Grande Allée East, looks more like a fortress than a place of religious worship, with its large archways, bartizans, and towers. The church was built in 1919 for the Eudists.

Across the street, **Terrasse Frontenac**, 455-555 Grande Allée, is an interesting and unique row of Second Empire homes, built in 1895.

Cross Grande Allée and turn right, then left at Cours du Général de Montcalm. Note the **Monument Montcalm**, sculpted by Léopold Morice in 1911. Farther on, note the **Monument Charles de Gaulle**, erected in honor of the French statesman for his support in the development of franco-québecois relations in the 1960s.

Return to Grande Allée, cross the street, and turn left. Note the **Chapelle Franciscaines de Marie**, situated between Rue de Clairefontaine and Avenue Turnbull. The chapel was built in 1901 by a community of nuns devoted and dedicated to the adoration of the Lord. Note the small cupola supported by angels.

Continue walking along Grande Allée, admiring the varied and elegant architecture, to the corner of Avenue Cartier.

MAISON HENRY-STUART ⑥, 82 Grand Allée West, **T**:(418) 647-4347, **W**: cmsq.qc.ca. *Open for guided tours, late June through Aug. daily 11–5; Sept. to late June Sun. 1–5; other days upon reservation. Admission $5, tea included.*

This charming cottage, built in 1849, used to mark the border between the city and the country. It boasts an authentic Victorian interior, with period furnishings and a covered veranda. The guided tour is delightful, topped by a delicious afternoon tea.

Cross Grande Allée again and go right. Note the elegant Renaissance

Revival **Ladies' Protestant Home**, 95 Grande Allée West, built in 1862. Also note the **Monastère des Dominicains**, 175 Grande Allée West, built in the 20ᵗʰ century in the Gothic Revival style.

Turn left onto Avenue Wolfe-Montcalm. In the roundabout is the **Monument to General Wolfe**, built in 1832, who led the British to victory in the Battle of the Plains of Abraham. Legend has it that this is the exact spot where General Wolfe fell. The monument has been the object of numerous demonstrations by French Québecers. When it was rebuilt in 1963, after being toppled over again, it was finally inscribed in French.

MUSÉE du QUÉBEC ⑦, 1 Avenue Wolfe-Montcalm, **T**:(418) 643-2150. *Open Sept.–May Tues.–Sun. 11–5:45, Wed. 11–8:45; June–Aug. daily 10–5:45, Wed. 10–9:45.*

Québec's national art gallery is situated in three buildings, connected via a glassed-in corridor. The main part of the museum was built in 1933; one of its buildings is an old prison. The museum displays an extensive collection of Québec art, from colonization to modern day, including a wide variety of paintings, sculptures, photographs, and decorative art. Temporary exhibits include international artists and shows, themed by artist, subject and era.

The **Battlefields Park Interpretation Center** has a fantastic multimedia presentation that explains the great battles fought on the Plains of Abraham from 1759–60. There is also an exhibit on the American Invasion from 1775 to 1776.

To end your tour you have two options. Either stroll leisurely back through the **Battlefields Park** (see trip 4), overlooking the Saint Lawrence River. Or, meander back along Grande Allée, drinking in the history and culture of this lively neighborhood and perhaps stopping for a bit more to drink in one of the many cafés.

The Citadel and Ramparts

Because of its strategic location, Québec played a crucial role in the defense of northeastern French America during the 17th century. Throughout its history, fortification projects have taken place, implemented by both the French and British. This tour brings visitors up close to Québec's tumultuous military history, while providing stunning views of the city, parks, gardens and the Saint Lawrence River.

Start on the Plains of Abraham, where the fate of Québec was determined through a number of battles, and where today visitors and residents of Québec can enjoy one of the most magnificent urban parks. At the end of the park, sitting solidly atop Cap Diamant, is the impressive Citadel — a military fortification built during peacetime that has never seen battle. From the Citadel, follow the ramparts around the city, inspect the city's defenses, and admire many of the other military establishments throughout Québec.

The fortifications of Québec stand, preserved, today as they had in the 17th, 18th, and 19th centuries when they were being built. They are constant reminders of the important role the city had in the development of French Canada and make Québec the only remaining walled city in North America. UNESCO recognizes the fortification walls as a World Heritage site.

GETTING THERE:

Start the tour in **Battlefields Park**.

By Car, park near Battlefields Park on **Avenue Wilfrid-Laurier** and walk into the park.

By Bus, take Bus number **3** or **11** to reach the Battlefields Park. The fare is $1.75 for tickets purchased at a tobacco stand, or $2.25 (exact change only) on the bus.

PRACTICALITIES:

The Promenade des Gouverneurs is closed in winter.

The **Tourist Information Center** is located at 835 Avenue Wilfrid-Laurier, in the Discovery Pavilion of the Plains of Abraham. **T**: (418) 649-2608. Open late June through Sept. daily 8:30–7:30, Oct. to late June Mon.–Sat. 9–5, Sun. 10–4.

Audio-guided walking tours are available at the tourist information office, 12 Rue Sainte-Anne, for Artillery Park National Historic Site, as well as other areas of the city. **T**:(418) 990-8687. *Cost $10 per person, $15 for two.*

A combination ticket is available for access to many of the sites on this tour, including the Battlefields Park Interpretation Center, the Citadelle, Artillery Park and the Observation Tower for $23. Tickets can be purchased at the Battlefields Park Interpretation Center.

FOOD AND DRINK:

The Council of War at Martello Tower 2 (Rue Tachè) A mystery theater dinner set in 1814, with period costumes and authentic décor. Experience the tastes, sounds and business of the 19th-century military, while attempting to discover the traitor among the crowd. Open July and Aug., Fri. in English and Sat. in French. Reservation required. Bring your own wine. **T**:(418) 648-4071. $$$

La Petit Château Crêperie (5 Rue Saint-Louis, behind Château Frontenac) Offering a vast array of crêpes, sweet and savory, for breakfast, lunch, and dinner. **T**:(418) 694-1616. $$ and $$$

Le Vendôme (36 Côte de la Montagne, near Porte Prescott) One of the oldest restaurants in the city, featuring classic French dishes including Duck à l'orange and Chateaubriand. **T**:(418) 692-0557. $$$

Entrecôte Saint-Jean (1011 Rue Saint-Jean, near Porte Saint-Jean) A French bistro featuring steak, shoestring fries, and a house-special gravy. **T**:(418) 694-0234. $$$

There are numerous restaurants, cafés, and pubs along Grande Allée, not far from the Saint Louis gate and Battlefields Park.

SUGGESTED TOUR:

Circled numbers correspond to numbers on the map.

The **Battlefields Park** ① is on the spot where many battles took place between the French and British empires in the clash over the new territory. It was also here in 1759 that the Conquest took place, changing the course of Québec's history, and giving the British control of the city. Battlefields Park, comprising the Plains of Abraham and Des Braves Park, was created to honor the French and British soldiers who fought and died for the city.

The park has a network of trails for walking, cycling, and inline skating. There are also a number of fields used for local sporting events and games. In the evenings in fall, school kids hold soccer and football practice here. Note the peaceful **Joan of Arc Garden and Monument** near the Rue Tachè entrance, embracing both French and British gardening styles and featuring more than 150 species of flowers from May to October. The scenic lookout at the **Governor's Kiosk**, beside the Citadelle, affords excellent views of the park, the Saint Lawrence River and the Citadelle. An interesting collection of **military guns** is

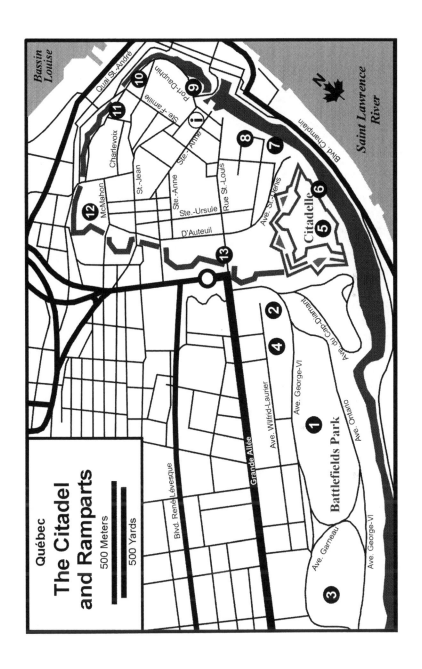

Québec

The Citadel and Ramparts

500 Meters

500 Yards

National Battlefields Park

spread throughout the park, including cannons, howitzers, mortars, and German guns.

Two **Martello Towers**, the only ones of their kinds, completed in 1812, are a credit to 19th-century British military engineering. **Martello Tower 1** stands in the middle of the park, overlooking the Saint Lawrence River. The tower houses an exhibit, with a number of sound stations depicting the life of soldiers in the 19th century. The exhibit also reveals the history of the towers, their architectural mystery and strategic inventiveness. *Open mid-June through Aug. daily 10–5:30; early June, Sept. and Oct. weekends 10–5:30.* **Martello Tower 2** stands on Rue Tachè, providing a defense from overland attacks.

The **Discovery Pavilion** ②, 835 Avenue Wilfrid-Laurier, was built in the fashion of French castles from the Loire Valley and was once home to the naval reserve. On the first floor is an interesting scale model of the citadel and battlefields park. **T**:*(418) 648-4071. Open mid-June to mid-Oct. daily 9–5:30; mid-Oct. to mid-June daily 9–5.*

Canada Odyssey is a multimedia presentation and exhibition illustrating the role that the Plains of Abraham played in the development of the city, its history, and geography. Using state-of-art-technology, the presentation is truly impressive and entertaining. **T**:*(418) 648-4071,* **W**: *ccbn-nbc.gc.ca/_en/odyssecanada.php. Open mid-June to mid-Oct. daily 10–5:30; mid-Oct. to mid-June daily 10–5. Admission $6.50 for adults, $5.50 for children 13-17, children 12 and under are free.*

A guided tour of the Plains of Abraham is available on **Abraham's Bus**, which operates from the Discovery Pavilion. This takes visitors through the park and offers some little-know information about the history of the site. **T**:*(418)*

THE CITADEL & RAMPARTS   44

648-4071. Scheduled mid-June through Aug. daily 10–5:30; early June, Sept. and Oct. weekends 10–5:30. Fee is $4 for adults, $3 for children 13–17, children 12 and under are free.

The **Battlefields Park Interpretation Center** ③, housed in an old jail, guides visitors through the history of the site. An impressive mural in the entryway, the work of Québec artist Aline Martineau, illustrates the varied vocations of the park throughout history. A multimedia presentation recounts the battles of 1759 and 1760. **T**:*(418) 648-5641. Open year-round daily 10–5:30; mid-Oct. to May closed on Monday. Admission $5 for adults, $4 for children 13–17, children 12 and under are free.*

MANÈGE MILITAIRE VOLTIGEURS de QUÉBEC and MUSÉE des VOLTIGEURS ④, 805 Avenue Wilfrid-Laurier, **T**:(418) 648-4422. *Call for schedule and admission fees.*

Built in 1885, the military compound building is listed as a major national architectural structure. The museum, housed in the compound, contains an expansive collection of items pertaining to life in the military.

Note the **Croix du Sacrifice** on Avenue George IV, erected in memory of soldiers killed during World War I. A commemoration ceremony is held here every year on November 11.

*THE CITADELLE ⑤, Côte de la Citadelle, **T**:(418) 694-2815, **W**: lacitadelle.qc.ca. *Open for guided tours Apr. to mid-May daily 10–4; mid-May through June daily 9–5; July–Aug. daily 9–6; Sept. daily 9–4; Oct. daily 10–3; Nov.–Mar. by reservation only. Admission $8 for adults, $4.50 for children 7–17, children 6 and under are free.*

Making up the east flank of the city's fortification walls, the star-shaped structure rests on Cap Diamant, high above the Saint Lawrence River. Construction of the Citadelle was started in 1820 by the British, and took more than 30 years to complete.

Catch the **changing of the guard**, held every day during the summer. This traditional military ceremony features the regimental band, "Batisse" the regimental goat, and security officers in full traditional uniform. At nightfall the traditional **Retreat** is enacted. During the ceremony, the night Guard pays tribute to the Canadian flag.

There are a number of interesting and historic buildings within the Citadelle. At the southeastern end you'll find the King's Bastion, Cap Diamant Redoubt (dating back to 1693), and the former military prison that now houses a museum.

The **Royal 22nd Regiment Museum,** located in the 1750 French army powder magazine, exhibits 17th- to 21st-century military medals and insignias, weapons, and uniforms. **T**:*(418) 694-2815. Guided tours Apr.–Oct. for the* *public, Nov.–Mar. for groups.*

Walk back along the edge of Battlefield Park, up the hill to the **Promenade des Gouverneurs** ⑥. This boardwalk follows the top of the cliff of Cap Diamant, along the edge of the Citadelle. The views of the Citadelle, city, and river are spectacular from here.

Dufferin Terrace ⑦, in front of the Château Frontenac, is the starting point for a stroll around the ramparts of the city. The boardwalk offers beautiful views of the Saint Lawrence River, the town of Lévis on its opposite shore, and the Château Frontenac. The terrace was built on the site of the former Fort Saint-Louis, built by Samuel de Champlain in 1620 and the site of his death in 1635. Champlain's successor, Montmagny, built a castle on the site known as Château Saint-Louis. It served as a residence to the governors of New France until it was destroyed by fire in 1834. In 1838, Lord Durham, governor at the time, had a promenade built on the site, which has since been enlarged several times.

Parc des Gouverneurs ⑧ sprawls uphill over the Dufferin Terrace. The **Wolfe-Montcalm Monument** was erected in honor of all the generals, victorious and defeated, who were killed during the battle of the Plains of Abraham. Walk up the hill, about 500 feet, to the **Bastion du Roy**, which offers a spectacular view of the Saint Lawrence River, its south shore, Île d'Orléans, and Mont Sainte-Anne.

Continue walking to the end of Dufferin Terrace. In the large square, stop to admire the **Samuel de Champlain Monument**, a tribute to the founder of New France. This is also the location of the **funiculaire**, which links the upper and lower towns. At the far end of the square, take the **Frontenac staircase**.

Cross over **Porte Prescott**, built in 1797 and named for the governor at the time. This was the first gate built in the ramparts. The original gate was demolished in 1871 and was not rebuilt until 1983.

Just on the other side of the gate, note the large **cross** in a small field outside the fortification walls. This space was formerly a cemetery.

The beautiful **Parc Montmorency** ⑨ affords sweeping views of the Old Port and Saint Lawrence River. Note the statues of Louis-Hébert, Québec's first settler, and Sir Georges-Étienne Carter, one of the founding fathers of the confederation. Walk across Côte de la Montagne, to see the memorial to Bishop Laval.

Cross back to Parc Montmorency and continue along **Rue des Remparts** ⑩, originally a dirt path running along the inside of the fortification walls, connecting batteries and bastions. The Sault-au-Matelot and Clergé batteries, located across from the seminary buildings, were constructed in 1711 to protect the Québec harbor. Black cannons, of varying types, and interpretive panels are placed along the route, educating visitors on Québec's battlements and giving an authentic feel of military readiness.

The **Hope Gate** once stood at the intersection of Rue Sainte-Famille and Rue des Remparts, closing off access between the upper and lower towns at this point. The gate was permanently opened in 1871.

Note the **Maison Montcalm** ⑪, 45–51 Rue des Remparts, on the corner of Rue Saint-Flavien. Originally the home of the Marquis de Montcalm, during the Battle of the Plains of Abraham, this was a very large single home until 1727. Today, the house is separated into three homes.

Across the street from the Maison Montcalm is the **Bastion des Montcalm**, a small square with views of the Old Port, Québec harbor, and the ramparts.

The **Bastion des Augustine**, located across from the Augustine Monastery at 75 Rue des Remparts, affords views of the Saint Charles River. This northern section of the fortification walls had long been neglected, because it was believed that the cliff itself provided adequate defense. However, with the American Invasion of 1775–76, this section of the wall was finally completed.

The **Palace Gate** originally stood in front of the Augustine Monastery, until it was demolished in 1871. Note also the former powder magazine in the monastery garden, which was used to supply ammunition to the northern cannon batteries.

Continuing along the ramparts, note the **Gare du Palais** train station and **Old Post Office** buildings to the left of the Old Port.

ARTILLERY PARK NATIONAL HISTORIC SITE ⑫, 2 Rue d'Auteuil, **T**:(418) 648-4205, **W**: parkscanada.gc.ca/artillerie. *Open Apr.–Oct. daily 10–5. Admission $4 for adults, $2.75 for children 6–16, children under 6 are free.*

Commemorating nearly three centuries of French, British, and Canadian military history from Québec's past, this military stronghold was used by French soldiers until 1747 and by the British Garrison after the conquest. In the 19th century, the site became a munitions factory for the Canadian Army, the first ammunitions factory in Canada, known as the Dominion Arsenal.

The **Old Foundry**, where the munitions were manufactured until 1964, houses a reception and information center offering four floors of exhibits on Québec's military history. Exhibits include a model of Québec City built between 1795 and 1810. The ruins of a powder magazine and its protective wall, as well as other archeological objects dating back to 1808, can be found on the lower level.

The **Dauphine Redoubt**, built beginning in 1712, is an interesting and imposing structure. After the conquest, the British Army constructed massive buttresses on the sides of the building to protect the masonry and prevent the vaults from collapsing. Intended as a fortified structure for troops to retreat to for safety, the building was instead used as barracks. Inside, exhibits display uniforms, paintings, and other artifacts that immerse visitors in the life of soldiers during the 18th and 19th centuries.

The **barracks** were the primary military barracks used during the French Revolution. The long stone structure built in 1750 housed armories, supply rooms, guardrooms, and prison cells.

Sample bread and scones baked fresh in the traditional outside bread oven as guides in period costume move throughout the park bringing the military establishment to life. In July and August there are also daily musket demonstrations.

At the top of the hill, at the entrance to the park, note the **Celtic Cross**, commemorating the compassion the people of Québec showed the thousands of Irish immigrants fleeing the potato famine in the 1840s. Many of the immigrants died in passage and the families of Québec adopted the orphaned children. The cross is carved from Irish blue limestone and was donated to the city by the Strokestown Park Famine Museum, Roscommon, Ireland.

Leaving the Parc de l'Artillerie, walk along Rue d'Auteuil. The **Porte Saint-Jean** was originally one of the only three gates into the city, in 1693. The gate was reinforced in 1757 and then completely replaced in 1867 with a larger gate to facilitate the increased traffic flow between the different areas of Québec. The gate was subsequently demolished again in 1867 and not rebuilt until 1936.

Created in 1879, **Porte Kent** was named for the Duchess of Kent.

After Porte Kent, leave Rue d'Auteuil and meander through **Parc de l'Esplanade**, which stretches out along the base of the fortification wall.

At 100 Rue Saint-Louis, on the corner of Rue d'Auteuil, is an **1815 Esplanade Powder Magazine**. The historical building, originally used for storing and handling gunpowder, now houses an interpretive museum that illustrates the history of the city's fortification walls.

Fortifications de Québec Centre ⑬, 100 Rue Saint-Louis, is hidden beneath the ramparts near the Saint Louis Gate. The museum features a scale model depicting various fortification projects designed for the city. **T**:*(418) 648-7016.*

Porte Saint-Louis, like the other gates, no longer controls access to the city, but provides a sort of bridge for pedestrians, using the fortification walkway, to cross over the street. Reminiscent of a castle, complete with towers, turrets and battlements, this gate was designed by Irish architect William H. Lynn in 1878. This helped to influence the prevalent château-style architecture found throughout the city.

On the corner of Rue Saint-Louis and Rue d'Auteuil, note the monument in honor of soldiers who fought the Boers War.

From Porte Saint-Louis, walk up Grande Allée to return to Battlefields Park.

Section III

DAYTRIPS AROUND
QUÉBEC CITY

The rural areas surrounding Québec City were critical for the development and growth of both the town and New France. As the burgeoning city spread on and around Cap Diamant, resources were needed to support the inhabitants: farms to provide food, shipyards to build vessels for moving supplies, and a lumber industry to support construction.

Settlers quickly moved to the outlying areas, building farms, mills, shipyards, and villages. With them, missionaries spread out to convert and incorporate the native Amerindians into the faith and culture of New France. Military strongholds were established to protect the city of Québec, as well as the other cities of New France farther along the Saint Lawrence River.

The villages of the Saint Lawrence River Valley that surround and support Québec City were the first rural areas to develop in New France. Vestiges of these supporting roles can still be found in the towns outside of Québec City, along the Beaupré Coast, and on Île d'Orléans. Today, these quaint villages, most of which maintain their original charm and character, provide additional support for the region — urban zones for city workers and tourism.

In addition to a rich history, the Beaupré Coast and Île d'Orléans are renowned for their breathtaking scenery — steep valleys, rolling hills, monumental cliffs, and the ever-present Saint Lawrence River. Farms, maintained with as much care as the day they were built, and the remnants of locally built wood ships, greet visitors along their route.

Trip 5

Sillery and Sainte-Foy

Sillery was originally settled in 1637 as a Jesuit mission to evangelize the Amerindians, but epidemic diseases and alcoholism led to its abandonment in the 1680s. With the British conquest Sillery became a popular spot for its beauty and location. British administrators, military officers, and wealthy merchants built large estates with immense English gardens.

The protected coves along the shores of Sillery were ideal for shipbuilding, and numerous shipyards were opened. For a time, the shipbuilding industry prospered as wooden ships were in great demand for supplying the British Navy during Napoleon's blockade in 1806. However, by the time Boulevard Champlain was built in 1960, running along the shore of the Saint Lawrence River, the shipyards had closed and disappeared.

The drive through Sillery could easily be named the "Heritage Estates" tour. You will be able to see some of the opulent estates, still preserved throughout this wealthy suburb, and their vast gardens. The cute town center bustles with galleries, boutiques, restaurants, and cafés.

Nearby Sainte-Foy is a busy, modern suburb of Québec, and home to Laval University.

GETTING THERE:

By Car, Sillery borders the City of Québec. Follow **Grande Allée** west, which becomes **Boulevard Laurier**.

Turn right on **Chemin Saint-Louis**.

To reach Laval University, turn right on **Rue Jean de Quen** and then right on **Boulevard Laurier**. Turn left on **Rue du Vallon** (Route 740 north) to the university.

Leaving the university, turn left on **Chemin Sainte-Foy** to Parc de la Visitation. Return along **Chemin Sainte-Foy** and turn right on **Rue du Vallon** (Route 740 south). At the end, turn right onto **Boulevard Laurier** and left onto **Rue Jean de Quen**. At the end, turn right onto **Chemin Saint-Louis** and then left onto **Avenue de Parc**.

Leave the aquarium by **Boulevard Champlain** and turn left onto **Côte de Gignac**. Turn right onto **Chemin du Foulon**.

Continue along **Chemin du Foulon** to Saint Michael's Church. Turn right on **Côte de l'Église** and then left, continuing on **Boulevard Champlain** back to Québec.

PRACTICALITIES:

Spring and summer are ideal times to visit Sillery, when the many English gardens are in bloom and spectacular.

Bureau d'Information Touristique de Sainte-Foy. 3300 Avenue des Hôtels. Open late June to mid-Oct. daily 8:30–7; mid-Oct. to late June Mon.–Sat. 9–5, Fri. 9–6, Sun. 10–4.

FOOD AND DRINK:

Montego (1460 Avenue Maguire, Sillery) Festive and colorful décor featuring "gastronomy, from California to Asia, via Italia." **T**:(418) 688-7991. $$$

Le Cochon Dingue (1326 Avenue Maguire, Sillery) In a sunny solarium, with views of the busy shopping district and great food, renowned for their breakfasts and elaborate homemade desserts. **T**:(418) 684-2013. $$$

Foccacia Café (2382 Chemin Sainte-Foy, Sainte-Foy) An innovative pasta bar concept, enabling diners to create their own dish from over 300 possible combinations. **T**:(418) 650-9449. $ and $$

La Tyrolienne (2846 Rue du Bois-Gomin, Sainte-Foy) Authentic alpine atmosphere with Swiss specialties, featuring fondue, seafood, and steaks — like dining in Switzerland without leaving Canada. **T**:(418) 651-6905. $$

LOCAL ATTRACTIONS:

Circled numbers correspond to numbers on the map.

PARC du BOIS-de-COULONGE ①, 1215 Chemin Saint-Louis, Sillery, **T**:(418) 528-0773. *Open year-round daily. Admission is free.*

Originally called Spencer Wood in the mid-19th century, the sprawling gardens were once the property of Henry Atkinson, the Governor General of the Province of Canada. A major fire destroyed the main residence in 1966, but the gardens have remained intact and thriving. At the eastern end of the park, the Saint-Denys stream cuts through a picturesque ravine. British troops were able to gain access to the Plains of Abraham by climbing through this ravine, signaling the beginning of the battle of the Plains of Abraham.

Several old buildings remain on the grounds, including the **Guardian's House**, a quaint château-style building built in 1891. The sides are covered with decorative cedar shingles, while the beautiful gardens also afford breathtaking views of the Saint Lawrence River.

VILLA BAGATELLE ②, 1563 Chemin Saint-Louis, Sillery, **T**:(418) 688-8074. *Open Mar.–Dec. Tues.–Sun. 10–5. Admission $3 per person, children under 12 are free.*

This neo-Gothic residence, built in 1848, has an exquisite British-style garden, featuring over 350 indigenous and exotic plants. The villa features temporary exhibits, and can be toured upon request.

Continuing into **Sillery** ③, stop along Chemin Saint-Louis and stroll through the bustling little town. Enjoy a break at one of the many outdoor cafés along the streets and browse in the boutiques and galleries.

DOMAINE CATARAQUI MUSÉE-JARDIN ④, 2141 Chemin Saint-Louis, Sillery, **T**:(418) 681-3010. *Open late June through Aug. daily 10–5; Sept. to late June Tues.–Sun. 10–5. Admission $5 for adults, $4 for students 12–17, children under 12 are free.*

This beautiful museum and garden, situated in a historic home built in 1851, offers art exhibits and music concerts. The estate was originally built by the wealthy businessman, Henry Burstall, atop the cliff overlooking his business on the river's shore. Today, the magnificent nine-building complex is the official residence of the Government of Québec. The main villa houses eleven exhibition halls relating the history of the estate and highlighting Québec culture. The grounds also feature a winter garden and several greenhouses. A stroll through the garden provides access to peaceful wooded areas, flowerbeds, and rock gardens, along with extensive views of the Saint Lawrence River.

In the fall, catch one of the many concerts held on the estate during the **Festival de Musique Ancienne de Sillery**.

MAISON HAMEL-BRUNEAU ⑤, 2608 Chemin Saint-Louis, Sainte-Foy, **T**:(418) 654-4325. *Open year-round Tues.–Sun. 12:30–5, Wed. 12:30–9. Admission is free.*

This quaint cottage-style house, built in 1858, features flared eaves and a low wraparound veranda. Once a private residence, the property is now home to the **Cultural Center of Sainte-Foy**, which focuses on visual arts and music and offers a varied cultural program.

Continue on Chemin Saint-Louis and turn right onto Rue Jean de Quen. Turn right onto Boulevard Laurier and then left onto Route du Vallon (Route 740).

UNIVERSITÉ LAVAL ⑥, Sainte-Foy, **T**:(418) 656-2571, **W**: ulaval.ca. *Guided tours of the campus are available upon reservation, Sept.–June. Admission is free.*

Founded in 1852, Université Laval was the first French-language Catholic university in North America. It was originally a part of the Séminaire de Québec, founded by Monseigneur de Laval in 1633. The university split and relocated to its current site in 1946.

The university, with 13 departments, 9 specialty schools and numerous research facilities, is attended by more than 40,000 students each year.

Points of interest on the campus include: the General Library in the Pavillon Jean-Charles-Bonenfant, The Geology Collection at the Pavillon Adrien-Pouliot, and the Roger Van den Hende gardens.

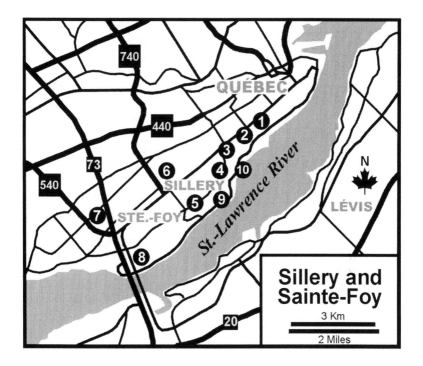

Sillery and Sainte-Foy
3 Km
2 Miles

The **Musée de Géologie** contains a large collection of minerals and fossils from around the world. With over 30,000 specimens (only one-quarter displayed at a time) this is one of the major geological collections in Québec. **T**:*(418) 656-2131. Open daily 8:30–4:30. Admission is free.*

The **Jardin Roger Van den Hende** botanical garden covers 15 acres and contains more than 5,000 plants and flowers. The garden was created in 1966 by Professor Roger Van den Hende and is used for teaching, research, and the promotion of the art of horticulture. **T**:*(418) 656-3410. Open May–Sept. daily 9–8. Admission is free.*

Follow Chemin Sainte-Foy west to the corner of Route de l'Église. Note the **Parc de la Visitation** ⑦, 801 Route de l'Église, which has the ruins of two Notre-Dame-de-Foy churches. A tower erected on the spot where the steeple once stood offers excellent views of the surrounding area and the ever-present Saint Lawrence River. The site occasionally is host to concerts and exhibits. **T**:*(418) 654-4576. Open mid-May through Oct. daily afternoons and evenings. Admission is free.*

Return back along Chemin Sainte-Foy and turn right on Rue Jean de Quen. Cross Boulevard Laurier and then turn right onto Chemin Saint-Louis. Turn left onto Avenue de Parc.

SILLERY & SAINTE-FOY   53

AQUARIUM du QUÉBEC ⑧, 1675 Avenue des Hôtels, Sainte-Foy, **T**:(418) 659-5264, **W**: *spsnq.qc.ca. Open Oct.–May 10–4, June–Sept. 10–5. Admission $15 for adults, $10 for children 6–12, $5 for children 3–5, children under 3 are free.*

This magnificent park highlights the various ecosystems of the Saint Lawrence River and Arctic. A multimedia presentation in the welcome center takes visitors on a virtual tour of the Saint Lawrence River, on land and under water. Throughout the park, the habitats of the marshland and lakes of the Saint Lawrence are represented. The Arctic habitat is home to polar bears, walrus, and seals in their natural environments. Fresh and saltwater aquariums proudly exhibit the wildlife of the Saint Lawrence River and its associated bodies of water. The park is also home to marine research facilities dedicated to studying the aquatic systems of the Saint Lawrence and to assisting the reproduction of endangered species.

The main pavillion, new in 2002, is home to over 3500 fish species. An acrylic tunnel allows visitors to become submersed in the arctic water, surrounded by the fascinating life of the Pacific Ocean and more than 600 specimens.

Follow Boulevard Champlain along the Saint Lawrence River. Turn left on Côte de Gignac and right on Chemin du Foulon.

MAISON des JÉSUITES ⑨, 2320 Chemin du Foulon, Sillery. **T**:(418) 654-0259. *Open June–Sept. Tues.–Sun. 11–5; Apr.–May and Oct.–Dec. Wed.–Sun. 1–5; Feb.–Mar. Sun. 1–5. Small suggested donation.*

This was the site of a Jesuit mission for the Indians in New France, founded by Father Paul LeJeune in 1637. Built between 1699 and 1733, it is one of Canada's oldest houses, and one of the first to be declared an historical monument in Québec Province. The first novel written in Canada, *The History of Emily Montague* by Frances Brooke, was written in this house when she occupied the residence with her husband, an Anglican bishop.

In the 17th century, the mission complex included a stone fortification wall, a chapel, priest's residence, and housing for the Aboriginal population. Through its history, the main house has served many functions, including a brewery and offices for some of the nearby shipyards. Today it houses a small museum telling the colorful history of the complex. Exhibits explain the history of Sillery, the native people, and Jesuits who settled here; and display antique furniture, archeological finds, and everyday items. The chapel ruins, a native cemetery, and gardens can still be observed on the grounds.

Continue on Chemin du Foulon. Note the old wooden houses along this road and compare them to the immense estates seen earlier in this trip. The simple houses along this road were home to the shipyard workers.

POINTE-à-PUISEAUX and SAINT-MICHEL ⑲, corner of Chemin du Foulon and Côte de l'Église, **T**:(418) 527-3390. *Open year-round daily 8:30–8. Admission is free.*

This Gothic-style Catholic church was built in 1852. Five paintings from the famous Desjardins Collection (created in Paris by Abbot Louis-Phillipe Desjardins, former chaplain for the Ursuline Sisters) are hanging inside the church. Originally from churches in Paris, the paintings were sold after the French Revolution and brought to Québec by Abbot Desjardins.

In front of the church, a wide terrace with several beautiful white marble statues affords stunning views of the Saint Lawrence River.

Leaving Saint-Michel's Church, turn right on Côte de l'Église and proceed downhill. Turn left on Boulevard Champlain and continue back to Québec.

Statue at Pointe à Puiseaux

SILLERY & SAINTE-FOY 55

Trip 6

Charlesbourg

One of the first permanent settlements in Canada inhabited by Europeans, this area was founded by the Jesuits in 1626. With the growth of Québec City, Charlesbourg became one of its principal suburbs. Rapid expansion and modernization have erased most of the town's historical landmarks and charm.

Fortunately, a central section of the city was steadfastly protected and preserved. Known as the Trait-Carré, this historical neighborhood, with narrow tree-lined streets, still boasts quaint old homes.

Not far from Charlesbourg, the village of Wendake has maintained all of its Old World charm. The Huron-Wendat reserve gives visitors a trip into the past with the traditional village and old town.

GETTING THERE:

Charlesbourg borders Québec City to the northwest.

By Car, take **Route 73** north out of the city to **Exit 150**. Follow **Rue 80th** to **Boulevard Henri-Bourassa**.

Park at the **Moulin de Jésuites**, on the corner of Rue 80th and Boulevard Henri-Bourassa, where you can find a map of the historic walking tour.

Leaving the Moulin de Jésuites, turn right and continue along **Boulevard Henri-Bourassa**. Turn left on **Rue de la Faune** and the zoo will be on your left.

From the zoo, follow **Rue de la Faune**, cross Route 73. The road becomes **Boulevard de la Rivière**. Turn right on **Rue Chef Max Gros-Louis**, then left on **Rue Loup**, and right onto **Rue Stanislas-Kosca**, to reach the Traditional Huron Village.

Leaving the village, return along Rue Stanislas-Kosca and Rue Loup, to **Rue Chef Max Gros-Louis**. Turn right on **Rue du Buisson** and then left onto **Rue Cloutier**. Park the car and walk through the village.

Leaving the parking lot, turn right on **Rue Cloutier**, then right on **Rue Théophile-Gros-Louis** and a quick left onto **Rivière du Serpent**. At the end turn right onto **Boulevard Maurice-Bastien**, cross the bridge, and continue to the intersection of **Route 573**. Take **Route 573** south to **Route 40** east, returning to Québec.

PRACTICALITIES:

Bureau d'Information Touristique, 7960 Boulevard Henri-Bourassa, located in the Moulin des Jésuites building, Charlesbourg, **T**:(418) 624-7720. Open mid-June to mid-Aug. daily 10–7; mid-Aug. to mid-June Sat.–Sun. 10–5.

Centre d'Information Culturelle et Touristique. 10 Rue Chef Alexandre-Duchesneau, at the Maison Aroüanne, Wendake. **T**:(418) 845-1241.

FOOD AND DRINK:

L'Amarelle Restaurant Traiteur (8000 Boulevard Henri Bourassa, Charlesbourg) Affordable, comfortable, and gourmet, featuring Amarelle specialties such as ostrich, game, and seafood. **T**:(418) 627-5526. $$ and $$$

NEKBARRE (575 Rue Stanislas-Kosca, Wendake, at the Huron Village) Traditional native Huron dishes are served, featuring caribou, trout, and deer, in a unique setting. **T**:(418) 842-4308. $$$

Le Piolet (103 Rue Racine, Loretteville, not far from Wendake) Homemade meals and sandwiches. **T**:(418) 842-7462. $$

LOCAL ATTRACTIONS:

Circled numbers correspond to numbers on the map.

Charlesbourg's Trait Carré ① is a historic neighborhood in the heart of Charlesbourg. The Jesuits implemented this unique residential zoning as a means of bringing settlers together and enabling quick organization of defenses in case of attack. A walking tour allows visitors to see the star-shaped layout of the area, dating back to 1660, and admire the French and Québécois architecture, typical of the 17th and 18th centuries. Tours start at the Moulin des Jésuites. Maps are available for self-guided tours or join a guided tour.

The **Moulin des Jésuites** ②, 7960 Boulevard Henri-Bourassa, is one of the three mills built by the Jesuits in Charlesbourg under the French Regime, around 1740. This is the oldest building in Charlesbourg. The mill offers interpretive exhibits and activities that address the history of the region and the role of the Jesuits in the development of Québec. **T**:*(418) 624-7720. Open mid-Aug. to mid-June Sat.–Sun. 10–5; mid-June to mid-Aug. daily 10–7. Admission is free.*

Maison Pierre-Lefebvre, 7985 Trait-Carré East, built in 1846, is a common wood home of the era. Restored in 1977, the house now features a gallery and cultural center. **T**:*(418) 623-1877. Open July–Aug. Wed.–Sun. 1–9; Sept.–June Thurs.–Fri. 7–9, Sat. 1–5, Sun. 11–5. Admission is free.*

In the center of the old Charlesbourg neighborhood, note the municipal library housed in the old **Saint Charles College**, built in 1903, and the **Bon Pasteur Convent**, built in 1883.

The **Église Saint-Charles-Borromée**, 135 Rue 80th West, dates back to 1828 and still retains its original design. The splendid interior was completed in 1833. Note the triumphal arch and the statues dating back to 1742. Influenced by English Palladian movement, the church features two steeples, an imposing

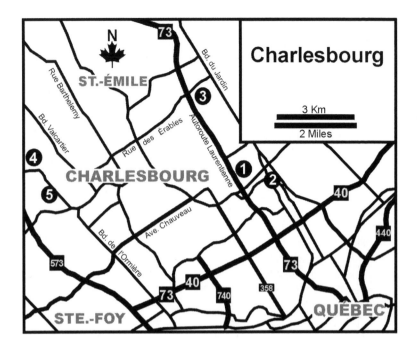

façade, and an unusual arrangement of windows. **T**:*(418) 624-7720. Open for guided tour by appointment only.*

Maison Ephraïm-Bédard, 7655 Chemin Samuel, was built early in the 19th century. The descendants of several of Québec's pioneer families have lived in this house, a typical example of the average farmer's home in Charlesbourg in the 18th century. The house was completely restored in 1988 and opened as a historical interpretation center. **T**:*(418) 628-8278. Open mid-June to mid-Aug. Wed.–Sun. 12–7; mid-Aug. to mid-June Tues.–Thurs. 1:30–4. Admission is free.*

JARDIN ZOOLOGIQUE du QUÉBEC ③, 9300 Rue de la Faune, **T**:(418) 659-5264 or 1-888-622-0312, **W**: spsnq.qc.ca. *Open daily Oct.–May 10–4, June–Sept. 10–5. Admission $10 for adults, $8 for children 6–12, $3 for children 3–5, children under 3 are free.*

Park visitors are treated to an impressive collection of animals from around the world, boasting over 750 specimens. Beautiful gardens, with fountains, ponds, and marshes adorn the park. Rare and exotic birds and primates are a delight. The tropical rainforests of Southeast Asia, Indonesia, and Australia are home to birds, reptiles, and small animals, including fishing cats and tree-dwelling kangaroos. In the African exhibit admire the acrobats of the chimpanzees. A vast North American forest, with aviaries and bodies of water, houses deer, bear, and lynx.

VILLAGE des HURONS ④, 575 Rue Stanislas-Kosca, **T**:(418) 842-4308, **W**: huron-wendat.qc.ca. *Open year-round daily 9–5 for guided tours. Admission $9 for adults, $7 for children 13–17, $5 for children 7–12, children 6 and under are free.*

This small traditional Huron village is both interesting and exciting. Friendly and informative guides, in traditional costume, welcome all visitors to experience their culture and heritage. Visitors are greeted with a traditional welcome dance. There is also an opportunity to try your hand with the bow and arrow.

Continue on to **Wendake** ⑤. A group of about 300 Huron-Wendat, originally native throughout Ontario and Québec and forced to leave their land by the Iroquois, settled near Québec City in 1697. They set up their village by a small waterfall on the Saint Charles River, which they named Kahir Kouba. Renowned for their negotiating and commercial skills they quickly adapted, becoming a modern and successful community.

This charming, tightly settled, village is an Amerindian Reserve. Park the car off Rue Cloutier and wander the winding, narrow streets. Many of the houses in the reserve are historically significant.

The **Église Notre-Dame-de-Lorette** is the first Amerindian Catholic chapel. The earliest church, completed in 1730, was destroyed by fire in 1862; the current church was built at the same site in 1865. Inside the chapel is a small museum depicting some of the history and legends of the tribe. The chapel also displays valuable artifacts left behind by the Jesuit missionaries.

Across from the chapel, **Maison Aroüanne**, 10 Rue Chef-Alexandre-Duchesneau, is home to the Huron-Wendat Cultural Center. Exhibits, arts, crafts, and videos unveil the history and culture of the Huron-Wendat people. **T**:*(418) 845-1241. Open May–Sept. daily 9–4; Oct.–Apr. by reservation. Admission is free.*

The **Parc de la Chute et de la Falaise Kabir Kouba** is not far from the church. Several hiking trails lead along the top of the cliff, overlooking the Saint Charles River and the Kabir Kouba falls. This is a picturesque and peaceful stop to end your tour, before heading back to the busy city.

Trip 7

Beaupré Coast

The area known as the Beaupré Coast consists of a narrow stretch of land squeezed between the Canadian Shield and the Saint Lawrence River, whose unique location gives it a rich and rugged texture. The name was taken from Jacques Cartier, who exclaimed upon seeing the meadows beside the river "Quel beau pré!" (What a fine meadow!).

Samuel de Champlain established his first farm on this fertile land in 1626. Settlers soon followed in the 1630s and established the first rural parishes of New France along this coast. The earliest maintained road in the New Colony was built from Beauport to Saint-Joachim and dubbed Chemin du Roy or King's Road.

This scenic drive winds past picturesque farms, quaint cottages, and historical villages settled during the French Regime, while offering sweeping views of the countryside, Île d'Orléans, and the Saint Lawrence River. If you are passing through in the evening you are likely to spot many families enjoying the fresh air and tranquil countryside while relaxing on their front porches.

GETTING THERE:

Beauport borders Québec City to the east.

By Car, take **Route 40** east from Québec, using the exit for **Avenue Saint-David** in Beauport. At the end, turn left and follow **Chemin Royal** to **Avenue Royale**.

Find parking in the **Bourg du Fargy** area and explore Old Beauport on foot.

Leave Beauport by **Avenue Royale** (Route 360). Follow Avenue Royale all the way to Sainte-Anne-de-Beaupré.

In Sainte-Anne, turn right on **Rue Régina**. Turn left onto **Boulevard Sainte-Anne** (Route 138) and park in the large parking lot behind the basilica.

Leaving the parking lot, turn right onto **Route 138** and follow that back to Québec.

PRACTICALITIES:

Bureau d'Information Touristique de Beauport, 550 Avenue Royale, Beauport. **T**:(418) 666-2325 or 1-800-351-4095, **W**: tourisme.ville.beauport.qc. ca. Open June daily 10–5; July 10–7; Aug. 10–6; early Sept. 10–5. Closed the rest of the year.

Bureau d'Information Touristique de la Côte-de-Beaupré, 9630 Boulevard Sainte-Anne, Sainte-Anne-de-Beaupré. **T**:(418) 827-5281. Open late June through Aug. and late Dec. through Feb. daily 9–9; Sept. to late Dec. and Mar. to late June daily 9–8.

When you arrive in Sainte-Anne-de-Beaupré, park in the large lot behind the basilica, on Route 138, and tour the town on foot.

FOOD AND DRINK:

Restaurant du Manoir Montmorency (2490 Avenue Royale, Beauport) With a spectacular view of the falls, a sophisticated atmosphere, and gourmet Québec cuisine. **T**:(418) 663-3330. $$$+

Au Sommet de la Chute (5014 Avenue Royale, Boischatel) Breakfast and lunch, fast and cheap, near the top of Montmorency Falls. **T**:(418) 822-1422. $

Auberge Les Volets Verts (9926 Avenue Royale, Sainte-Anne de-Beaupré) A comfortable little café on the first floor of an inn, serving home-cooked regional favorites. **T**:(418) 827-8170. $$

Marie Antoinette (9749 Boulevard Sainte-Anne, Sainte-Anne de-Beaupré) Family dining for breakfast, lunch, and dinner with roasted chicken, ribs, pizza, sandwiches and much more. **T**:(418) 827-3446. $$

SUGGESTED TOUR:

Circled numbers correspond to numbers on the map.

Beauport ① has played a number of roles in the development of the Greater Québec City area. Originally founded in 1634 by Robert Gifford, who built an enormous fortified manor, mill, and village, the town was primarily an agricultural settlement. In the 19th century it grew into an important industrial area, later evolving into a suburban community for Québec City.

The historic center of Beauport, **Bourg du Fargy**, is characterized by its "zigzag" arrangement of homes. The neighborhood was originally built as a fortified village in the 17th century.

Maison Bellanger-Girardin, 600 Avenue Royale, dates from 1673. Originally built with timber, the house was rebuilt with stone between 1727 and 1735. Today it houses a permanent exhibit on the historical district of Beauport, the town's founding families, and its architecture. *T:(418) 666-2199. Open year-round Tues.–Sun. 10–5. Admission is free.*

Note the "zigzagging" **Edwardian style houses** that climb up Rue du Convent, offering great contrast to the distinctly French architecture around them.

In the center of the historic district stands the imposing **Nativité-de-Notre-Dame Parish Church**. The current church was built in 1916 using the remains of the walls from the original church, which was destroyed by fire. Note the **presbytery**, next to the church — a stone structure built in 1903 in the French Provincial style.

Near the church you will see the **Couvent de Beauport**, built in 1886, with turreted façades and an elaborate mansard roof topped by a statue of the Virgin Mary.

*PARC de la CHUTE MONTMORENCY ②, 2490 Avenue Royale, Beauport, **T**:(418) 663-3330, **W**: *chutemontmorency.qc.ca/index_en.html. Open Apr.–Oct. daily 8:30–6, Oct.–Apr. 10–4. Parking $7.50. Cable car: Adults $5 one-way, $7.50 round-trip per person, children 6–16 $3 one-way, $4.50 round-trip, children under 6 ride free.*

The Montmorency River, flowing from the Laurentians, must make a large drop before reaching the Saint Lawrence River. This spectacular waterfall, 1½ times higher than Niagara Falls, is an amazing sight year-round. In the winter, the spray from the falls freezes, creating a cone of ice sometimes reaching 30 meters (98 feet) high, known as the sugarloaf.

In the early 19th century the falls were recognized for their industrial and economic potential. A mill was built at their base in 1811. In 1884 a power plant was added to the site, becoming the first hydroelectric plant in the world to transmit power for long distances. Eventually, a second power plant and a cotton mill were added. Today, however, there are only a few remains of these industries found at the park.

At the top of the cliff, overlooking the falls is the **Manoir Montmorency** with panoramic terraces, a café-bar, and a gourmet restaurant. The elegant estate rests on the site where Sir Frederick Haldimand, governor of Québec in 1780, made his home.

From the manor house, a cliff-side boardwalk leads along the edge to the top of the falls for breathtaking views and the suspension bridge spanning the top of the falls. Across from the manor, a cable car whisks visitors to the lower park. Walkways and trails lead around the falls and river. Close to the bottom is a masterpiece of rainbows, the sun reflecting in billows of spray.

Panoramic stairs scale the side of the gravely cliff to a park at the top for more views, a playground, walking trails, and the bridge crossing the fault gorge.

Don't miss the smaller **Bridal Veil Falls** west of the cable-car terminal.

Leaving Montmorency Falls, turn right and continue along Avenue Royale. Note the small **processional chapels** beside the road as you drive through l'Ange-Gardien, one of the oldest villages on the Beaupré Coast. The chapels, built during the French Regime around 1750, served as altars during the Corpus Christi processions.

Avenue Royale is lined with well-preserved cottages and picturesque farms as it passes through l'Ange-Gardien and Château-Richer.

CENTRE d'INTERPRÉTATION de la CÔTE-de-BEAUPRÉ ③, 7007 Avenue Royale, Château-Richer. **T**:(418) 824-3677. *Open June–Oct. daily 10–5;*

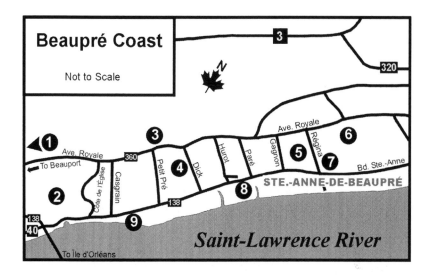

Nov.–May Mon.–Fri. 10–4:30. Admission $5 for adults, children under 16 are free.

Situated in the attic of Moulin du Petit-Pré, built in 1695, the center offers audiovisual presentations and exhibits on the geology, culture and history of the Beaupré Coast. Exhibits include interactive games, models, music and photographs. An evolutionary model illustrates geological changes in the region, from Amerindian times to current day.

Admire the vineyard and views at the **Vignoble Moulin du Petit-Pré** as well. A small shop offers a variety of regional products, gourmet foods, and wine accessories. Wine tasting and information about the vineyard are also available. **T**:*(418) 824-4411,* **W***: moulin-petitpre.com. Open mid-June to late Oct. daily 9–6.*

For a tasty and interesting break, stop at the **Érablière Sucre d'art**, 8515 Avenue Royale, Château-Richer. This traditional maple sugar shack introduces visitors to the art of making maple products. The site features certified organic maple syrup. Tasting is available. **T**:*(418) 824-5626. Open May to mid-Oct. daily; mid-Oct. through Apr. upon reservation. Admission and tasting are free.*

Make a stop at **Chez Marie**, 8706 Avenue Royale, Château-Richer, for local and regional treats and souvenirs.

Nearby is **Château-Richer** ④. A fortified castle, complete with a tower prison, was built on the hillside above the Saint Lawrence River in 17th century and named Château-Richer after a priory in France. During the British conquest the château was all but destroyed, and was finally demolished around 1860.

The **Église La-Visitation-de-Notre-Dame**, built in 1866, is perched high on the hill, watching over the charming village below. On a clear day, the view from the church takes in Cap Tourmente.

Note the quarry, carved out of the hillside above the town. Limestone from this quarry was used in the 18th and 19th centuries for many of the buildings in Québec City.

The **Atelier Paré Économusée des Légends**, 9269 Avenue Royale, displays a collection of more than 15 murals illustrating some of the most famous legends in Québec. The artists in this woodcarving museum and workshop welcome visitors to see their handiwork and watch them in action. **T**:*(418) 827-3992. Open mid-May to mid-Oct. daily 9–5:30; mid-Oct. to mid-May Mon.– Fri. 1–4, Sat.–Sun. 10–4. Admission is free.*

Continue on to **Sainte-Anne-de-Beaupré** ⑤. This small village is a world-renowned religious pilgrimage site, famous for the legendary miracles said to have taken place here. Tradition has it that sailors, who in 1658 prayed to Sainte-Anne, the Virgin Mary's mother, were saved from drowning during a storm on the Saint Lawrence River. The Catholic Church built on the site was dedicated to Sainte-Anne. It is also said that during construction of the church, one of the workers was miraculously cured of lumbago. As word of the miracles spread, the small village quickly became a pilgrimage site for people in need of divine help.

The **"Way of the Cross"** garden, on the hillside, is lined with life-sized bronze figures, cast in France between 1913 and 1946. On many evenings, candlelight processions take place on the hillside.

The **Memorial Chapel**, on Avenue Royale, built in 1878, displays a collection of remains from the old chapel including a bell tower dating back to 1696, a tabernacle from the altar dating back to 1700, and the tomb. The chapel commemorates the third Church of Saint-Anne that welcomed pilgrims from 1676 to 1876. **T**:*(418) 827-3781. Open May–Nov. daily 8–5. Admission is free.*

Scala Santa, beside the Memorial Chapel, is a beautiful white chapel built in 1891 with a stairway commemorating the one used by Christ to meet Pontius Pilate before his condemnation. *Open May to mid-Sept. daily 8–4:30. Admission is free.*

The **Musée Edison du Phonographe**, 9812 Avenue Royale, is an interesting museum dedicated to the invention of the phonograph, in 1877, by Thomas Edison. The museum has more than 200 cylinder phonographs on display, as well as three tin-foil phonographs dating back to 1878. Also on exhibit are a three-cylinder jukebox, a wax cylinder phonograph alarm clock, and cylinder recordings of celebrities such as Thomas Edison, Theodore Roosevelt, Sarah Bernhardt, and Pope Leo XIII. **T**:*(418) 827-5957,* **W**: *phono.org/beaupre-en.html. Open May–Sept. daily 10–6; Oct.–Apr. by reservation. Admission $4 for adults, $2 for children 7–12, children 6 and under are free.*

The **Musée de Sainte-Anne**, next to the basilica, illustrates the history of devotion to Sainte-Anne and memorializes moving stories of pilgrimages to the shrine since its origin. **T**:*(418) 827-6873 ext. 223. Open mid-Apr. to mid-Oct. daily 10–5. Admission $2 per person, children under 12 are free.*

BASILIQUE SAINTE-ANNE-de-BEAUPRÉ ⑥, 10018 Avenue Royale, **T**:(418) 827-3781, **W**: ssadb.qc.ca/en/index.htm. *Open year-round daily 8:30-4:30. Admission is free.*

A popular pilgrimage site, with more than 1½ million visitors each year, the original basilica was destroyed by fire in 1922. Reconstructed and covered with granite in the medieval style, the current structure is striking in size and beauty. Its interior features 240 stained-glass windows, a beautiful rose window, mosaics, and a number of artistic religious artifacts.

Take a peek at the **Immaculate Conception Chapel**, dedicated to the Virgin Mary. The rounded ceilings and bluish light give the chapel a peaceful, warm feeling.

The **Tomb of Father Alfred Pampalon** is said to help visitors with drug and alcohol dependencies.

Admire the **Pietà**, which is said to be an exact replica of the original sculpture by Michelangelo, housed in Saint Peter's Basilica in Rome.

CYCLORAMA de JÉRUSALEM ⑦, 8 Rue Régina, **T**:(418) 827-3101, **W**: cyclorama.com. *Open late May–Oct. daily 9–6; July–Aug. daily 8–8; Closed Nov.–Apr. Admission $7 for adults, $4 for children 6–15, children 5 and under are free.*

This fascinating panorama, the largest in the world, was painted in Munich, Germany from 1878 to 1882 and has been on display in Sainte-Anne-de-Beaupré since 1895. The painting is 14 meters (45 feet) high and 110 meters (365 feet) in circumference. The size and exquisite detail gives viewers, standing from a central viewing platform, a seemingly three-dimensional look at Jerusalem in biblical times.

MUSÉE de l'ABEILLE, HONEY ECONOMUSEUM ⑧, 8862 Boulevard Sainte-Anne, **T**:(418) 824-4411, **W**: musee-abeille.com/horaire.html. *Open July–Oct. daily 9–6; Nov.–June daily 9–5. Admission to the museum and boutique are free. Bee-safari is $2 per person over 12.*

A museum with interesting displays and activities educates visitors on the evolution of bee-keeping techniques. Watch the fascinating glassed-in hives, with millions of bees dancing for each other and making honey. On the "Bee Safari" an experienced beekeeper leads you on an adventure through a working bee farm.

End your tour with a special treat from **Chocolaterie de la Côte** ⑨, 6600 Boulevard Sainte-Anne, l'Ange-Gardien. **T**:*(418) 822-1666.*

Trip 8

Lévis

The steep southern shore of the Saint Lawrence River was taken by British General Wolfe in 1759 with the intent to bombard Québec City. In 1826, Henry Caldwell founded a town on that site, originally named Ville d'Aubigny. This was renamed in 1861 for the Duc de Lévis, who defeated the British at Sainte-Foy in 1760.

Development of the city was rapid toward the end of the 19th century with the building of railway lines in 1854. As there were still no tracks on the north shore of the river, Lévis took over some of the shipping business for Québec City, making it the center for timber exports to England. Today the city is known for its shipbuilding and lumber industry.

Lévis is also widely know as the birthplace of Alphonse Desjardins and headquarters for the Caisse Populaire Desjardins, the first credit union in North America. Desjardins implemented European banking practices, adapted to local needs and conditions, to form the widely popular cooperative savings and loan.

GETTING THERE:

By Ferry, on foot or by car, departing from **10 Rue des Traversiers**, daily, every 30 minutes during the day and every hour in the evening. **T**:(418) 644-3704.

By Foot, take the **ferry** from Québec to Lévis. The **Navette** tourist bus connects all of the major sites throughout the city. Minor sites are easily accessible by foot from one of the main bus stops.

PRACTICALITIES:

Tourist Information Office, 5995 Rue Saint-Laurent, at the ferry station. **T**:(418) 838-6026, **W**: ville.levis.qc.ca

The Navette runs from late June through Aug., Thurs.–Sun. 10–5; last two weeks of July daily. Tickets are $6 per person and include return ferry trip.

FOOD AND DRINK:

Restaurant l'Escalier (610 Rue Saint-Laurent) Quiet and charming, serving regional and gourmet cuisine. **T**:(418) 835-1865. $$$

L'Optionnel (123 Côte du Passage) Serving tasty vegetarian and vegan dishes beside an inviting fireplace or on a breezy terrace. **T**:(418) 833-0243. $$ and $$$

Café Gallerie de Vinci (4 Avenue Bégin) A casual café with a unique and thoroughly charming atmosphere — great for a snack, coffee, or light meal. **T**:(418) 838-4848. $$

LOCAL ATTRACTIONS:

Circled numbers correspond to numbers on the map.

Begin in the **Vieux-Lévis Business District** ①. Spanning several blocks beside Côte du Passage, the commercial heart of Old Lévis is thriving with businesses, restaurants, pubs, galleries, and boutiques.

Nearby is the **Centre d'Art de Lévis** ②. Resting beside the busy business district, along Rue Wolfe, is the city's cultural center. Stroll through **Parc Capitaine-Bernier**, a quiet green space perfect for relaxing or enjoying a picnic.

L'Anglicane, built in 1850, was originally an Anglican Church, but has since been converted into a concert and theater hall. The old-fashioned, intimate atmosphere and excellent acoustics make this a popular music hall.

Galerie Louise-Carrier, formerly the rectory for the church, later became a residence for painter Louise Carrier. The gallery displays a permanent collection of art works by regional artists. **T**:(418) 838-6001. *Open year-round Tue.-Fri. 11-5, Sat.-Sun. 1-5. Admission is free.*

MAISON ALPHONSE-DESJARDINS ③, 6 Rue du Mont-Marie, **T**: (418) 835-2090. *Open year-round Mon.–Fri. 10–12 and 1–4:30, Sat.–Sun. 12–5. Admission is free.*

The white clapboard house, built between 1882 and 1884, was the home of Alphonse and Dorimène Desjardins for nearly 40 years. The first branch of the Desjardins Savings and Loan bank was run from this home. An audiovisual presentation and exhibits introduce visitors to Alphonse Desjardins, describing his life and the beginnings of his bank.

Carré Déziel ④, off Rue Guénette, is an interesting group of buildings, with a monument to Joseph-David Déziel, the first parish priest of Lévis and founder of Lévis College. In the square, note the **Église Notre-Dame-de-la-Victoire** built in 1851. This church encompasses both French and English classical styles. On the grounds is a plaque marking the location of the English cannons used by Wolfe to bomb Québec City.

COLLÈGE de LÉVIS BIBLIOTHÈQUE PIERRE-GEORGES-ROY ⑤, 7 Rue Monseigneur Gosselin, **T**:(418) 838-4122. *Open year-round, Tue.–Fri. 1–9, Sat. 11–5, Sun. 1–5. Admission is free.*

The public library is housed in the college's former church. Admire the original structure of the chapel, restored and preserved, with the high vaulted ceilings, pillars, arches, and pristine white walls.

Église Saint-Joseph-de-Lauzon ⑥, Rue Saint-Joseph, built in 1673, is the

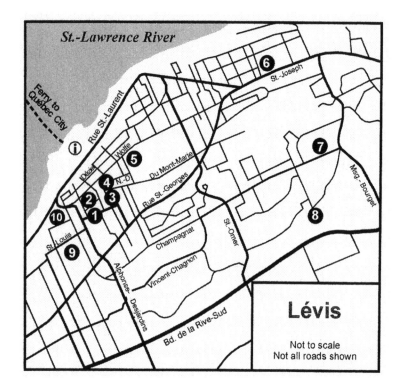

oldest parish church in Québec City's south-shore area. The original church was destroyed by fire in 1830 but was quickly replaced by the current church. Note the two processional chapels at either side of the church, dating back to 1789 and 1822.

Parc de la Paix ⑦, at the corner of Rue Monseigneur Bourget and Rue Champagnat, has an observation point affording excellent views of the river. An impressive Voodoo CF-101 plane is on display at one end of the park.

FORT NO. 1 ⑧, 41 Chemin du Gouvernement, **T**:(418) 835-5182, **W**: pc.qc.ca/levy. *Open mid-May through Aug. 10–5; Sept. 1–4. Admission $3.50 for adults, $2 for children 6–16, children under 6 are free.*

One of the three individual forts integrated into the fortification system of Québec, Fort No. 1 was built between 1865 and 1872. The British erected the fort in order to defend against the American invaders, should they attempt to take Québec via the railway linking Maine and Lévis. Any threat of such an attack faded in 1871 with the signing of the Treaty of Washington. The fort served as a munitions warehouse during World Wars I and II. It was later abandoned and finally restored in the 1970s.

Fort Number 1

A multimedia presentation introduces visitors to the history of the fort and highlights some of the architectural innovations in its construction. Explore the mysterious tunnels and blockhouses, then climb the embankments for an excellent view of the city. The fort hosts a wide range of activities throughout the day to entertain and thrill visitors of all ages.

Manège Militaire de Lévis ⑨, 10 Rue de l'Arsenal, **T**:(418) 835-0340, is a medieval-looking building erected in 1911 for the military. Today it houses an interesting museum that tells the history of the Régiment de la Chaudière.

Terrasse de Lévis ⑩, Rue William-Tremblay, affords a spectacular view of Québec City's lower and upper towns and the Citadelle, with perhaps the best view of Château Frontenac available. The Saint Lawrence River and the Laurentian mountains are also spectacular sites. The terrace was built during the Great Depression and inaugurated by George VI and Queen Elizabeth in 1939.

Trip 9

Île d'Orléans

The indigenous peoples of the area named this island Minigo, "bewitched," because they considered it to be the home of the spirit world. When Jacques Cartier first arrived on the island it was covered with wild vines, so he called it Île Bacchus. This was soon renamed to Île d'Orléans in honor of the Duc d'Orléans, son of King François I. Under the French Regime the land was parceled out in strips running along the length of the island and giving each parish optimal access to the river.

Development of the island was essentially stopped in 1970 when the government of Québec designated the entire island a historical district. Considerable expanses of farmland still stretch across the center of the island, producing berries, apples, and vegetables.

This peaceful green island is the largest historic area in Québec, still exuding Old World charm at every turn. The island is a feast for the senses with picturesque scenery, fresh air, natural wonders, and fabulous places to eat and relax. Local weavers, painters, and blacksmiths preserve traditional handicrafts, while fresh produce is sold at street-side farm stands.

GETTING THERE:

By Car, Île d'Orléans is 10 km (6 miles) northeast of Québec City. Follow **Route 138** or **Route 40** out of Québec City to Beauport. Take the **bridge** across the channel to the island.

At the top of the hill, by the tourist information office, turn right on **Chemin Royal**. Follow this road all the way around the island — it will change names as you move between villages.

PRACTICALITIES:

The **Tourist Information Office** is located at 490 Côte du Pont, soon after you cross the bridge. **T**:(418) 828-9411, **W**: iledorleans.com. Open late June through Aug., daily 9–7; Sept. to late June, Mon.–Fri. 9–5.

The best way to experience this island is to stop often, stroll through the historic villages, and meander through the many boutiques and galleries.

FOOD AND DRINK:

Buffet d'Orléans (1025 Route Prévost, Saint-Pierre) Touted to be the "best food on the island" since 1962, featuring traditional French Canadian, Québécois, and local dishes. **T**:(418) 828-0013. $$

Le Moulin de Saint-Laurent (754 Chemin Royal, Saint Laurent) Situated in an historic stone flour mill, serving gourmet regional cuisine with local produce. **T**:(418) 629-3888 or 1-888-629-3888. $$$

La Crêpe Cochonne (3963 Chemin Royal, Sainte-Famille) Café serving light meals, dinner and dessert crêpes, sandwiches, bagels, and salads, all with a view of the river. **T**:(418) 829-3656. $$

Les Ancêtres de la Petite Canadienne (391 Chemin Royal, Saint-Pierre) Traditional Québec country cuisine, mixed grill, and seafood. **T**:(418) 828-2718. $$$

SUGGESTED TOUR:

Circled numbers correspond to numbers on the map.

Begin at **Sainte-Pétronille** ①. Resting at the westernmost end of the island, known to locals as the "tip of the island," the smallest parish on the island was founded in 1870. This is the site of the island's first community, settled in 1648, long before the town became a parish. A mission was established at the point of the island welcoming Hurons in search of refuge. However, with ongoing Iroquois attacks, the mission was relocated to the opposite end of the island. The village did not begin to form as a community until the middle of the 19th century when it became a popular resort destination.

Vignoble de Sainte-Pétronille, 1A Chemin Royal, offers wine tasting in a picturesque setting. **T**:*(418) 828-9554.*

LES SOURCES d'ART & VITALITÉ ②, 41C Chemin Royal, Sainte-Pétronille, **T**:(418) 828-0569, **W**: art-vitality.com. *Open year-round daily 3–7 by appointment.*

This delightful sculpture garden is situated in the private gardens of the artist Gustin Keser and his wife. Bronze sculptures of fluid figures dance and do acrobats around the garden. Among the collection are the artist's own works and those of several of his sculptor friends. Large polyester statues move on water and in the air, bringing the exhibit to life.

The **Church of Sainte-Pétronille**, built in 1871, with its single towering spire is worth a look. Nearby is a convent built in 1875, and a presbytery as well.

Turn right onto Rue Horatio-Walker. **Maison Horatio-Walker**, (11 and 13 Rue Horatio-Walker) was home and studio to British-born painter Horatio Walker between 1904 and 1938.

As you pass through the quaint town, rounding the tip of the island, consider stopping for a treat at **Chocolateire de l'Île d'Orléans**, 150 Chemin du Bout-de-

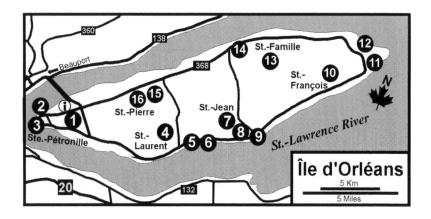

l'Île, which features homemade goodies such as chocolates and ice cream. T:*(418) 828-2250.*

Turn right onto Chemin du Quai. **La Goéliche** ③, 27 Chemin du Quai, built in 1880, is a massive Victorian hotel on the shores of the Saint Lawrence River.

Stroll around the wharf, which has several interpretation panels, and drink in the view of the river.

Before entering the next village you will pass **Club de Golf Orléans**, 246 Chemin du Bout-de-l'Île, the oldest golf course in North America.

Continue on to **Saint-Laurent** ④. This village, founded in 1679, has been traditionally known as the maritime center of the island, owning to its successful shipbuilding industry in the 19th century. At one time, about 20 family-owned shipyards spread out along the river shores, producing flat-bottomed boats called *chaloupes.* The boats were the primary means of transportation for islanders until the construction of the bridge in 1935. Traces of the abandoned shipyards and defunct industry can still be found along the river. The island's only marina, accommodating up to 130 boats, is in Saint-Laurent.

Maison Gendreau, 2387 Chemin Royal, was built in 1720. This beautiful residence is notable for its steep roof and unusual double row of dormer windows.

The **Forge à Pique-Assaut**, 2200 Chemin Royal, has traditional black-smithing demonstrations. Watch the artisans at work and take a guided tour of this preserved old blacksmith shop. T:*(418) 828-9300. Open June–Oct. daily 9–5; Nov.–June Sat.–Sun. 9–5.*

Nearby is **Parc Maritime** ⑤, 120 Chemin de la Chalouperie, T:(418) 828-9672. *Open June–Sept. 10–5, Oct.–May by reservation. Admission is free.*

This small park illustrates the history and craft of making the small wooden boats common on the island. Take a stroll along the river's edge, watch crafts-men building and sanding boats, and admire the model ships in the museum.

The **Église Saint-Laurent** ⑥, built in 1860, presides over the center of the village, beside the marina. Nearby, note the charming **processional chapel**. Both buildings have interpretive panels relating their history and the history of the parish. Also check out the **Exposition d'Art Religieux,** which has a fine collection of religious art and artifacts.

The **Moulin Gosselin**, 754 Chemin Royal, is a beautiful 18th-century stone flourmill that has been converted into a fine restaurant. The rugged **Chute du Moulin** provides a scenic backdrop for the mill, the restaurant, or just strolling the grounds.

Continue on to **Saint-Jean** ⑦. This village, founded by Monsignor Laval in 1679, has a long-standing maritime tradition. From its first days, the town has been a favorite of local seafaring pilots and navigators, who erected handsome homes overlooking the Saint Lawrence River.

Saint-Jean has a pleasant, long stretch of **beach**, popular with locals and visitors alike.

MANOIR MAUVIDE-GENEST ⑧, 1451 Chemin Royal, **T**:(418) 829-2630. *Open mid-June through Aug. daily 10–5; Sept. to mid-Oct. Tues.–Sun. 11–5, guided tours every half-hour. Admission $5 for adults, $2 for children 12–16, children under 12 are free.*

This French Regime manor house was built in 1734 by Jean Mauvide, surgeon to the King. The beautiful stone house has a coat of white roughcast in the traditional Norman style. By the middle of the 18th century Mauvide had amassed a large fortune through business ventures in the Caribbean. He used the money to purchase a large portion of land along the southern part of Île d'Orléans, building a large estate. Mauvide later sold the estate to his son-in-law.

In 1926, the property was purchased by Judge Camille Pouliot who restored it, adding a summer kitchen and chapel. Today the manor is still considered one of the finest examples of rural New France architecture. The house is now a museum illustrating the life of a landowner during the French Regime. Exhibits include period furniture and everyday objects from the era.

ÉGLISE de SAINT-JEAN ⑨, on Chemin Royal, **T**:(418) 829-3182. *Open mid-June to mid-Sept. daily 10–5. Admission is free but donation is requested.*

Built in 1736, the church is topped with a bright red tin roof. The décor and art of the interior reflect the village's dedication to seamen. The **Seamen's Cemetery**, at the water's edge, commemorates the lives of those who have perished traversing the mighty Saint Lawrence River.

Farther down the road is **Saint-François** ⑩. Founded in 1679, this is the smallest parish on the island. Its location at the eastern-most tip gives it a unique, rugged, and windswept landscape. The wild vine that covered the island when Champlain first landed here can still be found at this end of the island. Note the **processional chapels** marking the edges of the town.

VIEUX PRESBYTÈRE de SAINT-FRANÇOIS ⑪, 341 Chemin Royal, Saint-François, **T**:(418) 829-3614. *Open June–Sept. daily 10–5, Oct.–May by appointment.*

This old presbytery is studio, gallery, and sculpture garden for local artists. Stroll through the garden admiring the stone sculptures and watch the artists at work.

Walk across the street and take a look at the old stone **church** with its single slender steeple. *Open year-round Thurs.–Sun. 12–5.*

Nearby is **La Pointe d'Argentenay et sa Tour d'Observation** ⑫. At the tip of the island, the observation tower offers visitors beautiful views of the island, Saint Lawrence River, the Charlevoix coast, and Mont Sainte-Anne. Not far off the shore are the Îles Madame and Ruaux, which mark the area where the Saint Lawrence River changes from fresh to salt water.

Sainte-Famille ⑬, the oldest parish on the island, founded by Monsignor Laval in 1666, is virtually an open-air museum, with the highest concentration of authentic French Regime stone houses. Drive slowly and be prepared to stop a lot to admire the well-preserved homes, picturesque farms and fields, and sweeping views of the countryside and river.

ÉGLISE de la SAINTE-FAMILLE ⑭, 3915 Chemin Royal. *Open July–Aug. daily 12:30–5; June and Sept.–Oct. weekends 12:30–5.*

The church, dating back to 1743 and having undergone several changes through its history, is unique and architecturally significant. Towers stand at each corner of the façade; each topped with a steeple, giving the church the unusual number of three steeples. The church also features five alcoves, while its interior holds a number of significant pieces of religious art, including paintings and statues.

Nearby note the **Presbytery and the Musée de Patrimoine**, which houses exhibits and artifacts relating the history of the parish and the ancestral heritage of the island.

Saint-Pierre ⑮, the most developed and most populated parish of the island, greets visitors as they arrive and thanks them before leaving the island. The village is most well known as the home of poet and singer Felix Leclerc (1914–88) who was the first musician to introduce Québécois music to Europe. A monument to Leclerc and his grave can be found in the cemetery.

Stop at **Domaine Steinbach**, 2205 Chemin Royal, Saint-Pierre, for an interesting look at a traditional cider house and vinegar factory. Costumed hosts help to create an authentic New France atmosphere. An interpretation center and free samples make this stop both entertaining and delicious. **T**:*(418) 828-0777,* **W***: domainesteinbach.com. Open May–Oct. daily 10–7; Nov.–Apr. weekends by appointment. Closed January. Admission is free.*

Stop by the old **Église de Saint-Pierre** ⑯, built in 1717 and the oldest church on the island. The church was damaged during the British Conquest, then restored and enlarged in 1775. Inside, the church boasts three altars and a carved wood sanctuary lamp. At the front and back of the church stand the wood stoves, with sheet metal pipes, that were used to heat the nave.

The **Corporation des Artisans de l'Isle d'Orléans** is located in the sacristy, selling a wide selection of traditional crafts including quilts, furniture, and pottery. **T**:*(418) 828-9824. Open daily May–Oct.*

Church of Sainte Pétronille

Section IV

DAYTRIPS ON THE
CHARLEVOIX COAST

Lumberjacks and boatsmen first settled the Charlevoix Coast in the 17th century, with some of the more remote communities along the shore remaining inaccessible by road into the 20th century. Due to the rugged landscape and mighty Saint Lawrence, it is easy to understand why the Charlevoix's history is steeped in maritime lore.

Small schooners, called *goélettes*, were built along the Charlevoix for generations. The boats, originally equipped with sails and later with small motors, were used to transport food, supplies and wood along the Saint Lawrence to the isolated communities of the Charlevoix Coast. The schooners, used until the 1960s, were known locally as *"voitures d'eau"* — water cars.

By the later half of the 19th century the Charlevoix Coast became a popular tourist destination for city dwellers attracted by the stunning landscapes. Wealthy tourists refurbished traditional homes, constructed vacation cottages, and built elegant summer manors. Steamship companies transported tourists to the remote villages of the Charlevoix and contributed to the development of the area with construction of luxury hotels.

Where the Saint Lawrence River begins to widen to meet the sea, the land raises dramatically from the water's edge into a fluid series of peaks and valleys. Charming hamlets and artist villages hide amidst pristine forests and harbors. Wonders wait to surprise visitors around every corner in this spectacular region. It's easy to be caught up in the charm, beauty, and drama of the Charlevoix Coast.

Mont Sainte-Anne and Cap Tourmente

The Charlevoix Coast is world renowned for its natural beauty and splendor, and Mont Sainte-Anne and Cap Tourmente have some of the region's most spectacular landscapes. Discovered primarily for recreational uses, the sites in this tour have also been popular with artists and moviemakers attracted by the striking beauty and breathtaking scenery.

GETTING THERE:

By Car, Mont Sainte-Anne lies about 40 km (25 miles) east of Québec City. Take **Rte. 440** or **Rte. 40** east out of Québec, then follow **Rte. 138** east along the Saint Lawrence River toward Beaupré.

Bear left on **Rte. 360** for about 4 km (2½ miles) and turn right to reach Mont Sainte-Anne.

Return to **Rte. 138** in Beaupré. Follow **Avenue Royale** toward Saint-Joachim and continue to Cap Tourmente.

Turn left onto **Rue de l'Église** to reach Saint-Joachim.

Return to **Rte. 138** in Beaupré again and continue east for about 4 km (2½ miles), until you see the signs for Canyon Sainte-Anne on the left.

Leaving Canyon Sainte-Anne, take a left back onto **Rte. 138** heading east for about 14 km (9 miles). Turn left onto **Rte. 360** toward Saint-Ferréol-les-Neiges and look for signs for Les Sept Chutes.

Return to **Rte. 138**, turn right, and follow it back to Québec.

PRACTICALITIES:

Bureau d'Information Touristique de la Côte-de-Beaupré, 9630 Boulevard Sainte-Anne, Sainte-Anne-de-Beaupré. **T**:(418) 827-5281. Open late June through Aug. and late Dec. through Feb. daily 9–9; Sept. to late Dec. and Mar. to late June daily 9–8.

Tourist information is also available at the visitor center at Cap Tourmente.

This tour is focused primarily on outdoor and natural attractions and is best done in good weather. Some of the activities will not be available in the harsh winter months.

FOOD AND DRINK:

Casse-Croûte Chez Chantale (17 Rue de l'Église, Saint Joachim) A family restaurant with a menu featuring over 100 local dishes and regional favorites. **T**:(418) 827-4652. $$

Au Café Suisse Mont Sainte-Anne (1805 Boulevard Les Neiges, Saint-Ferréol-les-Neiges) The sister of the Swiss restaurant in Old Québec, featuring fondues, steaks, seafood, and alpine specialties. **T**:(418) 826-2184. $$$

Château Mont-Sainte-Anne (500 Boulevard Beau-Pré, Beaupré) This charming hotel offers several dining opportunities, including gourmet regional favorites. Enjoy fresh pasta dishes by the fireplace. **T**:(418) 827-5211. $$ and $$$

AREA ATTRACTIONS:

Circled numbers correspond to numbers on the map.

MONT SAINTE-ANNE ①, **T**:(418) 827-4561, **W**: mont-sainte-anne.com. *Open year-round daily. Mountain bikes are available for rental May–Oct. Mon.–Fri. 9–5, Sat.–Sun. 8:30–5.*

This recreational area, spreading leisurely over the slopes of Mont Sainte-Anne and into the Jean-Larose River Valley, was originally created in 1969 as a sports center for the residents of Québec City. Boasting impressive snowfall each year, especially on the north face, the mountain is renowned for skiing. The park offers more than 192 km (120 miles) of cross-country ski trails and 50 downhill runs.

In the warmer months the park is popular with sports and outdoors enthusiasts who enjoy hiking, mountain biking, mountain climbing, horseback riding, and golf. In fall, the mountain is host to the **Festival of Colors**, celebrating the spectacular colors of the season. *Open mid-Sept. to mid-Oct.* When the snow falls, the skiers and dog-sledders arrive.

The park is well worth the visit, even for those not looking to partake in outdoor sports. This well-preserved natural wonderland holds boundless beauty. The **summit** of Mont Sainte-Anne, accessible by gondola, offers sweeping views of the Saint Lawrence River, the Beaupré Coast, the Sainte-Anne-de-Beaupré Basilica, Île d'Orléans, and Québec city. On a clear day you can also see the Appalachian Mountains to the south and the Laurentian Mountains to the north. *The gondola runs late June through Aug., daily 10–4:45; Sept. to mid-Oct. weekends 10–4:45.*

From the ski chalet, follow the trail for the **Chutes Jean-Larose**, hidden in the forest. The Jean-Larose River drops more than 67 meters (220 feet) through a narrow canyon, racing to meet the Sainte-Anne River. The picturesque trail has a steep incline with nearly 400 steps.

Continue on to the **Réserve Nationale de Faune du Cap-Tourmente** ②,

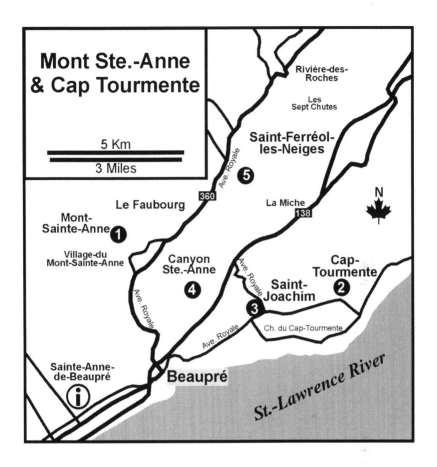

Mont Ste.-Anne & Cap Tourmente

5 Km
3 Miles

T:(418) 827-3776. *Open Jan.–Oct. daily 8:30–5, closed Nov.–Dec. Admission $6 for adults, $5 for students, children 12 and under are free.*

The word "tourmente" translates roughly to "windswept." The cape was named in honor of the strong winds that sweep through this part of the valley. Every year, in April and October, thousands of snow geese swarm this stretch of land above the Saint-Lawrence River. The river, wetlands, and mud flats are an ideal spot for the large birds that stop here during their spring and winter migrations. In the winter, the snow-covered walking trails are lined with bird feeders.

With more than 290 species of birds making their homes here, the cape was designated a wildlife reserve in 1979. An **interpretation center** with exhibits and films tells the history of the cape, the wildlife reserve, and the snow geese that frequent it.

The **Maison de la Chasse** (hunting lodge), located at the entrance to the reserve, was built on the land where Samuel de Champlain began the first farm of New France in 1626.

Nearby is **Saint-Joachim** ③, a quiet village founded soon after the British Conquest. The British fleet, on its way to Québec, burned all of the villages along the Saint Lawrence River. Fearing that history could repeat, the community of Saint-Joachim rebuilt their village inland rather than directly on the river's shore.

The **Église Saint-Joachim**, built in 1779, is dedicated to the father of the Virgin Mother. The church's interior, not completed until 1825, is spectacular. François and Thomas Baillairgé, charged with completion of the interior, sculpted the gold statues that decorate the church. **T**:*(418) 827-4020. Open mid-May to mid-Oct. daily 9–5. Admission is free.*

*CANYON SAINTE-ANNE ④, Route 138, **T**:(418) 827-4057, **W**: canyonste-anne.qc.ca. *Open May–June daily 9–5; July–Aug. daily 8:30–5:45; Sept. to late Oct. daily 9–5. Admission: $6.95 for adults, $2.40 for children 6-12, children under 5 are free.*

John Travolta's action movie, *Battlefield Earth*, was filmed in the canyon, which attracts more than 100,000 visitors annually. The park was visited by Henry David Thoreau in 1850 and received an award of "Responsible and Durable Tourism 1999" for the Québec City area.

The force of the Sainte-Anne River carved this deep canyon in the rock of the Canadian Shield during the Ice Age. Walking trails and three suspension bridges, one of which is 55 meters (180 feet) above the gorge, provide easy and exciting exploration of the site, which has been carefully preserved in its natural splendor. The Giant's Cauldron is a large pool of water on the cliff above the waterfall. Some of the rocks at the site have been identified as being over 600 million years old.

LES SEPT CHUTES ⑤, 4520 Avenue Royale, Saint-Ferréol-les-Neiges, **T**: (418) 826-3139. *Open mid-May through June. daily 10-5; July-Aug. daily 9-6; Sept. daily 10-5. Admission $6.50 for adults, $4 for children 6-12, children 5 and under are free.*

This hydroelectric plant dates back to 1916 and features an historic village, an interpretation center, and spectacular views of the falls. Walking trails allow visitors to explore the neighboring environment. Guided tours of the power plant and dam are available.

Around Baie-Saint-Paul

Baie-Saint-Paul is nestled in a picturesque bay, surrounded by high mountains and steep cliffs, where the Gouffre River meets the Saint Lawrence. Noël Simard, a farmer from the Beaupré Coast, settled beside the Gouffre River, clearing and farming the fertile land.

In the 1970s, Baie-Saint-Paul was a popular destination for a group of clowns, acrobats, jugglers, and contortionists who went on to found the famous Cirque du Soleil circus troupe.

The area has long been a magnet for artists who draw inspiration from the rolling green hills, surrounding mountains, and beautiful bay. Today the town boasts more than a dozen galleries, artist studios, an exposition hall, and art center. Each August, young artists from across Canada arrive in town, producing large-scale art works in a public exposition at the Canada Young Painters Symposium.

GETTING THERE:

By Car. Baie-Saint-Paul is 95 km (59 miles) northeast of Québec City. Follow **Rte. 138** east. At the intersection of **Rte. 362** turn right to reach the town center.

Follow **Rte. 362** east, just outside of town for a scenic overlook.

Return back through the village along **Rte. 362**. Turn right on **Rte. 138** east. Bear left at **Rte. 381** north to Parc des Grands-Jardins.

Return along **Rte. 381** to the intersection of **Rte. 138**. Turn right on **Rte. 138** and follow it back to Québec City.

PRACTICALITIES:

Baie-Saint-Paul is best seen on foot, with the exception of the two scenic overlooks, the Natural History Center, and the Parc des Grands-Jardins.

The **Tourist Information Office** has two locations in Baie-Saint-Paul. On Route 138, just before you reach the town, follow the signs that lead up a small hill to the office. A deck around the office provides a great view of the Gouffre Valley and Baie-Saint-Paul. Another office is located in the Art Center, 4 Rue Ambroise-Fafard.

Consider combining this trip with a tour of Les Éboulements and Île aux Coudres (Trip 12) and stay overnight in one of the many cozy Inns or Bed and Breakfasts in Baie-Saint-Paul.

FOOD AND DRINK:

Al Dente inc. (30 Rue Leclerc) A wide variety of pastas, in every shape and flavor, with an equally wide variety of sauces, olives, a salad bar, and excellent deserts. T:(418) 435-6695. $$

Restaurant Balsamo Café (1020 Boulevard Mgr. De Laval) Casual atmosphere with excellent Italian dishes. T:(418) 435-6504. $$

Saint Pub (2 Rue Racine) Excellent microbrewery and bistro with a festive atmosphere and sunny terrace. T:(418) 240-2332. $$$

Auberge La Pignoronde (750 Boulevard Mgr. De Laval) Gourmet French and Charlevoix regional cuisine in an excellent decor. T:(418) 435-5505. $$$

LOCAL ATTRACTIONS:

Circled numbers correspond to numbers on the map.

CENTRE d'HISTOIRE NATURELLE de CHARLEVOIX ①, 444 Route 138, T:(418) 435-6275. *Open late June through Sept. daily 9–5; Oct. to May by request only. Admission is free but donations are requested.*

A slide show, interpretive panels, and exhibits highlight the human and geological history, natural environment, and wildlife of the area.

The **village center** ② has a warm, festive atmosphere with small wooden buildings, tightly situated and brightly painted, which are today home to numerous art and craft galleries, boutiques, cafés, and restaurants. The many galleries throughout the center specialize in a wide variety of arts, including watercolors, pastels, etchings, and sculpture. The narrow streets bustle with activity as people leisurely stroll and shop. **Rue Saint-Jean-Baptiste** has a number of beautiful old houses.

Nearby is **Église de Baie-Saint-Paul** ③, Place de l'Église, T:(418) 435-2118. Dominating the center of town and the skyline, this imposing twin-steeple church dates back to 1962.

Stroll over to the **Chapelle Sacré-Coeur à la Maison-Mère des Petites Franciscaines de Marie** ④, 63 Rue Ambroise-Fafard, T:(418) 435-3520. The chapel of the mother house of the Franciscan sisters is quite impressive.

MAISON RENÉ-RICHARD ⑤, 58 Rue Saint-Jean-Baptiste, T:(418) 435-5571. *Open year-round daily 10–6. Admission $2.50 per person.*

In the 20th century, the family of François-Xavier Cimon lived in this house. Over the years a number of painters befriended the family and made their studios on the property. In 1942, Swiss-born painter René Richard married one of Cimon's daughters and took ownership of the house. Today, the quaint house is used as a museum depicting life on the Charlevoix Coast in the 1940s.

CENTRE d'ART de BAIE-SAINT-PAUL ⑥, 4 Rue Ambroise-Fafard,

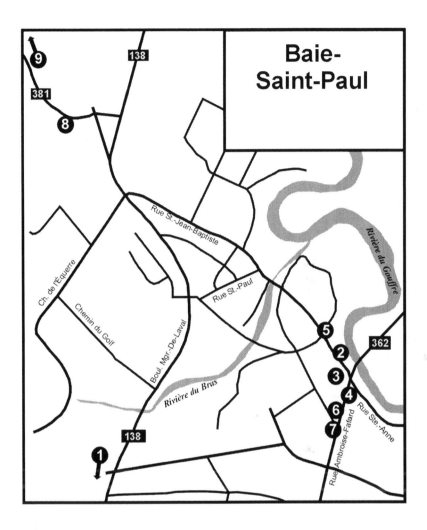

Baie-Saint-Paul

T:(418) 435-3681, **W**: centredart-bsp.qc.ca. *Open late June through Aug. daily 10–6; Sept. to late June daily 10–5. Admission is free.*

This beautiful museum features artists from the Charlevoix Coast. Various galleries display the different art genres that are practiced in the region, featuring traditional and modern techniques.

CENTRE d'EXPOSITION de BAIE-SAINT-PAUL ⑦, 23 Rue Ambroise-Fafard, **T**:(418) 435-3681, **W**: centredart-bsp.qc.ca. *Open late June through Aug. daily 10–5; Sept. to late June daily 9–5. Admission $3 for adults, children under 12 are free.*

Temporary and traveling art exhibits from around the world are featured at this center. A gallery dedicated to René Richard has several of his paintings on permanent exhibit.

Explore around the **wharf** and note Île aux Coudres at the mouth of the bay.

Drive east out of town on Route 362 and round the bay. A **scenic overlook** appears on the right, affording breathtaking views of the town, surrounding mountains, and rivers.

LES JARDINS SECRETS du VIEUX-MOULIN ⑧, 4 Chemin du Vieux-Moulin, **T**:(418) 240-2146, **W**: jardinssecrets.com. *Open July–Aug. daily 9–5; Sept. to mid-Oct. Sat.–Sun. 9–5. Guided tours run 10–4. Tour prices $7 for adults, $5 for children 4-12, children 3 and under are free. Archeology participation, call for reservations (418) 240-2146. Storytelling prices $5 for adults, $3 for children.*

The site is alive and bustling with archeologists, busily unearthing the secrets of the past. The old mill, more than 300 years old, dates back to the settlement of New France. Storytellers will entertain and thrill visitors with tales of the past and the ghost of the old mill.

PARC de GRANDS-JARDINS ⑨, Route 381, Saint-Urbain, **T**:(418) 457-3945. *Open late May to mid-June daily 9–5; mid-June to Aug. daily 8–10; Sept. to mid-Oct. daily 9–5. Admissions $3.50 for adults, $1.50 for children 6-17, children under 6 are free.*

Part of the Laurentides Natural Reserve, this is a beautiful protected park with an array of lush flora. Many animals make the park home, including a number of caribou. The park features hiking trails that enable visitors to enjoy the natural splendor of the area and possibly meet some of the local wildlife.

Les Éboulements and Île aux Coudres

A massive earthquake in 1663 triggered a number of large landslides *(éboulements)*, bringing down much of the mountainside. The land, atop a cliff of earth overlooking the river, was granted to Pierre Tremblay in 1710, who settled the town and built a mill.

The villages along this part of the Charlevoix Coast and Île aux Coudres have always had strong ties to the maritime. Traces of its shipbuilding heritage, fishing industry, and the schooners that once frequented the waters can be found throughout the area.

This is not only a trip along the scenic coast or through picturesque villages. This is a trip through time!

GETTING THERE:

By Car, Les Éboulements is about 128 km (80 miles) northeast of Québec City.

Take **Rte. 138** east to Baie-Saint-Paul. Turn right onto **Rte. 362** through the town, continuing to Les Éboulements. Return back along **Rte. 362** west. Turn left, following the road toward **Saint-Joseph-de-la-Rive**. At the bottom of the hill, turn left, following the signs for the **ferry**. Park by the ferry to explore this small hamlet on foot.

The **ferry** provides free transport to Île aux Coudres.

Return to Saint-Joseph-de-la-Rive on the ferry, and return to **Rte. 362**. Turn left and continue on **Rte. 362** west, through Baie-Saint-Paul. Turn right onto **Rte. 138** west and follow it back to Québec City.

PRACTICALITIES:

Consider combining this trip with a tour of Baie-Saint-Paul (Trip 11) and stay overnight in one of the many cozy Inns or Bed and Breakfasts in Baie-Saint-Paul.

Tourisme Île aux Coudres, 21 Rue Royale West, is open mid-June through Aug. daily 10–7. **T**:(418) 438-2930.

FOOD AND DRINK:

Chez Ti-Coq (29 Rue du Port, Île aux Coudres) Casual family dining with French Canadian dishes, pizza, sandwiches, and grill. **T**:(418)438-2944 or 1-877-438-2944. $$

La Mer Veille (160 Chemin des Coudriers, Île aux Coudres) Popular with locals and visitors alike, light meals and a casual atmosphere. **T**:(418)438-2149. $$

Auberge de nos Aïeux (183 Rue Principale, Les Éboulements) Regional Charlevoix dishes and local specialties. **T**:(418)635-2405. $$$

La Maison Sous les Pins (352 Rue Félix-Antoine-Savard, Saint-Joseph-de-la-Rive) Gourmet French and regional cuisine in a charming historic setting. **T**:(418)635-2583. $$$

SUGGESTED TOUR:

Circled numbers correspond to numbers on the map.

Les Éboulements ① rests atop a cliff created during a massive rock and landslide that was caused by an enormous earthquake in 1663. The peaceful village has maintained its charming and historic appearance with preserved old houses and a stone church. Surrounded by rolling hills, farms, and fields, and overlooking the river, the town is also popular with artists.

Moulin Banal ②, 157 Rue Principale, sits beside the Du Moulin River, just before the junction of the road that leads to Saint-Joseph-de-la-Rive. Resting at the top of a waterfall, the stone mill was built in 1790. The well-preserved flourmill still operates with its original equipment, and visitors are able to watch as grain is ground into flour. **T**:*(418)635-2239. Open May–Oct. daily 10–5. Admission $2 per person, children 12 and under are free.*

Nearby is the **Manoir de Sales-Laterrière**, 159 Rue Principale, providing an example of the manor houses and life-styles of the landowners in the early 19th century. Interpretive panels give the history of the site. **T**:*(418) 635-2666. Open year-round daily 9–11 and 2–4. Admission is free. Only the exterior of the site is available to the public.*

Also nearby is the **Église de les Éboulements** ③, 280 Rue Village. This massive church, built in 1930, towers over the small village that spreads out before it. Inside, don't miss the black marble altar imported from Italy.

Continue on to **Saint-Joseph-de-la-Rive** ④. With a population of little more than 225 people, this village was once one of the main shipbuilding towns for the traditional Charlevoix schooners. Remnants and ghosts of these schooners still rest along the shores of the village as testimony to the village's long history with the river. Today, traditional local crafts and tourism are the economic base of the village. The village also features a traditional cottage bakery and general store.

There is a beautiful **sandy beach** along the river, east of the ferry dock. The water of the Saint Lawrence River is salty and cold at this point.

LES ÉBOULEMENTS & ÎLE AUX COUDRES 86

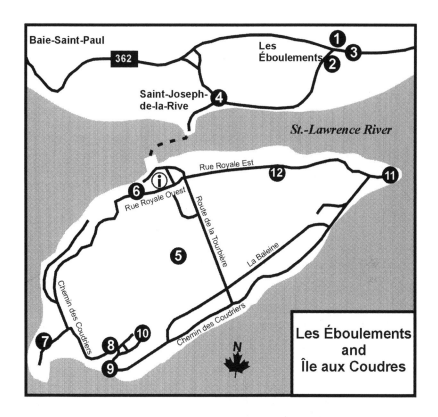

Les Éboulements
and
Île aux Coudres

Église Catholique Saint-Joseph, 252 Chemin d'Église, is interesting for its maritime décor. The baptismal fountain is a large shell and anchors support the altar. An audio presentation, started with the button to the right of the entrance, explains the church's ornamentation.

The Musée Maritime de Charlevoix, situated in a former shipyard, has a number of old boats for visitors to explore. The museum recounts the glorious days when Saint-Joseph was a busy shipbuilding town. Navigation equipment, two impressive schooners, and other maritime artifacts are ready for exploration. T:(418)635-1131, W: musee-maritime-charlevoix.com/. Open mid-May through June and Sept. to mid-Oct., Mon.–Fri. 9–4, Sat.–Sun. 11–4; July–Aug. daily 9–5. Admission $3 for adults, children under 15 are free.

Craftspeople of Saint-Joseph-de-la-Rive have been making the Santons de Charlevoix. The terracotta figurines, representing the nativity scene, complete with villagers and the manger, are thoroughly unique. The characters are dressed in traditional Québec costumes and miniature buildings are representative of typical Charlevoix and Île aux Coudres homes. T:(418) 635-2521 or (418) 635-1362. Open mid-May through June and Sept. to mid-Oct., Sat.–Sun. 10–5;

July–Aug. daily 10–5:30. Admission is free.

Board the ferry for the trip to **Île aux Coudres** ⑤. When Jacques Cartier landed on the island in 1535 he found several hazel trees, laden with hazelnuts, which he found to be as large as those in France, but tastier. He dubbed the small landmass "Hazel Island" (l'isle es coudres). The island was originally only a stopping point for ships before it became a shipbuilding center. Isolated by the harsh weather and the Saint Lawrence, the islanders were forced to be self-sufficient from the first settlements. Because of this, the islanders have made their own clothing, linen, and supplies.

The **Monument Jacques Cartier** ⑥, Chemin du Mouillage, marks the spot where Jacques Cartier and his crew celebrated the first mass in Canada in 1535.

Pointe de l'Islet ⑦, accessed by turning right on Chemin de l'Islet, at the western-most tip of the island, affords beautiful views of the Saint Lawrence River.

The **Centre d'Observation et Musée les Voitures d'Eau**, 203 Chemin des Coudriers, has an interpretation center and observation tower. The small museum exhibits maritime artifacts that bring to life the era when the island and Saint Lawrence River were bustling with schooners and seamen. The first Columber Motor, built in 1925, which replaced the sailed schooners, is on display at the museum. **T**:*(418)438-2208 or 1-800-463-2118. Open mid-May to mid-June and mid-Sept. to mid-Oct., Sat.–Sun. 10–5; mid-June to mid-Sept., daily 10–5. Admission $4 for adults, children 10 and under are free.*

Continue on to **Église Saint-Louis** ⑧, 280 Rue des Coudriers, **T**:(418) 438-2442. This impressive church was built in 1885 from the same plans as the basilica in Sainte-Anne-de-Beaupré. Inside are several beautiful sculptures.

Note the **Chapelle de Procession Saint-Isidore** and **Chapelle de Procession Saint-Pierre** along Rue des Coudriers. These charming chapels, used for religious processions, are classified as historical monuments.

MUSÉE de l'ISLE aux COUDRES ⑨, 231 Chemin des Coudriers, **T**:(418)438-2753. *Open May–June and Sept.–Oct., daily 8:30–6:30; July–Aug. daily 8–7. Admission $4 for adults, $3 for children 7–15, children under 7 are free.*

The Alfred-Desgagnés Exhibition Gallery transports visitors back in time to experience the islander's way of life. Other rooms display the natural wonders of the island, introducing visitors to the insects, flowers, animals, minerals, and fossils found on the Charlevoix Coast. Temporary exhibits include some borrowed from other museums across Canada and in France.

LES MOULINS de l'ISLE aux COUDRES ⑩, 247 Chemin du Moulin, **T**:(418) 438-2184, **W**: charlevoix.qc.ca/moulins. *Open mid-May to late June, daily 10–5; late June to late Aug., daily 9:30–6:30; late Aug. to early Oct., daily 10–5. Admission $3 for adults, $2.50 for students, children 12 and under are free.*

Île aux Coudres

Built in the early 19th century, the water-powered mill stopped frequently due to insufficient water flow. In an attempt to improve productivity and reliability a windmill was built nearby in 1836. The mills were stopped in 1948, and designated as historical monuments in the 1960s. Today, visitors can watch as millers grind wheat and buckwheat for flour in the traditional ways. Also of interest on the site are several pieces of old farming equipment.

There are several old houses around the island that are worth a look. **Maison Bouchard**, located on Chemin du Ruisseau Rouge, is a beautiful whitewashed house with a striking red roof.

Maison Leclerc is among the oldest houses on the island, built at the end of the 18th century. The simple stone building features a roof of painted red shingles.

Maison Croche is a large old stone farmhouse.

Pointe du Bout d'en Bas ⑪, the eastern-most tip of the island offers spectacular views of the river and Charlevoix Coast.

Église Saint-Bernard ⑫ boasts a large painting depicting the first mass celebrated on the island. *Open year-round daily 9–6.*

Trip 13

La Malbaie-Pointe-au-Pic and Saint-Irénée

In 1608, Samuel de Champlain discovered the small bay along the Saint Lawrence River. Anchoring his ships for the night, he was surprised to find them grounded in the morning — and so proclaimed this a *"malle baye"* (bad bay). After the British Conquest it was renamed Murray Bay for General James Murray.

In the early 20th century wealthy French Canadians, Americans, and Englishmen came to the area of La Malbaie and Saint-Irénée to vacation, where they built summer houses with cedar shingles and manor houses in the style of 17th century France.

In 1995, the communities of La Malbaie and Pointe-au-Pic were merged and incorporated to form La Malbaie-Pointe-au-Pic.

Nestled snuggly between the Saint Lawrence River and rugged landscape, Malbaie, Pointe-au-Pic, and Saint-Irénée are peaceful and picturesque destinations.

GETTING THERE:

By Car, La Malbaie-Pointe-au-Pic is about 140 km (87 miles) northeast of Québec City.

Take **Rte. 138** east from Québec. At La Malbaie, bear right onto **Rte. 362**. Follow **Rte. 362** along the river and through La Malbaie-Pointe-au-Pic.

Continue on **Rte. 362,** leaving La Malbaie to the south. Follow **Rte. 362** to Saint-Irénée.

Return along **Rte. 362** through La Malbaie. Turn right on **Rte. 138** across the bridge. Take a left after the bridge and follow **Chemin de la Vallée** for 1.6 km (1 mile) up the hill. Turn right, following signs for the campground, to reach the Fraser Falls.

Return down the hill to La Malbaie and turn right onto **Rte. 138**, across the bridge. Turn right on **Rte. 381** to Parc Règional des Hautes-Gorges de la Rivière Malbaie. Note that part of the road to the park is not paved.

Return along **Rte. 381** and turn right on **Rte. 138**, following it back to Québec City.

PRACTICALITIES:

The **Tourist Information Office** is on Route 362 as you enter La Malbaie. This has information for the Charlevoix Coast Region. Open mid-June through Aug. daily 9–9; Sept. to mid-June daily 8:30–4:30. **T**:(418) 665-4454 or 1-800-667-2276, **W**: *tourisme-charlevoix.com*

FOOD AND DRINK:

L'Artichaut (100 Boulevard de Comporté, La Malbaie) Grill specials, fondue, sandwiches, and roasted chicken in a casual family atmosphere. **T**:(418) 665-7453. $$

Allegro (53 Rue John-Nairne, La Malbaie) Italian trattoria with fresh pasta and gourmet pizza in a comfortable Mediterranean setting. **T**:(418) 665-2595 or 1-888-775-2595. $$

Auberge des 3 Canards (115 Côte Bellevue, La Malbaie Pointe-au-Pic) For a wonderful gastronomic experience, a five-course gourmet French meal, featuring regional favorites and homemade sorbet. **T**:(418) 665-3761 or 1-800-461-3761. $$$+

Le Saint-Laurent Café (128 Rue Principale, Saint-Irénée) Good international fare, light meals, and casual dining. **T**:(418) 452-3408. $$

SUGGESTED TOUR:

Circled numbers correspond to numbers on the map.

As you enter La Malbaie, the small **Parc du Casgrain** ① is on the right, sitting beside the rocky mouth of the Malbaie River. A walk along the small bay and Saint Lawrence River offers a great opportunity for stretching your legs after the long ride.

ÉGLISE PROTESTANTE de MURRAY BAY ②, 200 Boulevard de Comporté. *Open mid-June to mid-Sept. daily.*

This beautiful stone church was built in 1867. The grave of lawyer and writer William Hume Blake (1809–70) is on the grounds.

Also worth seeing are the **Église de Pointe-au-Pic**, 118 Rue Richelieu, and **Église de la Malbaie**, 353 Rue Saint-Étienne. Both of these beautiful 20th-century churches boast stunning stained-glass windows.

MUSÉE de CHARLEVOIX ③, 10 Chemin du Havre, **T**:(418) 665-4411, **W**: museedecharlevoix.qc.ca. *Open late June through Aug., daily 10–6; Sept. to late June, Tues.–Fri. 10–5, Sat.–Sun. 1–5. Admission $5 for adults, $4 for students, children under 11 are free.*

A large permanent collection features paintings, sculptures, and textiles done by local artists. Particularly fun for the whole family is the display of carousel and toy horses. Temporary exhibits represent a wide variety of themes.

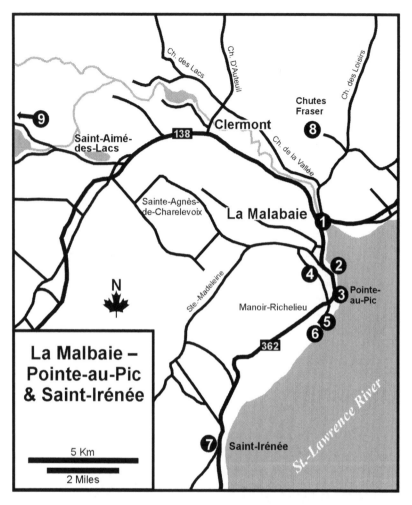

La Malbaie –
Pointe-au-Pic
& Saint-Irénée

5 Km

2 Miles

Chemin des Falaises ④ has a number of 20th-century houses, built as summer homes for wealthy vacationers. Shingled beach cottages, houses in the style of 17th-century English manors, and several local architectural styles all mingle along this quaint street.

Turn left and follow **Rue de Quai,** parking at the end. A small wharf reaches out into the river and provides a nice view of the rocky beach and the sharp cliffs of the shoreline. Across from the wharf, a row of brightly painted buildings overshadowed by a stark cliff today houses artist studios, shops, and inns.

Continue on to **Manoir Richelieu** ⑤, Chemin des Falaises. One of the original grand hotels, built in 1899, it welcomed visitors to the newly popular resort destination. The original building was destroyed by fire and rebuilt in 1929. The château-style hotel has hosted a number of famous guests through its history, including the Vanderbilts, Charlie Chaplin, and the King of Siam. Today, the hotel welcomes visitors to wander its elegant hallways and explore the various salons and gardens, even if they are not staying at the manor.

CASINO de CHARLEVOIX ⑥, 183 Avenue Richelieu, **T**:(418) 665-5300 or 1-800-665-2274, **W**: casinos-quebec.com. *Open year-round, summers daily 10–3, winters Sun.–Thurs. 10–1, Fri.–Sat. 10–3. Proper dress is required.*

With 22 gaming tables and more than 800 slot machines, the casino offers excitement for all tastes.

Domaine Forget, 5 Saint-Antoine, Route 362, Saint-Irénée, was the former summer home of Rudolphe Forget, who built the railway along the north shore of the Saint Lawrence River. The property had its own power plant, in addition to an impressive château and several other interesting buildings. This pleasant country estate is now a cultural center for the performing arts. **T**:*(418) 452-8111 or 1-888-336-7438,* **W**: *domaineforget.com. Schedule and ticket prices vary.*

Now head southwest to **Saint-Irénée** ⑦. The birthplace of Adolphe-Basile Routhier, lawyer and poet, who write the French lyrics to *Ô Canada*, the Canadian anthem, Saint-Irénée has a long tradition as an artist colony. The picturesque village, at the bottom of a steeply sloping hill, is bordered by rolling fields and the Saint Lawrence River.

A beautiful church, **Église de Saint-Irénée**, 124 Rue Principale, is perched atop a hill overlooking the small village. The simple white wooden church, dating from the mid-19th century, offers sweeping views of the village and river.

There are many fabulous **artist studios and galleries** throughout the town.

Drive to the end of **Rue de Quai** where a little wharf and port village sit quietly on the water's edge. A collection of quaint houses, cutely painted, rest at the bottom of a cliff along a narrow brick street. The homes now house small shops, cafés, artist studios, and inns.

The **Chutes Fraser** ⑧ on the Comporté River is in a beautiful setting. The river gradually drops for 98 feet, giving the impression of fluid lace moving over the rocky river bed.

PARC RÉGIONAL des HAUTES-GORGES de la RIVIÈRE MALBAIE ⑨, Route 381, Saint-Aimé-des-Lacs, **T**:(418) 439-4402 for the park, (418) 665-7527 for cruise information and reservations. *Open June through mid-Oct., daily 9–5. Scenic cruises run July to mid-Aug. 10–4 five times a day; mid-June through July and mid-Aug. to mid-Oct. a limited number run. Reservations are required. Admission $7 per car, cruises are $24.33 for adults, $14.76 for children 6–17, children under 6 are free.*

Riviére Malbaie

Massive mountain peaks and dramatic gorges, the Malbaie River, and the Martres River Valley are the setting for this stunning park. A breathtaking **cruise**, departing from the wharf at the end of the dirt road, affords a close look at the steep sides of the Malbaie River.

White water rafting on the Rivière Malbaie makes an unforgettable adventure amidst dense forests, high mountainsides, and the rocky river bed. *Descente Malbaie, 316 Rue Principale, Saint-Aimé-des-Lacs,* **T***:(418) 439-2265.*

Port-au-Persil to Baie Sainte-Catherine

Inaccessible by road until the 20th century, this stretch of the Charlevoix Coast is rugged and stunningly beautiful. The drive along the coast treats visitors to a feast of heart-stopping views as steep peaks give way to glimpses of isolated bays, and pristine forests hide quaint villages. Here, nature is preserved, honored, and incorporated into everyday life.

Baie-Sainte-Catherine is a popular destination for whale watching and tours of the Saguenay Fjord. Many species of whales can be seen in the area, drawn to the deep waters at the mouth of the fjord, including minke whales, finbacks, blue whales, and other marine mammals.

GETTING THERE:

By Car, Port-au-Persil is about 168 km (105 miles) and Baie-Sainte-Catherine is about 208 km (130 miles) northeast of Québec City.

Take **Rte. 138** out of Québec, following it north past La Malbaie. About 6.5 km (4 miles) after Saint-Fidèle-de-Mont-Murray turn right following the sign for Port-au-Persil.

Bear right back onto **Rte. 138**, through Saint-Siméon. Turn right on **Chemin Baie-des-Rochers** and follow it to the bay at the end.

Return to **Rte. 138**, turn right and continue to Baie-Sainte-Catherine.

Follow **Rte. 138** west back to Québec City.

PRACTICALITIES:

If you are interested in doing a whale watch, you may want to do this tour in the reverse order. Drive straight to Baie-Sainte-Catherine to meet the boat for the whale watch and then work your way back to Québec City. If you do it this way, the left turn for Port-au-Persil will be shortly after Saint-Siméon, just before the Port-au-Persil Pottery gallery.

Seasonal **Tourist Information Offices** are located in Saint-Siméon at 494 Rue Saint-Laurent and in Baie-Sainte-Catherine at 308 Rue Leclerc. Open mid-June to Labor Day daily 10–7. **T**: 1-800-667-2276, **W**: tourisme-charlevoix.com

FOOD AND DRINK:

Auberge sur Mer (109 Rue du Quai, Saint-Siméon) Popular family restaurant with a vast menu, including light meals and regional specialties. **T**:(418) 638-2674. $$

Auberge Petit Madeleine de Port-au-Persil (400 Route Port-au-Persil) Featuring home-cooked French and regional Charlevoix cuisine in a country setting. Open seasonally. **T**:(418) 638-2460. $$$

Hotel Motel Baie-Sainte-Catherine (294 Route 138, Baie Sainte-Catherine) Casual family restaurant with steaks, Canadian food, and basic fare. Open all day year-round. **T**:(418) 237-4271. $$

SUGGESTED TOUR:

Circled numbers correspond to numbers on the map.

Begin at **Port-au-Persil** ①, a quaint hamlet nestled around a small picturesque bay. As you approach the village the road leads past charming farms with brightly painted barns and well-maintained homes.

A small **cascade** of water tumbles down a rocky river bed into a peaceful little harbor. Park in the scenic overlook and follow the easy walking path to see the river and waterfalls.

Just past the scenic overlook, turn right on Rue du Quai for the quiet **wharf**. Leave the car on the pier and stroll along the rocky shore, admiring the quiet that surrounds you.

The **Chapelle de Port-au-Persil**, 128 Rue du Quai, beside the wharf, is accessible by foot via the rocky beach. The Protestant chapel was built in 1897 by Scottish Presbyterian pastor John McLaren.

Continue on to **Saint-Siméon** ②. The village, situated at a crossroads between forests and the Saint Lawrence River, has a steep history of ecological awareness. Saint-Siméon is a popular stopping point for nature lovers enroute to the Park de Saguenay, the Saguenay Fjord, and the Saint Lawrence River.

Farther up the road is **Baie des Rochers** ③. Although it seems somewhat out of the way, a visit to this little bay is well worth the trip and highly recommended. Deep in a pristine forest, surrounded by high rugged cliffs, an isolated pier reaches into a small bay. An island, which appears to block access to the bay, is accessible on foot at low tide. Many hiking trails start along the road to the bay, leading into a wild natural environment.

Head northeast to **Baie-Sainte-Catherine** ④. At the mouth of the Saguenay River and fjord, this little village rests on a sand-and-clay plateau looking out at the sea.

A splendid hike, the **Sentier des Chutes**, about 11 km (7 miles), is near the village.

Nearby is the **Église de Baie-Sainte-Catherine** ⑤, 294 Rue Leclerc. This beautiful white church with sky blue trim was built in 1908, beside the wharf, to serve the workers of the Price sawmill.

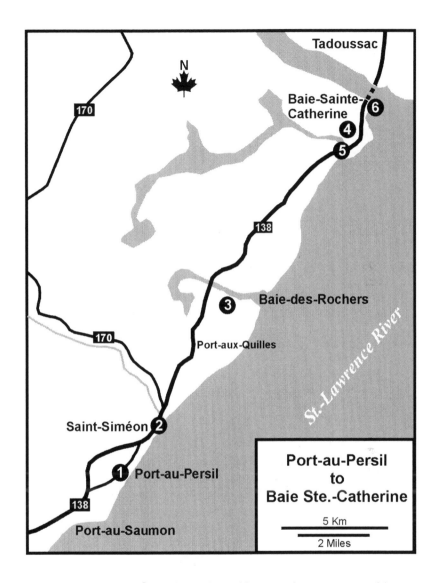

Port-au-Persil
to
Baie Ste.-Catherine

5 Km

2 Miles

At **Pointe-Noire** ⑥, an observation and interpretation center treats visitors to breathtaking views of the Saguenay and Saint Lawrence Rivers and the mouth of the fjord, and introduces visitors to the marine ecology of the area. Watch the free ferry that makes up the stretch of Route 138 between Baie-Saint-Catherine and Tadoussac, across the Saguenay River. A wooden walkway affords views of the deep waters at the mouth of the Saguenay River — you may be able to see some of the whales that feed here. **T**:*(418) 237-4383 or (418) 235-4703. Open*

Port-au-Persil

mid-June through Aug., daily 9–6; Sept. to early Oct., Fri.–Sun. 9–5. Admission $2 per person, $5 per family, children 5 and under are free.

Whale watching tours and cruises of the Fjord du Saguenay are available from **Croisières Baleines**, departing from the wharf in Baie-Sainte-Catherine. The catamaran *Katmar* offers underwater observation. On-board naturalists give an informative and entertaining presentation during the tour. **T**:*(418) 627-4276 or 1-800-694-5489,* **W***: baleines.ca. Tours run May–Oct. at 9:30, 12:45, and 4, duration of 3 hours. Adults $52, children 6–13 $22, children 5 and under are free.*

Whale watching is also available from **Croisières Dufour**, **T**:*(418) 692-0222 or 1-800-463-5250,* **W***: familledufour.com. Tours run daily at 9:45 and 1:45, and a sunset tour at 5, which includes whale watching and a tour of the fjord. Fares $52 for adults and $22 for children 6-12. Children 5 and under are free.* Also available is **extreme whale watching** aboard their Zodiac-style craft. *Tours run daily at 9:15, 12:45, and 3:45. Call for fares.*

For the truly adventurous, try whale watching in Zodiacs with **Croisières AML**, departing from Quai Baie-Sainte-Catherine. **T**:*(418) 237-4274 or 1-800-563-4643. Two-hour tours run at 7 and 5, $45 for adults, $30 for children 6-12. Three-hour tours run at 9:30 and 1:30, $52 for adults, $35 for children 6-12. Children under 6 are not permitted.*

Section V

DAYTRIPS NORTH OF
QUÉBEC CITY

Mountains and jagged cliffs drop dramatically to dark lakes and wild rivers. Nature thrives here, undaunted by modernity, untouched by technology.

Jacques Cartier discovered the vast area of the Saguenay and Lac Saint-Jean in 1535 and called the area a "kingdom." This marked the beginning of a working relationship between the native Montagnais people and the French settlers. The countless rivers and lakes enabled the region to become a busy fur-trading district for nearly 200 years, until the area was opened to colonization.

Around the middle of the 19th century, William Price and a number of businessmen from the Charlevoix region formed a coalition to mine the forests of the Saguenay region for lumber.

Today, all of the natural resources of the area are being harvested for thriving pulp and paper, hydroelectric, and aluminum industries.

A devastating fire swept through the region of the Fjord du Saguenay in 1870, flattening much of the forest. As the land recuperated, wild blueberries were the first plant life to grow and flourish. The region is now renowned for its abundance of fresh blueberries. Local specialties frequently include these and the people of the region affectionately refer to themselves as "Bleuets."

Understanding the wealth of nature that thrives in these areas, the people of Québec founded a number of reserves and parks to protect and care for their treasures. The Parc du Saguenay and Park Marin du Saguenay-Saint-Laurent were founded to protect and understand the ecology of the Fjord du Saguenay and the sea mammals that live there. The Reserve Faunique de Laurentides is dedicated to preserving the vast forests, lakes and rivers of the Laurentides, stretching north from Québec City.

Trip 15

*Tadoussac

A stronghold of provincial history, Tadoussac is the birthplace of New France. Jacques Cartier dropped anchor in the deep waters of the Saguenay-Saint-Jean in 1535, enchanted by the beauty of the site. Pierre Chauvin followed suit in 1599, and then Samuel de Champlain in 1603. The first fur-trading post of New France was erected at the location in 1600, sparking the beginning of the colonization of New France.

It wasn't long before cruise ships began bringing vacationers to the area, in search of a peaceful seaside holiday and a glimpse of the magnificent animals that frolic offshore. The inviting town has been welcoming tourists for more than 100 years. In the summer, it bustles with outdoors sports enthusiasts, open-air concerts, and storytellers.

Bordered by the nature reserves Parc du Saguenay and Parc Marin du Saguenay-Saint-Laurent, Tadoussac is a paradise. The village is also the hub for whale watching and boat tours of the Fjord du Saguenay.

GETTING THERE:

By Car, Tadoussac is about 218 km (136 miles) northeast of Québec City. Take **Rte. 138** from Québec to Tadoussac. Free ferries transport cars across the mouth of the Saguenay River, between Baie-Saint-Catherine and Tadoussac.

Follow Rue des Pionniers through town to Baie du Moulin-Baude.

By Boat, take the catamaran *Famille Dufour II* from Québec's Quai 19, departing at 8. The return trip departs from Tadoussac around 6. The trip includes lunch onboard, an amazing look at the Saint Lawrence River, and whale watching. **Croisières Dufour, T**:*(418) 692-0222 or 1-800-463-5250. Tours run June and Sept. $119 for adults, $75 for children 6-12; July and Aug. $149 for adults, $75 for children; children under 6 are free.*

PRACTICALITIES:

It cools off early in this region and can be cold even in July and August. It is wise to bring warm clothes with you at any time of year, especially if you plan to take advantage of a whale-watching cruise, which are best in June when the whales are most plentiful.

To get a full appreciation for the natural splendor of the area, consider staying overnight and including a tour of the Fjord du Saguenay (Trip 17). If you chose to stay, **Hôtel Tadoussac** welcomes visitors in Old World resort elegance. **T**:1-800-561-0718.

Tadoussac Maison du Tourisme, 197 Rue des Pionniers, Tadoussac. Open year-round Mon.–Fri. 8:30–12 and 1:30–4:30. **T**:(418) 235-4744.

Additional tourist information is available on the Internet at **W**: tadoussac.com and **W**: tourismsaguenaylacsaintjean.qc.ca

Most of Tadoussac is best explored on foot. You will need to drive out to Baie du Moulin-Baude to explore the sand dunes.

FOOD AND DRINK:

Restaurant Le Bateau (246 Rue des Forgerons) Popular regional cuisine in a comfortable, casual atmosphere. **T**:(418) 235-4427. $$

Coverdale (165 Rue Bord-de-l'Eau, at Hôtel Tadoussac) Fine regional and provincial specialties in a charming setting. **T**:(418) 235-4421. $$$

La Bolée (164 Rue Morin) Offers a variety of delicious, light, and casual meals. A bakery on the site is perfect for a snack or treat. **T**:(418) 235-4750. $$

Restaurant de Hôtel le Béluga (191 Rue de Pionniers) A large menu offers Canadian, Italian, Continental, and Vegetarian meals. **T**:(418) 235-4784. $$

LOCAL ATTRACTIONS:
Circled numbers correspond to numbers on the map.

MUSÉE MARITIME de TADOUSSAC ①, 145 Rue du Bateau-Passeur, **T**:(418) 235-4657. *Open June–Oct. daily 9–6. Admission $2 for adults, $1.50 for children.*

This museum illustrates the maritime history of Tadoussac, navigation along the Saint Lawrence and Saguenay Rivers, and the local shipbuilding industry. See how the first tourists arrived to the town by cruise ship. The museum has some impressive models, photographs, and audiovisual displays.

La Chapelle des Indiens de Tadoussac ②, Bord-de-l'Eau, is a quaint white wood chapel with red trim and shingled roof. Built in 1747 by a Jesuit missionary, this is the oldest wood church in Canada. The interesting interior has a nice collection of religious artifacts and artworks, while the antique furniture and wood paneling of the interior are reminiscent of 19th-century French Canada.

Stroll along the boardwalk and admire the grandiose **Hôtel Tadoussac**, dating back to 1941, lumbering along Bord de l'Eau and overlooking the Saint Lawrence River. This long white hotel, with its striking red roof, is the symbol of Tadoussac.

The log **Poste de Traite Chauvin** ③, 157 Rue du Bord-de-l'Eau, re-creates Pierre Chauvin's busy trading post from 1600. Audiovisual displays and exhibits bring to life the beginnings of New France and enable visitors to relive the active commercial relationship between the people of the First Nations and the European settlers. T:*(418) 235-4446. Open late June through Sept. daily 9–9; May to late June and Oct. daily 9–12 and 3–6. Admission $3 for adults, $1.50 for children, children under 6 are free.*

CENTRE d'INTERPRÉTATION des MAMMIFÈRES MARINS ④, 108 Rue de la Cale-Sèche, **T**:(418) 235-4701. *Open mid-May to mid-June and Oct. daily 12–5; mid-June to Sept. daily 9–8. Admission $5.50 for adults, $3 for children 6–12, children 5 and under are free.*

This museum is a must, especially if you are planning to go on a whale watch. Broadcasts from below the surface of the Saguenay River serenade visitors with the songs of whales. Experience the life and work of marine biologists, ask experts about the whales that inhabit the deep waters of the rivers, and watch an interesting documentary on whales. Skeletons and models of whales give a close look at the enormous size of these animals. Up-to-date "whale news" gives visitors current information on the numbers and locations of whales in the Saguenay-Saint-Laurent.

There are several nice **hiking trails** that depart from around the village, affording views of the town, surrounding landscape, and rivers. The **Pointe de l'Islet** tour is a pleasant, short hike at the junction of the Saint Lawrence and Saguenay Rivers. It is frequently possible to spot marine mammals from this trail.

Around the Baie du Moulin-Baude, admire the large sand plateaus of **Les Dunes de Tadoussac** ⑤. A welcome center, Les Maison des Dunes, offers interpretive exhibits and information that explains the formation of the dunes thousands of years ago as the glaciers receded. The center also introduces visitors to a number of birds-of-prey known to the area. Stairs and walking paths afford sweeping views of the Saint Lawrence maritime estuary. T:*(418) 235-4238. Open June to mid-Aug. daily 10–6; mid-Aug. to early-Oct. daily 9–5. Admission $3.50 for adults, $1.50 for children 6-17, children 5 and under are free. Family rates are available.*

*Whale watching ⑥ tours and cruises of the Fjord du Saguenay offer a close look the marine mammals that call the Saguenay-Saint-Lawrence home. The deep waters provide a rich feeding ground for a number of whale species, including Minke, Finback, Blue, and Beluga whales, and grey seals.

Tours are available from **Croisières Baleines**, departing from the wharf. The Catamaran *Katmar* offers underwater observation. On-board naturalists give an informative and entertaining presentation during the tour. **T**:*(418) 627-4276 or 1-800-694-5489,* **W**: *baleines.ca. Tours run May–Oct. at 9:15, 12:30, and 3:45, duration of 3 hours. Adults $52, children 6–13 $22, children 5 and under are free.*

Whale watching is also available from **Croisières Dufour, T**:*(418) 692-0222 or 1-800-463-5250,* **W**: *familledufour.com. Tours run daily at 9:30 and 1:30, and a sunset tour at 4:45, which includes whale watching and a tour of the*

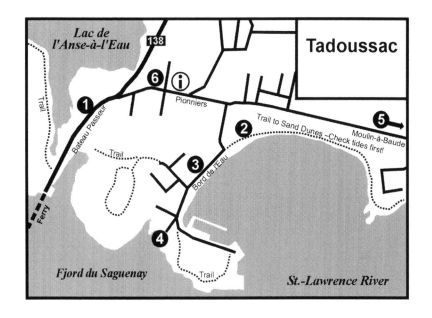

fjord. Fares $52 for adults and $22 for children 6–12. Children 5 and under are free. Also available is **extreme whale watching** aboard their Zodiac-style craft. *Tours run daily at 9, 12:30, and 3:30. Call for fares. Children under 6 are not permitted.* Or, try a trip along the fjord and back through time aboard the historic schooner *Marie Clarisse. Tours run daily at 10 for the fjord and 2 for whale watching. Fares $52 for adults, $22 for children 6–12, children 5 and under are free.*

For the truly adventurous, try whale watching in Zodiacs with **Croisières AML,** departing from Marina Tadoussac. **T:***(418) 237-4274 or 1-800-563-4643. Two-hour tours run at 7 and 5, $45 for adults, $30 for children 6–12. Three-hour tours run at 9:30 and 1:30, $52 for adults, $35 for children 6–12. Children under 6 are not permitted.*

Trip 16

Parc de la Jacques-Cartier Area

Commonly known as Québec's "best kept secret," at the back door of Québec City, not twenty minutes north, this vast natural oasis offers a bounty of natural beauty and outdoor sports activities. Country living and breathtaking scenery await among countless rivers and lakes.

With abundant wildlife in the dense forests and lush meadows, and oxygen-rich lakes full of fish, the area was a popular hunting, fishing, and trapping region for the Huron and Montagnais nations. The Huron and Montagnais would commonly guide the Jesuits from Québec to Lac Saint-Jean in the 17th century — a much shorter route than the Saint Lawrence River.

The 259-square-mile Parc de la Jacques Cartier is surrounded by the Réserve Faunique des Laurentides. Nearby is the pristine Montmorency Forest. In the 19th century the region was in danger from extensive logging that threatened to disrupt the wildlife and ecosystem. Parc de la Jacques Cartier was established in 1981 as part of an effort to preserve the natural treasures of the area.

The park is home to an array of wildlife including black bear, raccoon, white-tailed deer, lynx, moose, and wolf. Over 100 species of birds have been spotted in the park including osprey and barred owl. The waterways are popular for fishing, with their speckled trout, Arctic char, and Atlantic salmon.

Many of the towns surrounding the park have anglophone names, such as Stoneham and Shannon, reflecting the first settlers of the region who came from England, Ireland, and Scotland.

GETTING THERE:

By Car, the wilderness of Parc de la Jacques-Cartier begins only about twenty minutes north of the city. Follow **Rte. 73** north from Québec City, which becomes **Rte. 175**.

At the **Vallée Jacques-Cartier** sector of Parc de la Jacques-Cartier, turn left onto **road 4** to reach the entrance and visitor center.

Return to **Rte. 175** north. A number small roads, some unpaved, reach off in different directions, leading to hiking trails, rivers, and lakes. Turn right on

road 33 to explore the Montmorency Forest.

Continuing on **Rte. 175** north, Lac Jacques-Cartier will be on the right.

Return along **Rte. 175** back to Québec City.

PRACTICALITIES:

Tourisme Jacques-Cartier, 60 Saint-Patrick, Shannon. **T**:(418) 844-2358 or 1-877-844-2358, **W**: jacques-cartier.com

FOOD AND DRINK:

Vending machines and snacks are available at the Vallée Jacques-Cartier visitor center. There are many places to rest and enjoy a scenic **picnic** throughout the park. Make a picnic from one of the many bistros, cafés, or grocery stores around Québec City.

Le Tiffany (99 Chemin le Tour-du-Lac, Lac Beauport, at Le Manoir Saint-Castin) Gourmet and traditional French and Québec cuisine with beautiful lake views. **T**:(418) 841-4000. $$$

Restaurant Le Feu Follet (1420 Chemin du Hibou, Stoneham) Overlooking the ski slopes of Stoneham and featuring seafood and grill. **T**:(418) 848-2411. $$$

ATTRACTIONS:

Circled numbers correspond to numbers on the map.

PARC de la JACQUES-CARTIER ①, **T**:(418) 848-3169, **W**: sepaq.com. *Open late May to early Sept. Mon.–Fri. 8–5:30, Sat.–Sun. 7–5:30; early Sept. to mid-Oct. Mon.–Fri. 9–5, Sat.–Sun. 8–5:30.*

The park, which has been a forest reserve for more than 100 years, is renowned for its spectacular scenery. The Jacques-Cartier River winds tumultuously through the park, some days calm and some days raging. Over 2,000 lakes are spread across the region, providing numerous water activities year-round.

In summer, canoeing, kayaking, and rafting are popular on Rivière Jacques-Cartier, and the countless other lakes and rivers. More than 60 km (37 miles) of hiking trails extend through the forests and along the rivers. Former logging roads have been converted into six mountain-biking trails that cover over 80 km (50 miles) of wilderness.

In the winter the region is alive with skiing, snowshoeing, snowmobiling, and dog sledding.

The **Centre d'Interpretation de la Jacques-Cartier** ② welcomes visitors to the park, providing maps, information, and activity schedules. Exhibits and an audiovisual presentation address the history and geography of the area. Mountain bikes, rafts, and canoes are available for rent. Permits, required for fishing, can be purchased at the visitor center as well.

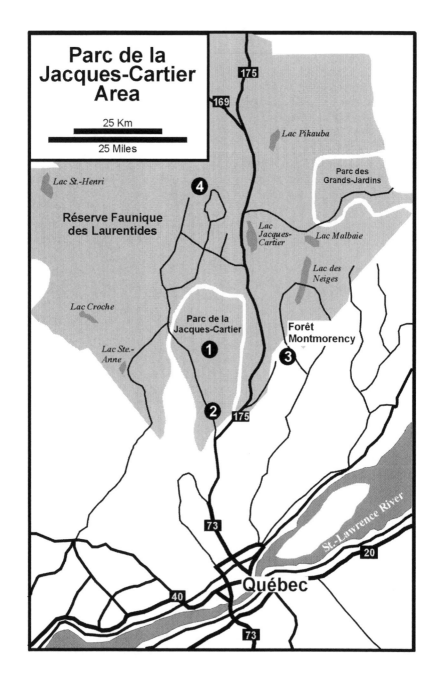

Parc de la Jacques-Cartier Area

25 Km

25 Miles

Lac Pikauba

Lac St.-Henri

Parc des Grands-Jardins

Réserve Faunique des Laurentides

❹

Lac Jacques-Cartier

Lac Malbaie

Lac des Neiges

Lac Croche

Parc de la Jacques-Cartier

❶

Forêt Montmorency

❸

Lac Ste.-Anne

❷ 175

St-Lawrence River

73

20

Québec

40

73

PARC DE LA JACQUES-CARTIER AREA   106

Join a **Safaris d'Observation de l'Original** moose safari, led by the knowledgeable park experts, to search out the large, lumbering animals in their natural habitat. **T**:*(418) 848-5099. Tours run mid-Sept. to mid-Oct. Reservations are required. Admission $15 per person.*

Other guided tours available include Rabaska canoe excursions, "rock shelter" hikes, and naturalist-led visits to spawning grounds.

The road behind the visitor center leads into the park, to the Jacques Cartier River. The **Sentier des Loups**, located on the other side of the Jacques Cartier river, is a nice 8-km (5-mile) hike that affords spectacular views of the park, river, and valley.

Follow **road 4** along the Jacques Cartier River for some spectacular views of the river and rapids.

The hiking trail **La Scotora** allows visitors to follow the same path the Huron and Montagnais used to lead the Jesuits between Québec City and Lac Saint-Jean.

Returning to Route 175, turn left to go farther into the park. There are many dirt and gravel roads reaching off the main throughway, leading to picturesque, isolated lakes and hiking trails.

Turning right on road 33 leads to **Forêt Montmorency** ③ and the **Chute de la Rivière Noire**. This dense fir, white birch, and pine forest, which boasts the highest annual snowfall in Québec Province, is home to an experimental forestry station for Université Laval, which established the forest reserve more than 30 years ago.

Continuing along Route 175 brings you deeper into the Laurentides wildlife reserve and to **Réserve Faunique des Laurentides** ④. This vast forest land and wildlife reserve is home to a number of animals, fish, and birds, including speckled trout, black bear, caribou, and moose. A variety of resort and outdoor sports activities are available throughout the park.

As you drive north along Route 175, the road hugs riverbanks and passes lakes, meadows, and forests. The scenery along this route is some of the most spectacular in the province. Small roads, many of them unpaved, fan off from Route 175 leading to the hiking trails, isolated beaches, and mountain cliffs. It is worthwhile exploring several of these roads as the mood hits you.

Trip 17

*Fjord du Saguenay

The Fjord du Saguenay is a spectacular natural wonderland, protected by the Parc du Saguenay and Parc Marin du Saguenay-Saint-Laurent. Solid walls of rock drop to the dark cool waters of the river, while picturesque villages rest snuggly between the river's edge and mountains.

The Rivière Saguenay, which stretches for over 152 km (95 miles), is the only river draining Lac Saint-Jean. From Saint-Fulgence, about 48 km (30 miles) from Lac Saint-Jean, to the Saint Lawrence River in Tadoussac, the Saguenay River flows through this awesome fjord.

Cut in Precambrian rock during the last Ice Age, the deep fjord is bordered by striking cliffs, some of which are over 450 meters (1,500 feet) high. The river is as much as 1476 meters (4,920 feet) in places and averages 236 meters (787 feet) deep.

GETTING THERE:

By Car, L'Anse-Saint-Jean and Tadoussac (the start and ending points of the tour) are each about 248 km (155 miles) north and northeast of Québec City. The tour around the fjord is also about 248 km (155 miles) long.

Take **Rte. 138** east from Québec City to Saint-Siméon. Turn left onto **Rte. 170**.

Turn right and follow signs to **L'Anse-Saint-Jean**.

Return to **Rte. 170** and turn right. At Rivière-Éternité turn right into the Parc du Saguenay.

Return to **Rte. 170** and turn right. At Saint-Félix-d'Otis, turn right and follow the rough road to Nuevo France.

Continue on the old road until it meets with **Rte. 170** again. Turn right and continue on **Rte. 170** to La Baie.

Bear left, continuing on **Rte. 170** to Chicoutimi. Turn right onto **Rte. 175** and follow it to the center of town and the old port. Cross the bridge to the opposite side of the river. Turn right onto **Rte. 172** east.

Turn right, descending to the river, for Sainte-Rose-du-Nord.

Return to **Rte. 172** and continue to Tadoussac. Turn right onto **Rte. 138**. A free ferry service brings you across the mouth of the Saguenay River. Continue on **Rte. 138**, returning to Québec City.

PRACTICALITIES:

This is a long tour, with a lot of driving involved, so it is recommended that you get an early start to do it in one day. Or, consider taking two days to move at a more leisurely pace. There are places to stay in Chicoutimi (the halfway point of the tour) and in Tadoussac. You may also want to combine this trip with a tour of Tadoussac (Trip 15).

The weather can be cool in the area around the Fjord du Saguenay, even in August. It is wise to have warm clothes with you when visiting the area, just in case they are needed.

Tourisme Chicoutimi-Valin, 295 Rue Racine, Chicoutimi. Open year-round Mon.–Fri. 8:30–12 and 1:30–4:30. **T**:(418) 698-3167 or 1-800-463-6565.

Société Touristique du Fjord, 1171 Avenue 7th, La Baie. Open year-round Mon.–Fri. 8:30–12 and 1:30–4:30. **T**:(418) 697-5050 or 1-800-263-2243.

Additional tourist information is available on the Internet at **W**: tourismsaguenaylacsaintjean.qc.ca

FOOD AND DRINK:

Cactus Rock Café (200 Boulevard Grande-Baie North, La Baie) Casual restaurant-bar serving an extensive menu of international, Canadian, vegetarian, and seafood dishes. **T**:(418) 544-9310. $$

La Sauvagine (122 Rue Jacques-Cartier East, Chicoutimi) Fine French cuisine and regional game dishes. **T**:(418) 690-2255. $$$

Restaurant Bistro La Cuisine (387 Rue Racine East, Chicoutimi) Delicious and satisfying French, International, grill and seafood, popular with the local crowd. **T**:(418) 698-2822. $$ and $$$

SUGGESTED TOUR:

Circled numbers correspond to numbers on the map.

Start the tour in perhaps one of the most beautiful villages of the Fjord du Saguenay, **L'Anse-Saint-Jean** ①. This charming town, founded in 1828, with beautiful ancestral homes and a preserved **covered bridge**, will win your heart. Resting on the edge of the Saguenay River and surrounded by mountains, the village is a peaceful place offering a wide variety of nearby activities.

For an adventurous look at the Fjord du Saguenay, try **Fjord en Kayak**, 359 rue St-Jean-Baptiste. A number of expeditions are available, offering a close look at all of the beauty and splendor of the fjord. The Islet Saint-Jean tour is a memorable three-hour journey by small islands, waterfalls, and steep cliffs. The outfitters supply weatherproof clothing free of charge. **T**:*(418) 272-3024. Tours run mid-May through Sept. Three-hour tours depart at 9:30, 2 and 5:30. Rates start at $42 per person. Not recommended for children under 3.*

Cross the covered bridge, continue for about 4.8 km (3 miles) and turn right to access **Anse de Tabatière** for amazing views of the area.

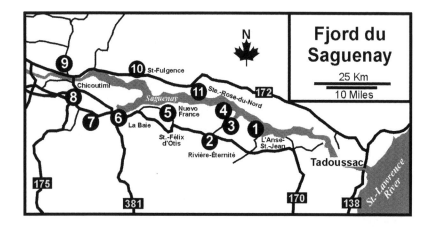

Fjord du Saguenay
25 Km
10 Miles

The village of **Rivière-Éternité** ② has been called the Bethlehem of the snow. A number of life-size religious scenes are displayed in the peaceful municipal park. The **Exposition Internationale de Crèches de Rivière-Éternité**, held in the basement of the church at 418 Rue Principale, has a charming exhibit of more than 250 nativity scenes created by artists from Québec and around the world. **T**:*(418) 272-2807. Open July–Sept. daily 9–7; late Nov. to early Jan. daily 12:30–7:30, Sun. 10:30–7:30. Admission $5 for adults, $2 for children, children under 5 are free.*

PARC du SAGUENAY ③, **T**:1-877-272-5229, **W**: sepaq.com. *Open mid-May through June daily 9–5; July–Labor Day daily 9–9; Sept. to early Oct. daily 9–5. Admission $3.50 for adults, $1.50 for children 6–17, children 5 and under are free. Family rates are available.*

Founded in 1983, the park was established to protect the fjord, extending for over 96 km (60 miles) and covering more than 298 square kilometers (115 square miles).

The "Secteur Baie Éternité" has a welcome center at the gate that provides information and maps. At the end of the road, an **Interpretation Center** welcomes visitors and provides the base for outdoor activities in the park. Exhibits introduce visitors to the flora and fauna of the area and explain the formation of the fjord.

A scenic cruise on **Croisière du Cap Trinité**, departing from the visitor center, is the ideal way to see the stunning cliffs and capes of the fjord. **T**:*(418) 272-2591. Tours run late May to mid-Sept. 11 and 2:30, for 1½ hours. Admission $20 for adults.*

Cap Trinté ④ rises sharply at the confluence of the Rivière Éternité and the Fjord du Saguenay. The climb to the top of the cape is relatively short, but extremely steep. The round trip usually takes about three to three-and-a-half

Saguenay Fjord

hours. A statue of the Virgin Mary, known as Our Lady of the Saguenay, is perched 177 meters (590 feet) above the dark waters on the first ledge of the cape. The statue, created in 1881, is over 26 feet tall, carved from three blocks of pine and covered in lead. The 3,400-kilo (7,000-pound) statue turned out to be too heavy to bring up the cliff. It had to be separated into pieces, carried up individually, and then reassembled.

A stop at **Saint-Félix d'Otis** is a trip to the pristine and wild land of Québec's past. The virgin landscape has been popular with moviemakers. The site of **Nuevo France** ⑤, off Chemin du Vieux, transports visitors to the 17th century, when the first settlers inhabited the area. Professional guides in period costumes lead visitors through authentically re-created buildings representing a Huron Village, Québec City, a country house, and a Montagnais village. **T**:*(418) 544-8027*, **W**: *sitenouvellefrance.com. Open late June to mid-Aug. daily 9:15–4:30; late Aug.–Labor Day weekends 9:15–4:30. Admission $12 for adults, $6 for children, children under 5 are free. Call for times of English language tours.*

La Baie ⑥ sits at the end of the magnificent Baie des Ha! Ha!, known locally as "the sea." Legend has it that the bay was named after Ha! Ha! Street in 17th-century Paris. A group of settlers, dubbing themselves the Society of Twenty-One, set out to settle the Saguenay-Saint-Jean area and founded three villages at the end of the Baie des Ha! Ha! in 1838. The villages were later merged into the community of La Baie.

Parc Mars, running along the bay, affords spectacular views of the fjord. Near the park, gift shops and galleries await.

The **Musée du Fjord**, 3346 Boulevard de la Grande-Baie South, has a number of interesting natural science and art exhibits. A vast display of mounted insects give a close look at the mysterious world of Québec's worlds. The "Paysages dy Fjord" exhibit features the latest works of regional artists. A new exhibit and documentary commemorate the flood of 1996. **T**:*(418) 697-5077,* **W***: museedufjord.com. Open late June to Labor Day, Mon.–Fri. 9–6; Labor Day to late June, Tues.–Fri. 9–5, Sat.–Sun. 1–5. Admission $8.50 for adults, $5.50 for students and children 6–11, children 5 and under are free.*

Check out **La Pyramide des Ha! Ha!**, Saguenay-Lac Saint-Jean's monument to the millennium. The reflecting pyramid, made primarily of aluminum, was built by a group of citizens after the 1996 flood.

MUSÉE de la DÉFENSE AÉRIENNE de BAGOTVILLE ⑦, Route 170, Bagotville. **T**:(418) 677-4000 ext. 8159, **W**: bagotville.net. *Open mid-June through Aug. daily 9-5. Guided tours of the Canadian Forces Base at 9:45 and 2, by reservation. Admission, for museum and tour, $4 for adults, $3 for children, children under 5 are free.*

This is the only museum in Québec dedicated to the history of military aviation. Interesting and informative exhibits, featuring aviation artifacts and models, illustrate the history of Canadian military air defense and the Canadian Forces Base in Bagotville. During a tour of the base, get a close look at the CF-18 Hornet, as well as other military planes from Canada and around the world.

Continue on to **Chicoutimi** ⑧. Situated around three magnificent rivers (Chicoutimi, du Moulin, and Saguenay) Chicoutimi was the hub of the fur trade that thrived in the area for nearly 200 years, but was not founded as a community until 1842, when the first sawmill was erected at the site. Today, the city is a world leader in the pulp and paper industry. The city's name is derived from the Montagnais word "eshko-timiou" which means "edge of deep waters."

The **downtown** area of the city is alive with boutiques, galleries, pubs, and terraced restaurants.

The **historic basin** area of the city has a number of interesting sites and a scenic walkway. The basin was the area most effected during the massive flood of 1996 and has since been reconstructed. The **Petite Maison Blanc** (little white house) stands alone at the top of a rugged rock wall. Miraculously, this was the only house to survive the flood of 1996. The **Église Sacre-Coeur** presides over the area with its single elegant silver steeple. Also of interest is the **Abitibi-Consolidated Dam**.

The historic **Vieux Port** offers a variety of activities and attractions. The works of local artists and crafts people are on display at the **pARTerre**. A public market, **Halles du Marché** offers local produce and other locally-made products.

A beautiful park, the **Zone Portuaire**, stretches out along the river by the old port, on Rue Lafontaine. Fanciful fountains and statues of whales delight visitors and playgrounds give the younger set a place to let out some steam. From

June to September the park hosts a number of outdoor entertainment programs. T:*(418) 698-3025. Open May–Oct. daily. Market open May–Sept. daily 9–9. The pARTerre is open late June through Sept. Wed.–Sun. 1–9. Admission is free.*

For a relaxing way to see the city, take a **Tour de Calèche**, by the old port.

The imposing **Cathédrale Saint-François-Xavier**, 514 Rue Racine, stands watch over the old city and port. The cathedral, dating from 1915, has twin silver-topped towers and an impressive stone façade.

Perched high above the hill on the north shore of the river, **La Croix de Sainte-Anne** ⑨, on Rue de la Croix, is a reminder of the community's faith and commemorates the extensive fire of 1870 that destroyed most of the region, but left Chicoutimi standing. The location, at the top of Cap Saint-Joseph, offers sweeping views of the city and fjord. *Open May–Oct. daily 7–9. Admission is free.*

To the east lies **Saint-Fulgence** ⑩. Resting on the north shore of the Saguenay River, the town of Saint-Fulgence is committed to conservation and ecology. Sandbars weave along the river's edge welcoming an array of waterfowl. Wood boardwalks and trails provide a place to stroll and take in the wildlife. The drive along Route 172, on either side of the village, presents panoramic views of the Saguenay River, the Fjord, and Mont Valin which rises high to the north of the town.

At the end of April each year, more than 10,000 **Canadian geese** stop to rest and feed along the shores of Saint-Fulgence during spring migration. This is a truly spectacular site to see.

Sainte-Rose-du-Nord ⑪, founded in 1838, is a spectacular little village, wedged in a small valley, between steep mountainsides and the Saguenay River. The charming haven has long been popular with artists and tourists who are attracted by the breathtaking views of the fjord and the peaceful beauty of the village. The **wooden church** is worth a look with its thematic décor honoring the forest. From the wharf, a 1½ mile **hiking trail** leads to a scenic overlook on the fjord.

The **Musée de la Nature**, 199 Rue de la Montagne, is an interesting and unique little museum that exudes a love for nature. The museum proudly displays some of the nature and wildlife found in the region, including tree burrs, wild mushrooms, butterflies, and the Canadian Lynx. Two sharks, which were pulled from the frozen Saguenay River at Sainte-Rose-du-Nord, can be examined and touched. T:*(418) 675-2348. Open year-round daily 8:30–9. Admission $5 for adults, $1 for children 6–13, children 5 and under are free.*

Trip 18

Lac Saint-Jean

Rich, fertile plains meander to the edge of the lake, so vast that the opposite shores are only visible in clear weather. With so much water, numerous beaches, and lively towns the area offers a wide variety of attractions and activities.

The current lake, covering 1,350 square kilometers (521 square miles), is only a small remnant of the original one created by glaciers more than 10,000 years ago. Fed by a number of rivers, its sole outlet is the Saguenay River. With steep walls, and surrounded by high mountains, the area is likened to a large crater.

Named Piékouagami (flat lake) by the Montagnais, the lake was subsequently renamed for Jean Dequen, the first Frenchman to visit the area. A fur-trading post was established on its shores in 1676, on the site that was to become Desbiens. The area still did not begin to be settled until the mid-19th century, when sawmills and pulp mills were established.

Today the region is known for the granite found by the shore, landlocked salmon, and the wild blueberries found everywhere.

GETTING THERE:

By Car, Lac Saint-Jean is about 184 km (115 miles) north of Québec City.

Take **Rte. 175** north. Turn left onto **Rte. 169**. At Hébertville turn left, staying on **Rte. 169**. At the end, bear left, continuing on **Rte. 169** around the river.

In Roberval, turn right, following signs for Mashteuiatsh, for the lakefront area and Boulevard de la Traversée. Continue on Boulevard de la Traversée through Mashteuiatsh until the road rejoins **Rte. 169**. Turn right and continue to Saint-Félicien.

Turn right following **Rte. 169** and then bearing right onto **Rte. 373**. When the road intersects with **Rte. 169** again, turn right, following **Rte. 169** around the lake to Alma.

Continue on **Rte. 169** back to **Rte. 175**, and then continue on **Rte. 175** south to Québec City.

PRACTICALITIES:

Many attractions and services are closed in the winter months. Some of the roads along this route are also closed in bad weather, when immense snow and drifts can obscure the road. Flashing lights, located as you enter the Réserve Faunique des Laurentides from either end, warn of closed roads before you get too far.

This is a long tour and it is recommended that you leave early or consider staying overnight for a more leisurely pace. The trip around the lake is about 208 km (130 miles). If you are staying overnight, you may also want to consider including a trip to the Val-Jalbert Historic Village (Trip 19).

Tourisme Alma, 1671 Avenue du Pont Nord, Alma. Open year-round Mon.–Fri. 8:30–12 and 1:30–4:30. **T**:(418) 668-3611 or 1-877-668-3611.

Bureau d'Information Touristique de Saint-Félicien, 1209 Boulevard Sacre-Coeur. Open year-round Mon.–Fri. 8:30–12 and 1:30–4:30. **T**:(418) 679-9888.

Additional tourist information is available on the Internet at **W**: tourismsaguenaylacsaintjean.qc.ca

FOOD AND DRINK:

Hôtel Universel (100 Boulevard des Cascades, Alma) Fine French food and local specialties in a classic elegant atmosphere. **T**:(418) 668-5261. $$$

Resto Roberto (11 Rue Scott East, Alma) Popular, family-style restaurant with Canadian and Italian meals. **T**:(418) 662-2191. $$

SUGGESTED TOUR:

Circled numbers correspond to numbers on the map.

Begin at **Desbiens** ①. Until the mid-17th century the area was a popular gathering place for the Montagnais nations, then in 1676 it became a busy fur-trading post. The first settlers arrived in the middle of the 19th century, bringing with them forestry and farming. Ideally located at the junction of the Rivière Métabetchouane and Lac Saint-Jean, the area has played an important role in the history of the region, and today plays host to a variety of outdoor activities.

Stop at the **Trou de la Fée**, Chemin du Trou de la Fée, off Avenue 7th, for a hike through spectacular natural surroundings. Hiking through the "Fairy's Hole" feels like a trip below the earth. The trail, running along the Rivière Métabetchouane, leads past waterfalls, cascades, a dam, and an old power station. Legend has it that deserters, fleeing World War II, hid in the cavern and later claimed to have been saved by the fairies who lived there. **T**:*(418) 346-1242 or (418) 346-5632. Open mid-June to mid-Aug., daily 9–5:30; mid-Aug. to Labor Day daily 10–4; Labor Day to mid-June by reservation only. Admission $7.50 for adults, $4.50 for children under 12. Not recommended for children under 4 or mobility-impaired people.*

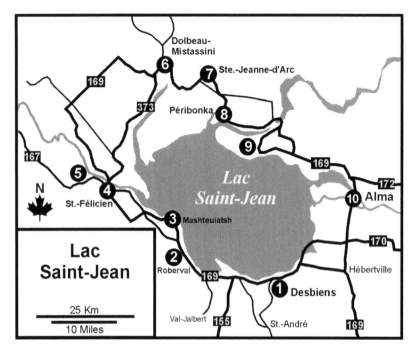

The **Centre d'Histoire et d'Archéologie de la Métabetchouane**, 243 Rue Hébert, is a nice little museum with interpretive and interactive exhibits illustrating local history. Visitors can see the working relationships between the Amerindian peoples and settlers at the mouth of the Rivière Métabetchouane, learn what they came to trade, how they worked the land, and how they grew together as a community. In July and August, archeological digs take place at the site. In the garden, a chapel and monument are dedicated to the Jesuits who came to the colony to convert the native people. **T**:*(418) 346-5341. Open late June to Labor Day daily 10–6; Sept. to late June upon reservation. Admission $5 for adults, $2.50 for children under 12.*

Beside the museum, follow the small road to a **scenic overlook** for a fine view of the lake and mouth of the Rivière Métabetchouane.

The road brings you through **Chambord**, a small farming village with a nice beach. The beautiful park has great views of the lake. Admire the panorama as the road hugs the shore.

Continue on to **Roberval** ②. The town was founded in 1855 and was the location of the prestigious resort, the Beemer Hotel, until it was destroyed by fire in 1908.

Renowned as the world's long-distance swimming capital, Roberval has been host to the **Traversée Internationale du Lac Saint-Jean** for more than 47 years.

LAC SAINT-JEAN 116

A peaceful **park** and **beach** welcome visitors to the water's edge and afford beautiful views of the immense lake. Galleries, boutiques, and pottery workshops rest along the edge of the lake.

Visit the **Centre Historique et Aquatique de Roberval**, 700 Boulevard de la Traversée, for a look at the history of Roberval and the marine environment of the lake. Exhibits educate visitors on the history and changes of the lake and the effects on its wildlife. A large aquarium proudly displays some of the fish and wildlife that can be found in Lac Saint-Jean. **T**:*(418) 275-5550. Open early June and late Aug., daily 12–5; mid-June to mid-Aug. daily 10–8. Admission $5.50 for adults, $3.75 for children, children under 6 are free.*

The **Église Notre-Dame-de-Roberval**, on Boulevard Saint-Joseph, built in 1967, is an interesting structure, shaped like a copper pyramid with a white steeple and brightly colored stained-glass windows. **T**:*(418) 275-0272. Open year-round Sat. 9:30–8, Sun. 8–12.*

Follow Boulevard de la Traversée to Mashteuiatsh. **Mashteuiatsh** ③, also known as Pointe-Bleue, was founded in 1856. Originally called Ouiatchouan and renamed in 1983, Mashteuiatsh is the only First Nation in the Lac Saint-Jean region. The village is home to the Pekuakamiulnuatsh (Lac Saint-Jean Montagnais) people, who live according to traditional values and customs.

As you drive through the village, note the small homes with **totem poles** decorating their front steps.

A **promenade**, situated along the lake, has a number of tepee-shaped monuments dedicated to the nation's leaders. In the village, enjoy the numerous arts and crafts shops, featuring traditionally crafts of the Montagnais people.

The **Musée Amérindien de Masheuiatsh**, 1787 Amishk, depicts the thousand-year history of the Pekuakamiulnuatsh people. Permanent and temporary exhibits illustrate the love this nation has for the land and lake. Marvel at the artifacts dating back to before the arrival of the settlers and admire the traditional art and crafts of this nation. **T**:*(418) 275-4842 or 1-888-875-4842. Open mid-May through Oct., daily 10-6; Nov. to mid-May, Mon.-Thurs. 9-12 and 1-4, Fri. 9-12 and 1-3, Sat.-Sun. for groups only with reservation. Admission $8 for adults, $6 for children, children 5 and under are free.*

At **Le Tipi**, 2204 Ouiatchouan, discover the Montagnais way of life before the European settlers arrived and take an interesting look at the parallels between the Montagnais and Iroquois people. Admire the tools, naturalized animals, and traditional handicrafts. **T**:*(418) 275-5593. Open May to mid-Oct., Mon.–Sat. 9:30–6, Sun. 12–6; mid-Oct. to Apr. with reservation only.*

The road continues through the beautiful farming town of **Saint-Prime**, known for its sandy beach and cheddar cheese. Stop at **La Vieille Fromagerie Perron, Musée du Cheddar**, 148 Avenue 15th, for an informative and tasty look at a 19th-century cheese factory. **T**:*(418) 251-4922 or 1-888-251-4922. Open June and Sept., daily 10:15–5:30; July–Aug., daily 9:15–5:30. Admission $6 for adults, $3 for children 6–12, children 5 and under are free.*

Farther along is **Saint-Félicien** ④. For thousands of years the Montagnais people have traversed the three rivers that border Saint-Félicien - Rivières Ashuapmushuan, Mistassini, and Ticouapé. When the first settlers arrived in 1865, they too found the location ideal for colonization.

Take a peek at the whimsical **Sacre-Coeur Park**, on Route 169. Fanciful statues, small buildings, cannons, windmills, fountains, and a miniature boat adorn this peaceful park. This is a nice place for a fun and relaxing stop.

As you leave town, follow the signs toward the zoo.

The wide **Chutes à Michel** on the Rivière Ashuapmushuan are a beautiful and picturesque place to enjoy the natural beauty of the area.

*ZOO "SAUVAGE" de SAINT-FÉLICIEN ⑤, 2230 Boulevard du Jardin, **T**:(418) 679-0543 or 1-800-667-5687. *Open mid- to late May, daily 9–5; June– Aug., daily 9–6; Sept. to mid-Oct., 9–5; late Oct. and early May by reservation only. Admission $28 for adults, $18 for children 6–14, $11 for children 4–5, children under 3 are free.*

Explore the wildlife of Canada, from coast to coast, in their natural habitats. Walking paths lead through a variety of environments where the animals roam and the people are behind fences. Different habitats represent forests, the arctic, mountains, and marshlands. A screened-in train brings visitors up close to some of Canada's more wild characters, such as families of bear, moose, and bison. The zoo is home to over 1,000 North American animals. Don't miss the polar bear feeding!

The Borealium brings you closer to the wildlife and nature of the reagion. This new visitor center includes nature exhibits, a discovery room, large screen theater, and documentation center. The beautiful exhibits and a spectacular film in the auditorium will entertain all of your senses.

Dolbeau-Mistassini ⑥ is nestled at the junction of two rivers, Rivière Mistassibi and aux Rats, and is host to a number of festivals each year. Each July **Les 10 Jours Western** celebrates country music. The **Festival du Bleuet** arrives in August in honor of the little blueberries that have become the symbol of the region.

Nearby, take a look at the **Chutes de Pères**, named for the Trappist Monks who settled at the site in 1892. The twin towers of the original monastery can be seen near the junction of the Mistassibi and Mistassini rivers. The monks moved out of the area in 1980, but the chocolate and other products they made are still for sale at the factory near the monastery.

The **Centre Astro**, 1208 Route de la Friche, is a nice planetarium and observatory with a number of attractions, including a computerized telescope, exhibits about the moon, a scenic lookout, and a playground. The lunar model is in the Guinness Book of World Records. **T**:*(418) 276-0919. Open late June to mid-Aug., 1–9, to midnight on clear nights. Admission $6 for adults, $3.50 for* *children, children 5 and under are free.*

Sainte-Jeanne-d'Arc ⑦ is a picturesque rural community and a great place to pick-your-own bushel of the infamous local blueberries. **Le Vieux Moulin,** 125 Rue du Vieux Moulin, dating back to 1902, is a fine example of the more than 200 mills that existed in the area during the colonization. **T**:*(418) 276-3166. Open mid-June through Aug., Mon.–Thurs. 10–5, Fri.–Sun. 10–7. Admission is free.*

The village of **Péribonka** ⑧, which means "where the sand shifts," is the locale for Louis Hémon's 1912 novel *Maria Chapdelaine.* The **Musée Louis Hémon,** 700 Route 169, is dedicated to literature and regional history. Exhibits chronicle the adventures of the author, look at the local history, and honor the arts. **T**:*(418) 374-2177. Open June through Sept., daily 9–5; Oct.–May, Mon.– Fri. 9–4. Admission $5.50 for adults, $3.50 for children, children 5 and under are free.*

Parc de la Pointe-Taillon ⑨, Rang 3 West, Saint-Henri-de-Taillon, has a number of outdoor activities. A large sandy beach welcomes visitors to enjoy the beautiful Lac Saint-Jean. Hiking, swimming, and aquatic sports are popular, and equipment rental is available.

Founded in 1864, the city of **Alma** ⑩ developed around the island of Alma that sits snuggly in the mouth of the Saguenay River. Started as a lumbering center, the city quickly became the industrialized capital of the region. Owing to its location between Lac Saint-Jean and Rivière Saguenay, and the abundant natural resources, the paper, electricity, and aluminum industries flourished.

MUSÉE d'HISTOIRE du LAC SAINT-JEAN, 54 Rue Saint-Joseph, Alma, **T**:(418) 668-2606. *Open late June through Aug., Mon.–Fri. 9–5, Sat.–Sun. 1–5; Sept. to late June, Mon.–Fri. 9–12 and 1–4:30. Admission $12 for adults, children under 14 are free.*

This delightful museum tells the history of Alma, the region, and its people through exhibits of everyday items. An extensive collection of old bicycles celebrates the history of cycling and illustrates the popularity of the bicycle as a mode of transportation and sport in the region.

There are two notable churches in the town. **Église Saint-Joseph,** 70 Rue Saint-Joseph, has a tall central spire with shorter side towers. The interior boasts several beautiful stained-glass windows. **T**:*(418) 662-6491. Open year-round Mon.–Fri. 9–5, Sat. 1–8, Sun. 9–12. Admission is free.* **Église Saint-Pierre,** Rue Harvey, built in 1963, is an interesting modern building with a freestanding bell tower and large triangular windows. **T**:*(418) 668-2496. Open year-round Mon.– Fri. 9–8.*

Trip 19

*Village Historique de Val-Jalbert

Spend the day in the early 1900s — time has literally stopped here. The village remains much the same as it was when abandoned in 1927. Val-Jalbert was founded in 1901 with the construction of a paper mill at the base of the massive waterfall. At its peak, the company-owned village was home to some 950 residents, 250 of whom worked the mill, which was producing as much as 50 tons of pulp a day.

Demand for pulp began to drop off in 1926 and the price fell. When the mill was closed in 1927 all of its residents were forced to leave. The chapel was moved, but the rest of the village was abandoned.

GETTING THERE:
By Car, the Val-Jalbert Historic Village is 259 km (162 miles) northwest of Québec City.

Take **Rte. 73** out of Québec. The road becomes **Rte. 175**, cutting through the Réserve Faunique des Laurentides. Bear left onto **Rte. 169** to Hébertville. Turn right, continuing on **Rte. 169** to the lake. Turn left again, staying on **Rte. 169**.

Ten kilometers (6 miles) after Chambord, turn left following the signs for Val-Jalbert.

PRACTICALITIES:
The village is open mid-May to mid-June and Sept.–Oct., daily 9–5; admission $10 for adults, $5 for children 7–14. Open July–Aug., daily 9–7; admission $16 for adults, $7 for children 7–14. Children 6 and under are free.

For information about the park: **T**:(418) 275-3132 or 1-888-675-3132, **W**: sepaq.com

FOOD AND DRINK:
There is a **café** in the old sawmill, serving light meals and snacks. The **general store** has light meals during the summer and snacks and ice cream all year.

Château Roberval (1225 Boulevard Saint-Dominique, Roberval) Gourmet regional, French and Canadian cuisine in elegant surroundings. **T**:(418) 275-7511. $$$

Brochetterie Chez Greco (979 Boulevard Marcotte, Roberval) Popular and casual restaurant serving Italian and Greek dishes, and seafood. **T**:(418) 275-5707. $$

ATTRACTIONS:

Circled numbers correspond to numbers on the map.

The Convent ① of Our Lady of Good Counsel, built in 1915, was home to the nuns and the village's school. Classrooms, living quarters, and a chapel are still set up as they were in the 1900s when the building was in full use.

Across from the convent, while you're waiting for the trolley, explore the foundations of the old church.

Start your visit of the historical village with an informative **trolley tour**. The knowledgeable guide gives an overview of the park and an in-depth look at its history. The trolley drops visitors off at the old sawmill.

Stop at the **Sawmill** ②. The hall has several interesting **scale models** of the village and mill. A **multimedia presentation** tells the history of the village and the production of wood pulp for manufacturing paper.

A **cable car** departs from the mill, whisking visitors up the steep mountain-side and presenting breathtaking views of the village, valley, and Lac Saint-Jean.

At the top of the mountain, follow the hiking path to the **Chutes Maligne** ③. A mill and lock once stood at the summit, preparing wood before sending it down the river to the lower mill. Stop to explore and admire the **trapper's hut** along the way and imagine what it would be like to be a trapper, alone in the woods, hunting for food.

The **Chutes Ouiatchouan** ④, higher than Niagara Falls, tumble roughly down the rugged mountain side, making a couple of twists and turns along the way.

Take the cable car to the top of the falls or climb the steep, panoramic stairs. The stairs have a number of observation decks, worth the effort for the descent.

Stroll along the river and admire the crashing water at its base. Walk uphill along Rue Sainte-Anne and wander through the housing neighborhoods that remain intact.

A **herb garden** ⑤ welcomes visitors to enjoy the sites and smells of the herbs found at the site. Imagine the women of Val-Jalbert picking the fresh herbs to season their daily meals.

A **theatrical presentation** ⑥ is given on Avenue Tremblay by experienced actors in period costumes, bringing the history and lifestyle of the village alive again, just as it had been before being abandoned. *Show runs late June through Aug. daily 10–5.*

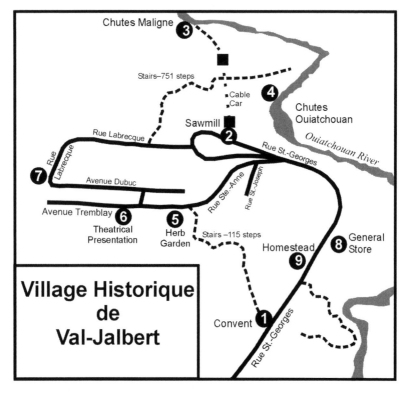

Village Historique de Val-Jalbert

Rue Labrecque ⑦ was one of the most progressive streets in Québec for its time, with a number of modern conveniences such as central heating, electricity, running water, and telephones. Note the old fire hydrants — a novelty for the beginning of the 1900s.

Most of the houses in the neighborhood have been restored to their original condition giving the feeling that the town is still alive and active today. Some houses have been left in a state of decay and deterioration to illustrate the ravages of time on the village after it was abandoned.

The **General Store** ⑧, originally the town's hotel for visitors, welcomes "towns people" and visitors to relax and have refreshments. If you're lucky you may be able to eavesdrop on a heated debate between some of the locals as they enjoy an afternoon respite on the porch.

Finish the day at the **daily gathering** of village folk. All of the costumed characters gather in front of the general store at the end of the day to socialize and mingle with visitors.

Grandma Galette welcomes visitors to explore her **homestead** ⑨ which once housed the families that worked the mill. Admire the small garden in the back.

Section VI

DAYTRIPS IN THE CHAUDIÈRE-APPALACHES REGION

Named for the Rivière Chaudière and Appalachian Mountains that dominate the region, the area reaches from the Saint Lawrence River to the United States Border. This vast expanse is rich and beautiful with lush green valleys and rolling mountains. The Chaudière River flows leisurely through the valley, its rocky bed providing miles of beauty. If you come here in the early morning hours, particularly in the fall, you may see them covered with a blanket of thick white clouds, the surrounding hilltops jutting up defiantly on either side. It is an amazing site.

In the early 19th century, numerous epidemics sweeping across Europe triggered a massive migration to the Americas. For years these immigrants moved out across Québec. Many Irish, British, and Scottish families settled in the Chaudière River Valley. The culture and heritage of these anglophone settlers is still seen in this region.

Herds of deer roam the land, and it is not uncommon to see them playing or grazing in the wide fields alongside the road. Keep an eye out, no only for safety reasons, but also to see these beautiful creatures.

Trip 20

La Beauce

The Rivière Chaudière winds leisurely through rolling hills and rich plateaus of greenery. Small villages rest along its shores, boasting heritage estates and manor houses. The wide river is rocky and calm, bringing a strong feeling of peace to the valley.

Strategically located between the capital city and the United States, the Beauce region was occupied by French settlers as far back as 1736. Resting in the heart of the Chaudière River Valley, the region has a diverse history of entrepreneurship, invention, and ingenuity.

Hugging the Chaudière River, cutting through the Beauce Region, Route 173 is called Route du Président Kennedy. It is estimated that hundreds of thousands of Americans take this route to Québec each year. They follow in the footsteps of Colonel Benedict Arnold, who led his troops along this way in 1775 in an attempt to conquer Québec City.

A gold nugget, reportedly the size of a pigeon's egg, was found on a tributary of the Chaudière River in 1846, triggering a gold rush that brought prospectors to the shores of the area. By the 20th century, more than a million dollars worth of gold ore had been found.

GETTING THERE:

By Car, the Chaudière River Falls are located on the opposite shore of the Saint Lawrence River, just a few miles from the city. Saint-Georges, the farthest point of this tour, is about 128 km (80 miles) south of Québec City.

Take **Rte. 73** south out of Québec and across Pont Pierre-Laponte. Take **exit 130** and follow the signs for Parc de la Chute de la Rivière Chaudière.

Leaving the park, cross Rte. 73 to Charny and follow **Rte. 175** south. Turn left following signs for Rte. 175. In front of the church, turn right, staying on **Rte. 175** (it may not be clearly marked).

In Saint-Lambert turn right onto **Rte. 218** west and then left onto **Rte. 171** south.

In Scott turn left onto **Rte. 173** south.

For the center of Sainte-Marie turn right onto **Rte. 218** again and then return to **Rte. 173**.

After Vallée Jonction, bear right for Saint-Joseph-de-Beauce. Continue back onto **Rte. 173**.

Turn right in Notre-Dame-des-Pins for the covered bridge.

Return to **Rte. 173** south and continue into Saint-George.

Follow **Rte. 173** back to Saint-Joseph-de-Beauce. Bear right and then turn right following signs for **Rte. 73**. Take **Rte. 73** back to Québec City.

PRACTICALITIES:

Office de Tourisme et Congrès de Beauce, 11700 Boulevard Lacroix, Saint-Georges. **T**:(418) 227-4642. Additional information is available on the Internet at **W**: chaudapp.qc.ca and **W**: destinationbeauce.com

FOOD AND DRINK:

Restaurant-Bar Le Sabreur (8585 Boulevard Lacroix, Saint Georges) Popular and trendy for its delicious selection of wood-oven pizza. **T**:(418) 227-5222. $$

Il Mondo (11615 1st Avenue, Saint-Georges) International cuisine and light meals in a comfortable contemporary atmosphere. **T**:(418) 228-4133. $$$

Le Table du Père Nature (10735 1st Avenue, Saint-Georges) Fine and imaginative French cuisine, commonly acknowledged as one of the best restaurants in Saint-Georges. **T**:(418) 227-0888. $$$

SUGGESTED TOUR:

Circled numbers correspond to numbers on the map.

PARC de la CHUTE de la RIVIÈRE CHAUDIÈRE ①, off Route 73, Charny. *Open year-round daily. Interpretation center open June–Sept. Admission is free.*

This magnificent crescent-shaped set of falls is breathtaking. Walking paths and hiking trails run along the river, affording a number of scenic viewpoints overlooking the river and falls. A suspension bridge, crossing high over the river, leads to more parkland on the far side. Interpretation panels along the walkways provide information on the geology and history of the river and falls.

From 1901 to 1970 a power station was in operation on the west bank of the Chaudière River Falls. A chunk of ice, breaking up on the river in the spring of 1970, destroyed a part of the dam and the power station shut down. A new dam and power plant were created on the site of the old and are accessible via hiking trails.

Route 175 through Breakeyville affords beautiful views of the Chaudière River. Spectacular estates and manor houses rest amongst sweeping lawns and trees.

Sainte-Marie ② is one of the oldest villages in the Beauce region, dating back to 1736. The town is also known as the birthplace of Marius Barbeau (1883–1969), writer and founder of the Québec Folklore archives at Laval University. Today, with the enormous success of the Vachon family bakery,

Sainte-Marie's economy is supported by the snack cake factory.

Église Sainte-Marie, built in 1856, dominates the heart of the city. The Gothic Revival exterior has a distinctly British feeling, while the ornate interior, reminiscent of Montréal's Notre-Dame Basilica, is distinctly French. T:*(418) 387-5467. Open year-round Mon.–Sat. 9–7:30, Sun. 9–12.*

Stroll along **Rue Notre-Dame**, which runs through the center of town and along the Chaudière River. Interpretation panels illustrate the history of the city with photographs and text. There are a number of houses of historical and architectural interest in Sainte-Marie.

Maison Dupuis, 640 Rue Notre-Dame South, has a small museum dedicated to pioneer pilots born in Sainte-Marie. A peaceful park and gardens on the estate welcome visitors to relax, stroll, and picnic. T:*(418) 387-7221. Open June–Aug., Tues.–Fri. 9–4:30, Sat. and Mon. 10–4, Sun. 1–3; Mar.-May and Sept.–Nov. by appointment only. Admission $5 for adults, $2 for children 12–18, children 11 and under are free.*

Also of interest is **Maison J. A. Vachon**, 383 Rue de la Coopérative, which houses the largest wedding cake on record in the Guinness Book of World Records. An interpretation center in the house tells the history of Pâtisserie Vachon, from a small family run bakery to Québec institution. Canada's largest snack cake factory is also located at the site. T:*(418) 387-4052 or 1-866-387-4052. Open Apr.–Oct., Mon.–Fri. 10–4:30; mid-June to mid-Oct. the house is also open on Sat. and Sun. Admission for house and factory $8 for adults, $6 for children 5–17, children under 5 are free. Reservations required for tour of factory.*

Maison Pierre-Lacroix, 552 Rue Notre-Dame North, is the oldest stone house in the Beauce region, built in 1821. Workshops illustrate traditional arts and crafts. Local handicrafts are sold in a boutique at the site. T:*(418) 386-3821. Open early June and Sept., Sat.–Sun. 1–5; mid-June through Aug., Tues.–Sun. 1–5.*

Nearby, don't miss the **Taschereau Manor**, 730 Notre-Dame North. This impressive white manor, with a grand columned entryway was built in 1809. Today the estate is a fine Bed and Breakfast. T:*(418) 387-3671. Open to the public for guided tour June–Aug., Tues.–Sat. 10–4.*

Vallée-Jonction ③ developed around a railway junction and is steeped in traditions and history of the railroad. Two local attractions pay tribute to the rails.

CENTRE d'INTERPRÉTATION FERROVIAIRE de VALLÉE-JONC-TION, T:(418) 253-6449. *Open late June to mid-Aug., Tues.–Sun. 9:30–4:30; mid-Aug. through Sept., Sat.–Sun. 9:30–4:30. Admission $3.75 for adults, $2.50 for children 6–17, children under 6 are free.*

Situated in the old stone railway building, built in 1917, the museum recounts the story of the railway system in the Beauce region. Exhibits display artifacts, a caboose, and a working model train.

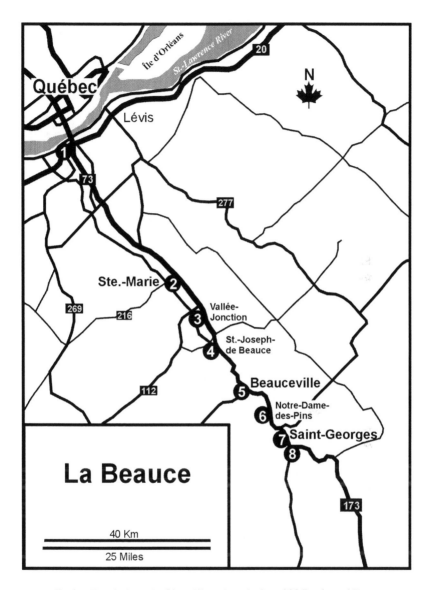

La Beauce

40 Km

25 Miles

Trains Touristique de Chaudière-Appalaches, 399 Boulevard Rousseau, take visitors off the beaten path, offering views of the region that are rarely seen. T:*(418) 253-5580 or 1-877-642-5580. Tours run May–Sept. Call for exact schedule, rates, and departure places.*

Saint-Joseph-de-Beauce ④ is nestled in a valley, on the river's edge. This quaint little village was founded in 1737. The heart of the town features a very well preserved grouping of religious and administrative buildings.

The **Église Saint-Joseph**, built in 1865, with its narrow façade and tall steeple, presides over the downtown area. Note the French château-style **presbytery** across the street, built in 1892. Also of note are the Second Empire-style **convent** and **orphanage**.

MUSÉE MARIUS-BARBEAU, 139 Rue Sainte-Christine, **T**:(418) 397-4039, **W**: museemariusbarbeau.com. *Open summer Mon.–Fri. 9–5, Sat.–Sun. 10–5; winter Mon.–Fri. 9–4:30, Sat.–Sun. 1–4. Admission $6 for adults, $5 for students, children under 5 are free.*

The museum, housed in a former convent, offers exhibits on the people of the Beauce region and more than 260 years of the region's history.

Beauceville ⑤ straddles the Rivière Chaudière, clinging to the steeply sloping valley. Admire the **Église Saint-François d'Assise** on the opposite shore of the river.

Île Ronde, in the middle of the Rivière Chaudière in downtown Beauceville, is a small flat island accessible via a staircase from the middle of the bridge. Benches are set up around the park, offering a peaceful location to stroll and enjoy the beauty of the river and the valley. The island is used for a number of festivals and the town is planning further development of the park with playgrounds and other attractions. **T**:*(418) 774-6252.*

The **Parc des Rapides du Diable** is located off Route 173, just past the village of Beauceville. Easy hiking trails meander through forests, to the edge of the Chaudière River and the Diable Rapids. Interpretation panels along the route reveal the history of the site to its gold-bearing past. **T**:*(418) 774-6252.*

Notre Dame des Pins, at the junction of the Chaudière and Gilbert Rivers, was commonly used as a starting-off point for gold-diggers in the 19th century. The pride of the town is its long **covered bridge** ⑥, built in 1929. This is the longest bridge of its kind in Québec and the second-longest in Canada.

Walk down through the picnic grounds to the rocky shore of the river. There is a great view of the covered bridge, in stark contrast with the more modern bridge beside it. The rich green farmlands on the hill across the river make a beautiful backdrop to the peaceful waterway.

Saint Georges ⑦ is the economic and industrial capital of the Beauce Region and Chaudière River Valley.

The **Parc des 7 Chutes** is a beautiful park along the Rivière Pozer on 49th Rue North. There are a number of wooded hiking trails offering views of the forest, river, and the many bird species living in the park. The Sentier des Gorges de la Rivière Pozer hiking trail affords magnificent views of the seven falls of the Pozer River and winds through a beautiful forest with white pines dating back over 200 years. Also available at the site are swimming and a small zoo. **T**:*(418) 228-8155. Open mid-May to Labor Day, daily 8–9.*

Chaudière River, Beauce

The **Église de Saint-Georges**, 1890 1st Avenue West, is a beautiful three-steepled church built in 1902. At the entrance note the copy of Louis Jobin's *Saint-George Slaying the Dragon*. The interior boasts a number of exceptional architectural and religious art works. **T**:*(418) 228-2558. Open June to early Oct., Mon.–Fri. 9–4, Sun. 12–3; late Oct. Mon.–Wed. 9–4, Sun. 12–3. Admission is free but donations are requested.*

CENTRE d'ART SAINT-GEORGES, 250 18th Rue West, **T**:(418) 228-2027. *Open year-round Tues., Wed., and Sun. 1–5, Thurs.–Fri. 1–8. Admission is free.*
The center has an art gallery dedicated to the artists of the Beauce Region. There is also an exhibition on local history. A boutique sells signed, locally-made arts and crafts.

MUSÉE de l'ENTREPRENEURSHIP BEAUCERON, 250 18th Rue, **T**:(418) 227-6176. *Open June–Sept., Mon.–Fri. 9:30–5, Sat.–Sun. 10–5; Sept.–May, Tues.–Fri. 1–4. Admission $4 for adults, children are free.*
Discover the significant social, political, and business achievements of prominent local families.

Village Miniature Baillargeon ⑧, 58th Avenue, is interesting for its fine collection of miniature houses. Buildings represent the wide variety of architectural types found throughout Québec, as well as farms and mills. Visitors will be amazed at the detail of the buildings and environment. **T**:*(418) 228-8796. Open mid-May to mid-Sept., daily 10–5; mid-Sept. to mid-Oct., Sat.–Sun. by reservation only. Admission $6 for adults, $4 for children 6–18, children 5 and under are free.*

Trip 21

Kinnear's Mills and Thetford Mines

This region was predominately settled by Irish and Scottish immigrants as far back as 1810. Much of the charm and culture of the area, including many of the location names, still reflect the heritage of these original settlers.

In 1876 asbestos was discovered in the area of Thetford Mines, forever changing the lives and landscape of the region — home to the first asbestos, chromium, and talc mines in Canada. The surrounding land has the appearance of the moon's surface, with deep craters and powdery hills. The round mounds that rise up around the area are actually hills of crushed rock taken from the mines.

Construction of the railroad in 1879 facilitated the transportation of raw and finished products, enabling the rapid development of the area.

GETTING THERE:

By Car, Thetford Mines is about 105 km (66 miles) south of Quebec City.

Take **Rte. 73** south from the city to the Vallée-Jonction exit. Turn right onto **Rte. 112**, through Vallée-Jonction.

At the Robertsonville/Thetford Mines town line, turn right onto **Rte. 269** north. In Pontbriand, bear right and then bear left, continuing on **Rte. 269** to Kinnear's Mills.

Return to **Rte. 112** and turn right to Thetford Mines.

Follow **Rte. 267** from Thetford Mines to Saint-Daniel for Parc du Frontenac.

Take **Rte. 112** north to **Rte. 73** and take **Rte. 73** north returning to Québec City.

PRACTICALITIES:

Tourisme Amiante, 682 Rue Monfette North, Thetford Mines. **T**:(418) 335-7141, **W**: tourisme-amiante.qc.ca

FOOD AND DRINK:

La Cage aux Sports (805 Boulevard Smith North, Thetford Mines) Popular chain restaurant with a variety of grilled, Canadian, and family-friendly dishes. **T**:(418) 338-5663. $$

Bravo Pizzeria (100 Rue Notre-Dame North, Thetford Mines) Family-style pizzeria in a pleasant atmosphere. **T**:(418) 338-4624. $$

La Maison D'Irlande (153 Rue de l' Église, Saint-Adrien-d'Irlande) Located just north of Thetford Mines in an ancient presbytere, serving home-made regional cuisine, with fresh local ingredients, in an elegant country setting. **T**:(418) 338-1351. $$$

AREA ATTRACTIONS:

Circled numbers correspond to numbers on the map.

Kinnear's Mills ① is a small, antique town with four churches situated around the town square. Several Scottish families settled here in 1842 and built the Presbyterian church. During the American Revolution, Loyalists moved into the town, building the Methodist and Anglican churches. Irish immigrants built the Catholic church in 1920. Guides in period costumes give visitors a lively tour of the historic hamlet, with its peaceful streets and Victorian houses all adorned with flowers.

Entertaining **guided tours** are available. **T**:*(418) 424-0480. Tours run late June to Aug., daily 10–5; Sept. Sat.–Sun. 10–5. Admission $7 for adults, $5 for children 13–17, $2 for children 7–12, children under 7 are free.*

Thetford Mines ② developed around the farmland where asbestos was first discovered. Reminders of the area's mining history can be seen at every turn.

The **town center** has all the charm of yesteryear with narrow streets, brick sidewalks, and old buildings. The imposing church dominates the main street.

MUSÉE MINÉRALOGIQUE et MINIER de THETFORD MINES ③, 711 Boulevard Smith South (Route 112), **T**:(418) 335-2123, **W**: mmmtm.qc.ca. *Open late June to Labor Day, daily 9:30–6; Sept.–Dec. and Mar. to late June, daily 1–5. Admission $7.50 for adults, $3.50 for children 7–17, children 6 and under are free.*

Multimedia presentations, interactive games, and thematic re-creations introduce visitors to the geology and mining history of the region. Other exhibits display a wide variety of rocks, crystals, and minerals.

Departing from the museum, don't miss the **mine tours**, for an extraordinary and unique trip. The guided tour of the mine includes a look at asbestos-based products, a trip into an open-air mine, and an overview of the workings of the mine. **T**:*(418) 335-7141. Tours run late June to Labor Day daily at 1:30; July–Aug. additional tours at 10:30 and 3:30. Reservations recommended. Admission $17 for adults, $10 for children.*

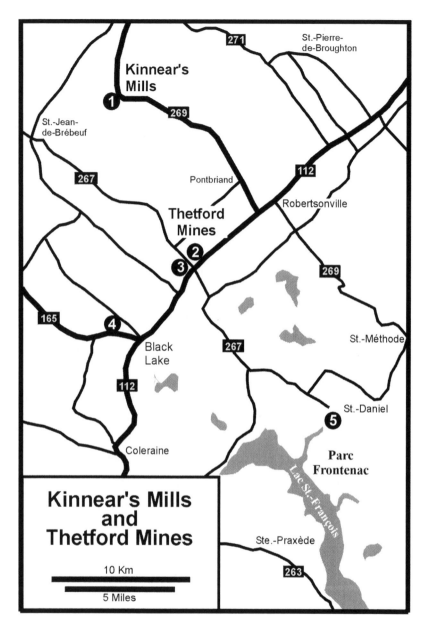

Kinnear's Mills and Thetford Mines

10 Km

5 Miles

Follow Route 112 south of Thetford Mines for the **Belvédère d'Observation de Thetford South** ④. This observation point affords sweeping views of the mine that is laid out below in circular plateaus.

Thetford Mines

Parc du Frontenac ⑤. 599 Chemin des Roys, Saint-Daniel. **T**:(418) 486-2300. *Open daily summer and fall.*

Resting on the shores of Lac Saint-François, the park offers a spectacular contrast to the barren landscape of the mining towns. A beach, water sports, and hiking trails greet visitors. Pedal boats and other equipment are available for rent at the site.

Trip 22

Lac Mégantic and Mont Mégantic

At the foothills of the northern Appalachians, amidst lakes and forests, lies a spectacular region. Lac Mégantic is actually in the Eastern Townships Tourist Region, but it is most easily accessed from Québec City. Discovered in 1646 for Father Druillettes, the lake region was originally settled by the Abenaki people in 1700. The name Mégantic is derived from the Abenaki word *"namesokanjik"* which means "place of fish." The area was popular with Abenaki hunters who found abundant fish and game along Rivière Chaudière and Lac Mégantic. Missionaries and adventures were attracted to the area, followed by Scottish and French Canadian settlers.

In 1877 Malcom Matheson, a businessman from Lewis Island, England, built a house and store at the site that would not become the town of Lac Mégantic until 1907. The village of Mégantic was founded in 1885. On the opposite shore of the Chaudière River, the village of Agnès was founded. The two villages were eventually merged to form the town of Lac Mégantic.

GETTING THERE:

By Car, Lac Mégantic is about 189 km (118 miles) south of Québec City.

Take **Rte. 73** south from Québec City. When the highway ends, turn right and then left onto **Rte. 173**.

Just past Saint-Georges turn right onto **Rte. 204** south to Lac Mégantic. Turn right onto **Rte. 161** for Baie des Sables and the Tourist Information Office.

Follow **Rte. 161** along Mégantic Lake and turn right onto **Rte. 212** to reach Mont Mégantic. Turn right and then left onto **Route du Parc** to reach the ASTROlab and mountains.

Return along **Rte. 212** and **Rte. 161**. Turn right onto **Rte. 204** and then left onto **Rte. 173**. Follow **Rte. 173** and then **Rte. 73** north returning to Québec City.

PRACTICALITIES:

Bureau d'Information Touristique Région Mégantic, 3295 Rue Laval

North. **T**:(819) 583-5515 or 1-800-363-5515, **W**: tourisme-megantic.com

A self-guided walking tour of Lac Mégantic gives visitors a good look at the charm and history of this lakeside town. An English-language map and guide are available at the tourist information office. Parking is available by the municipal wharf, off Rue Stearns and Boulevard des Veterans.

FOOD AND DRINK:

L'Extra sur la Rive (3502 Rue Agnès, Lac Mégantic) Casual restaurant serving a wide variety of international dishes including Cajun-style shrimp, Moroccan couscous, and filet mignon tournedos. **T**:(819) 583-2565. $$

Restaurant au Pied du Massif (187 Route du Parc, Notre Dame-des-Bois) Alpine ambiance in a mountain-chalet setting with light meals and casual snacks. **T**:(819) 888-2941. $$

Aux Berges de l'Aurore (139 Route du Parc, Notre-Dame-des Bois) Award winning and original dishes, regional and Québec cuisine, in a charming mountainside setting. **T**:(819) 888-2715. $$$ and $$$+

AREA ATTRACTIONS:

Circled numbers correspond to numbers on the map.

Ideally located on the shore of Mégantic Lake and the mouth of the Chaudière River, and in close proximity to the United States, **Lac Mégantic** ① has played a significant role in the history and development of the province. The location was central to a thriving lumber industry until the early 20th century. In 1775, American troops passed through the area, losing significant numbers in the treacherous waters and bad weather, in an attempt to conquer Québec City — they did not dare return through the area after their defeat.

Baie des Sables ② is located at the northern end of Mégantic Lake. A beautiful sandy beach is available to the public, and aquatic sports are popular.

The **marina and municipal wharf** ③ afford beautiful views of the lake. Located at the mouth of the Chaudière, it was here that logs were driven to the mills. In the late 19th century, the steamship "Lena" docked here, transporting visitors across the lake to neighboring towns. **Scenic cruises** of this beautiful lake still depart from this wharf aboard the "Capitaine Cap II."

The **Barrage du Lac Mégantic** ④, built in 1973, controls the flow of water from Lac Mégantic into the Chaudière River, which will eventually join the Saint Lawrence River. This is a popular site for fly-fishing.

In front of the Canadian Pacific Railway Station, built in 1925, on Rue Frontenac take a peek at the **Railway Station Park**. This small public garden usually has a beautiful display of flowers.

Note the Manoir Hotel, 5378 Rue Frontenac, which was once the **Old American House Hotel**. It was here in 1888 that Donald Morrison, known as the "outlaw of Mégantic," shot and killed the constable.

Farmington Park, squeezed between Rues Laval and Dollard, commemo-

LAC MÉGANTIC & MONT MÉGANTIC   135

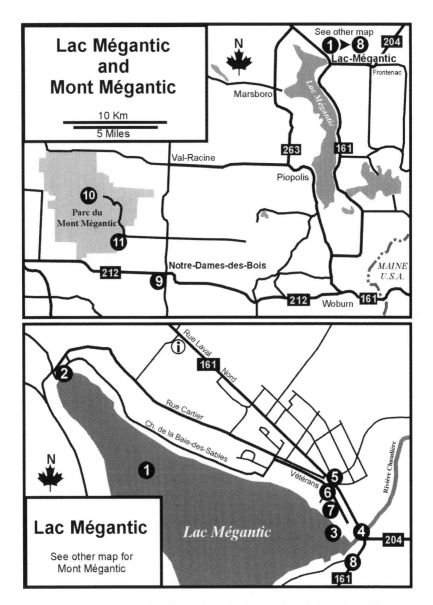

rates the formalized relationship between the towns of Lac Mégantic and Farmington, Maine.

Now visit **Église Sainte-Agnès** ⑤. This beautiful neo-Gothic Catholic church was completed in 1913. Inside, an impressive stained-glass window, made in 1849, depicts "Jesse's Tree," the genealogy of David. The window was originally installed in the Immaculate Conception Church of London. There is also a magnificent, large Casavant organ with 2,200 pipes.

Dr. Georges-Stanislas Grégire House ⑥ is a charming Queen Anne-style house with a large porch. The house was built in 1896 for Mégantic's first doctor.

Parc de Vétérans ⑦ is a beautiful park resting on the shores of the lake. A monument commemorates the soldiers of the two World Wars. Also of interest is a cannon from the German Imperial Army. In the summer, the park is host to outdoor music concerts.

Across the Chaudière River Bridge are a number of nice period houses along **Rue Agnès** ⑧. The Paul Cliche House, number 3522, was built in 1891 by Captain William Henry Smith, a marine officer for Queen Victoria, as a wedding present for his son, Henry Beaufiled Smith. The "turn-of-the-century" American-style house at 3502 was built by the Bank of Montréal in 1905 as a home for their local branch manager.

Parc de la Croix-Lumineuse, off Rue la Fontaine, affords sweeping views of the town and lake.

As you approach Mont Mégantic along Route 212 and Route du Parc, **Mont Joseph** and **Mont Mégantic** rise majestically, side-by-side. Locally and regionally they are referred to as the twin mountains or brothers.

Mont Joseph was named for Saint Joseph who, it was believed, saved the inhabitants of Notre-Dame-des-Bois from a devastating tornado. In 1883, Father Corriveault built a small sanctuary on the mountain in honor of Saint Joseph.

Notre-Dame-des-Bois ⑨ proudly perches in one of the steepest regions of the Appalachians, with the highest elevation of any village in the province. François-Xavier Dufresne first arrived in the area, clear-cutting a stretch of land in 1871 and establishing a smithy in 1875. With the Repatriation Act, a number of settlers moved to the area and the first mass was celebrated in 1876. The town was established in 1877 and was quickly inundated with gold-diggers, who soon traded their prospecting tools and plots for stakes in the colonization. Today the region is known for its natural beauty, outdoor sports, and astronomy center.

PARC du MONT MÉGANTIC ⑩, 189 Route du Parc, Notre-Dame-des-Bois, **T**:(819) 888-2941 or 1-866-888-2941, **W**: sepaq.com. *Open year-round, daily 9–5, until 11:30 during summer. Admission $3.50 for adults, $1.50 for children.*

Hiking trails and scenic overlooks await visitors in this spectacular mountain landscape. Route du Parc winds its way up Mont Mégantic to an **observatory**. The road also splits off for a breathtaking drive up Mont Joseph.

ASTROlab ⑪, 189 Route du Parc, Notre-Dame-des-Bois, **T**:(819) 888-2941 or 1-866-888-2941, **W**: astrolab.qc.ca. *Open mid-May to mid-June and Sept.–early Oct., Sat.–Sun. 12–5, observation night Sat. 7:30; mid-June through Aug., daily 12–11. Admission varies from $10.50 for adults, $8 for children 6–17, children under 6 are free.*

A fascinating astronomy center with guided tours of the observation tower. Lectures, multimedia presentations, and exhibits bring the stars to the Earth for a spectacular and memorable experience.

During the second week of July each year, the **Festival d'Astronomie Populaire du Mont Mégantic** makes the skies accessible to the public via the most powerful telescope in North America. The telescope is only available to researchers for the majority of the year.

Section VII

DAYTRIPS
NORTH OF MONTRÉAL

The regions of Mauricie, the Saint Lawrence Valley, and Lanaudiére are steeped in history and natural resources. Encompassing the Mauricie River Valley, the Mauricie region is home to two wildlife reserves, the Mauricie National Park and the Batiscan River Regional Park. The people who settled this region have taken full advantage of the natural resources throughout its history, developing successful wood and hydroelectric industries. The region was named Forest Capital of Canada for 2001.

The Saint Lawrence River Valley and Lanaudiére Region developed to support the growth of Montréal and Québec cities. Rich with natural resources, the regions feature a number of powerful rivers and dense forests. The people of Québec quickly harvested these resources, providing lumber and electricity to the province's cities.

Proud of the wild and beautiful land that covers much of this region, Québec enacted measures to preserve the landscapes and make the natural resources available for pleasure and recreation.

Trip 23

Mauricie Region

The Mauricie Region stretches north from Trois-Rivières through some of the most spectacular landscape in the province. This route moves through the region along Rivière Saint-Mauricie, hugging the shore closely in places.

The Saint Maurice River Valley has been an important industrial area since the 18th century, when veins of iron ore were first mined in the region in 1730. The forestry and lumber industry has dominated the region's economy since 1850. Beginning in the late 19th century, hydroelectric plants were constructed along the Saint Maurice River. Pulp mills and chemical plants soon followed making the Mauricie Region one of the most important industrial areas in the province.

Today the industry is contained and vast natural resources are preserved. The waterways, no longer needed to transport logs through the valley, have been returned to animals, nature lovers, and sports enthusiasts.

GETTING THERE:

By Car, the Mauricie Region extends north from Trois-Rivières, which is 85 km (53 miles) east of Montréal and 80 km (50 miles) west of Québec City.

Follow **Rte. 40** east from Montréal or west from Québec City to Trois-Rivière, and take **Rte. 55** north.

Take **Exit 191**, turn left and then right onto **Rue Saint-Michele**. At the end turn left to reach the forges.

Return to **Rte. 55** north and take **Exit 217** onto **Rte. 351** to reach Shawinigan.

Follow **Rte. 153** north to Grand Mère. Turn left on **8th Rue**, which becomes **4th Rue**. Turn right on **Chemin du Village**, which becomes **1st Rang**, and follow that into the Parc National de la Mauricie.

Return to **Rte. 55** and head north. At the end of **Rte. 55**, continue on **Rte. 155** north.

PRACTICALITIES:

This tour is about 335 km (210 miles), round trip from Trois-Rivières, and the driving is slow in places. Get an early start to the day to make the most of this trip. The scenery along the route is spectacular and worth the trip, but you can end the drive in Rivière Matawin and head back to Trois-Rivières if the drive gets to be too much.

Tourist Information Office of Grand-Mère, 2333 8th Rue, Grand-Mère. **T**:(819) 538-4883.

Additional information on the region is available on the Internet at **W**: icimauricie.com

The waterfalls are best seen in spring when the river is full with the melting snow.

FOOD AND DRINK:

Resto-Pub 57 (1st Rue, Shawinigan) With beautiful views of the river, a festive atmosphere, and good simple food, this is a favorite with locals and visitors. $$

Restaurant au Cénacle (2722 Boulevard Royal, Shawinigan) This popular restaurant, housed in an old Catholic church serves a variety of local favorites and a buffet. **T**:(819) 539-3939. $$$

La Cookerie (Route 155, Grande-Piles, at the Lumberjack Village) Serves traditional home-cooked Québec cuisine and local specialties in a unique setting. **T**:(819) 538-7895. $$ and $$$

Chez Marineau (Route 155, Rivière Matawin) Family style restaurant with a wide variety of popular foods, light meals, and regional cuisine. $

SUGGESTED TOUR:

Circled numbers correspond to numbers on the map.

LES FORGES-du-SAINT-MAURICE NATIONAL HISTORIC SITE ①, 10000 Boulevard des Forges, **T**:(819) 378-5116. *Open mid-May to early Oct. Admission $4 for adults, $2 for children 6–16, children under 6 are free.*

The first iron works in Canada, founded in 1730, was in operation for over 150 years. An interesting museum has exhibits depicting the history of the forge and displays of artifacts from the site. A scale model shows the layout of the forge and its supporting village during its heyday. Walking trails with interpretive panels wind through the park, past ruins of the forge and village.

By the river, the interesting little fountain, called the **Devil's Fountain**, is a natural phenomenon.

Continue on to **Shawinigan** ②. The name is derived from the Algonquin language, from *"achewenegan"* meaning "crest," referring to the majestic waterfalls that flow over a high crest of rocks near the town. The town, founded in

1901, is also nicknamed the "City of Lights" for the Shawinigan Water and Power stations. With an abundance of water and more than five waterfalls, Shawinigan has played a critical role in the industrialization of the province.

Saint Maurice Promenade stretches along the Saint Maurice River, providing a beautiful park for walking, roller blading, and relaxing. The **downtown** area is home to shops, galleries, boutiques, café, and restaurants.

PARC des CHUTES de SHAWINIGAN ③, Île Melville, **T**:(819) 536-0222. *Open year-round daily. Admission is free.*

The rushing water, particularly wide and fierce during spring thaw, provides a spectacular show. A short hiking trail leads to an observation deck. Other paths wander through the woods and along the river. Hikers may encounter a heard of deer that live in the woods.

LA CITÉ de l'ÉNERGIE ④, 1000 Avenue Melville, **T**:(819) 536-8516, **W**: citedelenergie.com. *Open late June, Tues.–Sun. 10–5; July–Aug., daily 10–6; Sept. to early Oct., Tues.–Sun. 10–5. Admission $14 for adults, $8 for children 6–12, children under 6 are free.*

This interesting, entertaining, and educational theme park introduces visitors to the industry that Shawinigan has dedicated itself to for more than 100 years. The observation tower, the second-highest in Québec, provides impressive views of the town, river, and surrounding area. Four interactive exhibits and two fascinating multimedia presentations present an in-depth look at hydroelectricity, electrochemistry, and the aluminum, pulp, and paper industries.

On the grounds, walking paths offer views of the river and lead across a suspension bridge. Ferry rides provide tours of the scenic river, while trolley rides bring visitors on a scenic tour of the gardens and surrounding area.

The village of **Grand Mère** ⑤, founded in 1898, derives its name from a nearby rock that resembles the head of an old woman. The town developed after the construction of a paper mill in 1888. Nearby, a **suspension bridge** was the first of its kind built in Canada.

The **Rocher de Grand-Mère**, which inspired the naming of the village, can be seen between 5th and 6th Avenues.

PARC NATIONAL de la MAURICIE ⑥ **T**: (819) 538-3232, **W**: parkscanada.gc.ca. *Open year-round daily. Admission $3.50 per person, $8 per family.*

This beautiful park of rolling hills, lakes, and rivers treats visitors to a peaceful interaction with nature. Naturalist guided tours introduce visitors to the flora and fauna of the area. The parkway, crossing through the heart of the park, leads to scenic viewpoints and numerous hiking trails.

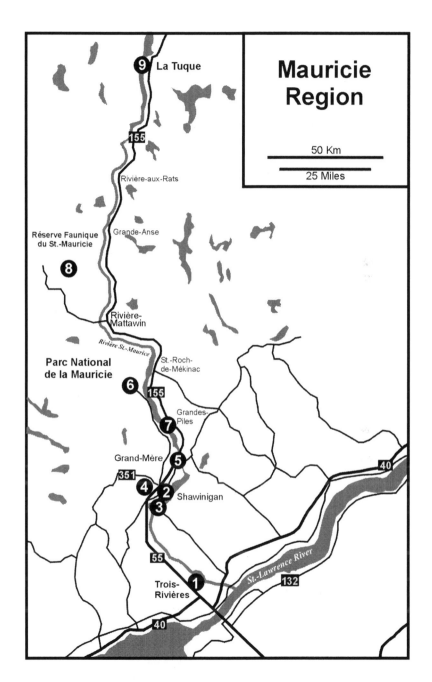

Mauricie Region

9 La Tuque

50 Km

25 Miles

155

Rivière-aux-Rats

Réserve Faunique du St.-Maurice

Grande-Anse

8

Rivière-Mattawin

Rivière St.-Maurice

Parc National de la Mauricie

St.-Roch-de-Mékinac

6 155

Grandes-Piles

7

Grand-Mère

5

351

4 2 Shawinigan

3

55

Trois-Rivières

1

St.-Lawrence River

132

40

40

Grandes-Piles ⑦, established in 1885 on the steep side of a mountain, provides spectacular views of the river. The village was named for the pile-shaped rocks located beside the nearby waterfall. A beautiful stone church dominates the village. This was once the hub of the region's forestry and logging industries.

The **Lumberman's Village**, on Route 155, provides an interesting look at the lumber camps of bygone days. This re-created turn-of-the-century lumber camp has more than 25 traditional log buildings and a number of other outbuildings. Imagine sleeping on the uneven wood cots; check out the fire tower and cookhouse. The "ice making" system is particularly interesting. **T**:*(819) 538-7895. Open mid-May to mid-Oct., daily 10–6. Admission $8 for adults, $6 for children 6–16, children under 5 are free.*

The road passes through the village of **Rivière-Mattawin**, founded in 1880, meaning "meeting of the waters." This is where the Mattawin and Saint Maurice Rivers meet.

The village of **Grande-Anse** is a tranquil hamlet in unforgettably beautiful surroundings.

RÉSERVE FAUNIQUE SAINT-MAURICIE ⑧, 3773 Route 155, Matawin, **T**:(819) 646-5687. *Open mid-May to mid-Oct. daily 8–10; mid-Oct. through Mar. daily 8:30–4:30. Some roads may be inaccessible in the winter months. The bridge toll across the Saint Maurice River is $12 per car.*

This wildlife reserve is a reminder of the wild lands of Québec, before settlement and industrialization. The vast expanse of land incorporates 245 lakes and 8 rivers. A number of animal species make the park their home, including moose, bear, rabbits, and hundreds of birds. The park is a popular destination for outdoor sportsmen and nature lovers alike.

Head on up to **La Tuque** ⑨. Named for a hill shaped like the woolen hats the French Canadians call "toques," the village was once a fur-trading center. The town was founded in 1911, beside a waterfall and the Saint Maurice River.

La Tuque is also famous as the birthplace of singer-composer Félix Leclerc (1914–88) who became the first songwriter from Québec to gain international fame.

Lac Saint-Louis stands in the heart of the village, a natural aquatic oasis.

Parc des Chutes de la Petit Rivière Bostonnais, on Route 155, affords views of a magnificent waterfall, surrounded by dense forests. A dam and hiking trails provide access and views along the river and through the woods. **T**:*(819) 523-5930. Open year-round daily. Admission is free.*

Trois-Rivières

Founded in 1634 at the mouth of the Saint Maurice River, Trois-Rivières is the second-oldest settlement in New France. The first steel plant was established on the outskirts of the river in 1730, solidifying the city's place in the economic and industrial development of Québec.

The city was named for the three channels that form the mouth of the Saint Maurice River, where it joins the Saint Lawrence. The location of the city, on the Saint Lawrence River, halfway between Montréal and Québec ensured Trois-Rivières' place in the history and development of the province.

A lot of history, architecture, and culture are packed in the compact space of the town center. The Laviolette Bridge, built in 1967, is the only bridge spanning the Saint Lawrence River between Montréal and Québec City.

GETTING THERE:

By Car, Trois-Rivières is 85 km (53 miles) east of Montréal and 80 km (50 miles) west of Québec City. Take **Rte. 40**, east from Montréal or west from Québec City.

By Boat, high-speed shuttle service is available from Montréal or Québec City on **Les Dauphins du Saint-Laurent**, **T**:(514) 288-4499.

PRACTICALITIES:

Don't let the industrial outer edges of this small city fool you — the center is a charming Victorian gem just waiting to be uncovered and enjoyed.

The **Tourist Information Office** is located right downtown at 1457 Rue Notre-Dame. **T**:(819) 375-1122 or 1-800-313-1123.

If time allows, don't miss Cap-de-la-Madeleine, just across the mouth of the Saint Maurice River. See Trip 25 for details.

FOOD AND DRINK:

Raphael Restaurant (10 Rue des Forges) Delicious and creative Italian dishes and regional favorites, in a comfortable, airy grotto-like atmosphere. **T**:(819) 376-2202. $$ and $$$

Portofino Restaurant (1300 Rue du Fleuve) Offering fine Italian cuisine with views of the Saint Lawrence River and the many people who mull around the riverside boardwalk. **T**:(819) 374-7272. $$$

Restaurant Menuet Oriental (324 Rue Bonaventure) Gourmet Asian cuisine in a beautiful garden-like décor. **T**:(819) 379-8754. $$$

Café Nord-Ouest (1441 Rue Notre-Dame) Drinks and light meals on an open terrace, affording excellent views of the pedestrian filled streets. **T**:(819) 693-1151. $ and $$

Patisserie Muscadin (60 Rue des Forges) Indulge in a sinfully decadent treat or put together a gourmet picnic. **T**:(819) 691-9080. $

LOCAL ATTRACTIONS:

Circled numbers correspond to numbers on the map.

Parc Portuoire ①, Rue du Fleuve, is a picturesque harbor front park, providing views of the river. The waterfront land was once the estate of Mayor Joseph-Édouard Turcotte who donated it to the city. Watch the cruise ships coming and going at the port, as well as the massive barges that traverse the river. The park is used to host numerous activities and exhibits throughout the year.

The **Centre d'Exposition sur l'Industrie des Pâtes et Papiers**, at the Parc Portuaire, has exhibits depicting all facets of the lumber and paper industries. Other displays illustrate the importance of recycling. **T**:(819) 372-4633. *Open June–Labor Day, daily 9–6; Sept. Mon.–Fri. 9–5, Sat.–Sun. 11–5; Oct.–Nov. and Feb.–May by appointment only. Admission $3 for adults, $1.50 for children 6–14, children 5 and under are free.*

Scenic Cruises on Croisières M/S Jacques-Cartier, departing from 1515 Rue du Fleuve, explore the shores of the Saint Lawrence and Saint Maurice Rivers. Guides are informative and entertaining, with abundant history and folklore. **T**:*(819) 375-3000 or 1-800-567-3737. Tours run May–Sept. at 1 and cost $12 for adults.*

URSULINES MONASTERY and MUSÉE des URSULINES ②, 734 Rue des Ursulines, **T**:(819) 375-7922, **W**: musee-ursulines.qc.ca. *Open May–Nov., Tues.–Fri. 9–5, Sat.–Sun. 1:30–5; Mar. and Apr., Wed.–Sun. 1:30–5; Nov.–Feb. by appointment only. Admission $3 for adults, $2 for students, children under 12 are free.*

In 1697, several Ursulines arrived in Trois-Rivières from Québec City with the goal of opening a school for the children of settlers and Amerindians. Because of the needs for health care at the time, they also took in the sick. The chapel and hospital, which now houses the museum, were built in 1715.

The **museum** has a nice collection of ceramics, textiles, prints, books, silver, furniture, and decorative arts, which relate to the history of the region. An interesting scale model shows the monastery as it appeared in the 19th century.

An elegant silver dome tops the chapel. The interior boasts a number of beautiful frescos and paintings by French Canadian artists.

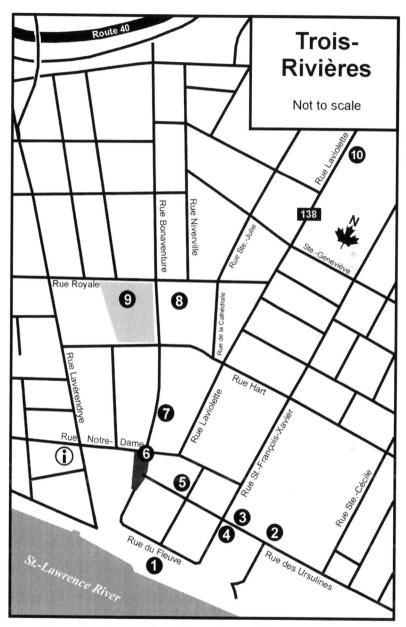

Trois-Rivières

Not to scale

Rue de Ursulines has some of the oldest buildings in the city, most of which survived the fire of 1908. The Maison Hertel-de-la-Fresnière 3, 802 Rue du Ursulines, dating back to 1824, is a perfect example of the urban architecture that was common in the 1820s. The estate originally included many out buildings such as a woodshed and stables. During the summer, a photography exhibit illustrates everyday life in the history of the city. *Admission is free.*

Note the **Maison de Gannes**, 834 Rue des Ursulines, was built in 1756 by a French officer.

Église Saint-James ④, 811 Rue des Ursulines, was built as a convent for the Récolets beginning in 1693. After the conquest it became a court of law and prison. In 1823 the chapel was permanently converted to an Anglican Church. **T**:*(819) 374-6010. Open June–Aug. Tues.–Sat. 10–5, Sun. 2–5; Sept.–May by appointment only.*

MANOIR de TONNANCOUR ⑤, 864 Rue des Ursulines, **T**:(819) 374-2355. *Open year-round Tues.–Fri. 10–12 and 1:30–5, Sat.–Sun. 1–5. Admission is free.*

Originally built in the early 18th century as a residence, the manor was rebuilt in 1795 after a devastating fire. The building now houses an art gallery and hosts a variety of cultural events.

Resting across from the Manoir de Tonnancour is **Place d'Armes**. Before the 19th century, the square was the camping ground for Algonquin Indians who came to the city to trade furs. From 1751 to 1815 it was reserved for military use.

The Flame ⑥, on Place Pierre Boucher, is a striking obelisk monument erected to celebrate the cities 325th anniversary.

Maison Hertel de la Fresnière

TROIS-RIVIÈRES 148

MANOIR BOUCHER de NIVERVILLE ⑦, 168 Rue Bonaventure, **T**: (819) 375-9628. *Open year-round Mon.–Fri. 9–5. Exhibit is open late June–Labor Day, Mon.–Fri. 9–5. Admission is free.*

This impressive manor house, built in 1730, is home to the Trois-Rivière Regional Chamber of Commerce. A thematic exhibit on the first floor illustrates the career of Maurice Duplessis, a significant politician in the history of Québec. A statue of Duplessis is located in the courtyard in front of the manor. The timbers, panels, and rafters of the roof are exposed and visible from the second level.

CATHÉDRALE de l'ASSOMPTION ⑧, 363 Rue Bonaventure, **T**:(819) 374-2409. *Open year-round Mon.–Sat. 7–11:30 and 2–5:30, Sun. 8:30–11:30 and 2–5. Admission is free.*

The neo-Gothic inspired cathedral is the only one in North America with elements of Westminster Abbey. The interior boasts 125 beautiful stained-glass windows made between 1925 and 1954.

Parc Champlain ⑨ is a beautiful green space, recently renovated, that invites locals and visitors to relax and enjoy the oasis in the heart of the city. A beautiful **fountain** seems to defy gravity with water appearing to be above the rim of the pool. **Monuments** in the park honor events and persons important to the town's history.

Séminaire de Trois-Rivières ⑩, 858 Rue Laviolette, originally built in 1860; it was rebuilt in 1920 after a fire. The long fieldstone building has a copper dome over the entrance. The Romanesque-style chapel, which survived the fire, has a nice collection of religious artifacts and art.

The **Musée Pierre-Boucher**, housed on either side of the seminary entrance hall, has a number of permanent and temporary exhibits illustrating highlights of the region's culture and history. **T**:*(819) 376-4459. Open year-round daily 1:30–4:30 and 7–9. Admission is free.*

Trip 25

Saint Lawrence Valley

Where the fertile agricultural lands narrow, squeezed between the foothills of the Laurentian Mountains and the Saint Lawrence River, the Saint Lawrence River Valley flourishes.

Rivers and lakes were referred to as "roads that walk" by the First Nations that lived in and traversed the region. The Saint Lawrence River, cutting a wide lane through the province, played an important role for the First Nations and settlers.

Route 138, running along the Saint Lawrence River from Montréal to Québec City, is called the *Chemin du Roy* (King's Highway). Inaugurated in 1737, this was the first permanent road built in the province, laid out over steep hillsides and through marshlands and swamps. The road improved trade throughout New France and facilitated the development of the colony.

Today, visitors are treated to picturesque farmlands, views of the mighty Saint Lawrence River, and historic villages.

GETTING THERE:

By Car, Cap-de-la-Madeleine is about 90 km (56 miles) east of Montréal and about 75 km (47 miles) west of Québec City.

Take **Rte. 40** east from Montréal or west from Québec City. Take **Rte. 157** south to Cap-de-la-Madeleine. Follow **Rte. 138** to the shrine.

Go back along **Rte. 138** west and turn right on **Rte. 363** to **Rte. 40**.

Take **Rte. 40** west to return to Montréal or east returning to Québec City.

PRACTICALITIES:

There aren't many restaurants through this area. You may want to stop in Trois-Rivières for dinner before heading back to the city.

Chambre de Commerce de Cap-de-la-Madeleine, 170 Rue de Chenaux. **T**:(819) 375-5346.

FOOD AND DRINK:

Café La Pérade (370 Boulevard Launadière, Sainte-Anne-de-la-Pérade) Casual café with breakfast, snacks, pizza, and Canadian favorites. **T**:(418) 325-2993. $$

Normandin (139 Rang 2, Deschambault) Family-style chain restaurant

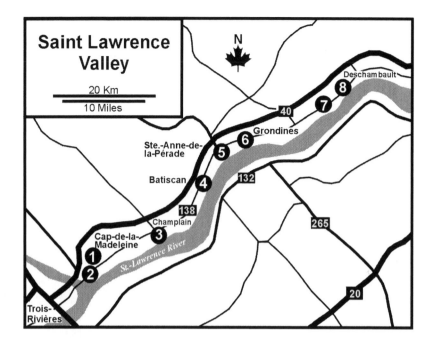

with popular foods, chicken, pastas, pizza, and Canadian foods. **T**:(418) 286-6733. $$

La Maison Deschambault (128 Chemin du Roy, Deschambault) Located in a historic house, built in 1790, surrounded by rivers and fields, and serving gourmet regional cuisine. **T**:(418) 286-3386. $$$

SUGGESTED TOUR:
Circled numbers correspond to numbers on the map.

Cap de la Madeleine ①, founded in the mid-17th century, rests on the banks of the Saint Maurice and Saint Lawrence Rivers opposite Trois-Rivières. The town is internationally renowned as a religious pilgrimage destination, and is also known for the annual **Festival des Amuseurs Publics**, a unique meeting and celebration of public entertainers.

*SHRINE de NOTRE-DAME-du-CAP ②, 626 Rue Notre-Dame, **T**:(819) 374-2441. *Open for guided tours June–Sept. daily at 2, fee $3 per person. Admission to the site is free.*

This prestigious pilgrimage site, founded in 1635 by Jesuit Father Jacques Buteux, who was later murdered by the Iroquois, is dedicated to the honor of the Virgin Mary. A chapel was started in the mid-17th century, but a formal church was not built until 1717. The parish began to grow and thrive by 1878 and Father

Luc Désilets planned to replace the chapel with a larger one. But the river didn't freeze and they were unable to transport the large stones needed for the new church. Father Désilets vowed to preserve the original church if the river would freeze and enable them to get the stones. The temperature dropped and the river froze, forming an ice-bridge dubbed the "Bridge of Rosaries," which lasted just long enough for all of the stones to be transported before it broke apart.

The first official pilgrimage to the site took place in 1883, with large wharves and railway stations being erected. A modern basilica was built in the 1950s to accommodate the increase in pilgrims. There are 350 spectacular stained-glass windows in the basilica, representing the Canadian provinces, Christ Triumphant, the rosary, prophets, and the Canadian pioneers.

The **Petit Shrine**, built in 1714, is the oldest stone chapel in Canada. It has been lovingly preserved in its original state. Visitors are welcome in this charming votive chapel.

The **grounds** are home to beautiful gardens, peaceful ponds, the Rosary Bridge, and statues representing the Way of the Cross.

The route through **Champlain** ③ brings you by many well-kept and utterly adorable cottages. There is an impressive church in the center of the village with twin spires.

The village of **Batiscan** ④, located at the junction of the Batiscan and Saint Lawrence Rivers, retains its original Amerindian name.

The **Old Presbytery of Batiscan**, built in 1816, is a nice place to stop for a peaceful walk. Paths lead around the gardens and interpretive panels tell the history of the site. Follow the path at the far end of the garden that leads through cornfields to a beautiful secluded beach on the shore of the Saint Lawrence River.

For a unique and exciting look at the region, consider a hydroplane tour. **Aviation Mauricie**, 1500 Route 138, offers an unforgettable look at the Saint Lawrence River, Batiscan River, maple orchards, and Trois-Rivière — from the air. T:*(819) 538-6454.*

Sainte-Anne-de-la-Pérade ⑤ is located at the confluence of the Sainte Anne and Saint Lawrence Rivers. This picturesque village takes pride in its beautiful streets, orchards, and rich architectural heritage.

The **Église de Sainte-Anne-de-la-Pérade**, 201 Rue Sainte-Anne, is an impressive neo-Gothic church, inspired by the basilica in Montréal, built between 1855 and 1869. T:*(418) 325-2025. Open summer daily 9–5, winter daily 9–11:30.*

Note the unique buildings neighboring the church with stone and stucco walls, and bright colors.

In the 18th century, the village of **Grondines** ⑥ was located directly on the banks of the river. It was relocated farther inland in 1831 to protect against flooding. Traces of the original village can still be found between Route 138 and the river. The village center has a number of charming Victorian buildings.

The **Moulin de Grondines**, 770 Rue du Moulin, is the oldest standing building of its kind. Originally built in 1672 for nuns working as nurses for the Québec City hospital, the mill was converted into a lighthouse.

Nearby, the remains of the **Église Saint-Charles-Borromée**, 490 Chemin du Roy, dating back to 1716, can be found. When the village was moved away from the river's edge, a new church was built.

The **Moulins de la Chevrotière** ⑦, are situated beside the Rivière de la Chevrotière. The smaller of the two mills dates back to 1767 and the larger one dates back to 1802. Temporary thematic exhibits are located inside the mill, displaying sculpture, painting, artifacts, and antiques. **T**:*(418) 286-6862. Open late June through Aug., daily 10–2. Admission $3.*

Nearby is **Deschambault** ⑧. Founded in the mid-18th century, this farming town has remained peaceful and charming. Turn right on Rue Church, following signs for the **Église Saint-Joseph**, built between 1835 and 1841. Circle behind the church to park. There is a small grassy park with several statues and great views of the river. A beautiful statue of Saint Joseph rests between the two steeples. Inside, magnificent statues adorn the choir. **T**:*(418) 286-3196. Open late June through Aug., Mon.–Sat. 10–4:30, Sun. 1–4:30.*

The former **presbytery**, built in 1815, stands in a nice park behind the church. The foundations of the original presbytery were built in 1735. **T**:*(418) 286-6891. Open June–Aug., daily 9–5; May and Sept.–Oct. Sat.–Sun. 10–5.*

Trip 26

Lanaudière

Rich in natural resources, with wild rivers, mountains, and forests, this region saw many villages built beside its rivers and waterfalls. Barthélemy Joliette established cities to harvest the forests and waterfalls, establishing one of Québec's first railroads to transport his lumber. Many diverse landscapes make up this vast region that reaches north from Montréal.

The area is rich in nature, history, and tradition — from the vast expanses of forest, mountains, and rivers to quaint villages and historic cities. There is also a long history and tradition of music.

GETTING THERE:

By Car, Terrebonne is 35 km (22 miles) north of Montréal.

Take **Rte. 25** north from Montréal to Terrebonne. Follow **Boulevard des Seigneurs** and turn right on **Rue Saint-Louis**. Turn right on **Boulevard des Braves**. At the end, turn left and park in the municipal lot.

From Terrabonne follow **Rte. 25** north to the end. Continue on **Rte. 125** north. Turn right on **Rte. 337** to Rawdon.

Continue on **Rte. 337** to Saint-Alphonse-Rodriguez. Bear left onto **Rte. 343** and then turn right onto **Rte. 347**.

At Saint-Émélie, turn left onto **Rte. 131** and continue to Saint-Michel-des-Saints.

Return along the same route back to Montréal.

PRACTICALITIES:

The river and falls along this route are at their best during the spring runoff. The Sept Chutes de Saint-Zénon all but stop flowing except during the spring. In addition, many sites are not available during the winter months and harsh weather may make some roads impassable.

Terrebonne Tourist Information Office, 775 Rue Saint-Jean-Baptiste, Terrebonne. **T**:(450) 471-4192, **W**: ville.terrebonne.qc.ca

Chambre de Commerce de Rawdon, 3590 Rue Metcalfe, Rawdon. **T**:(450) 834-2282, **W**: chambrecommercerawdon.ca. Open year-round Mon.–Thurs. 8:30–12 and 1–4:30.

FOOD AND DRINK:

Le Jardin des Fondues (186 Rue Sainte-Marie, Terrebonne) In a pleasant historic setting, serving a variety of fondues, French and Canadian cuisine. **T**:(450) 492-2048. $$$

Le Maison Staner (Route 343, Saint-Alphonse-Rodriguez) Gourmet deli and bakery with a wide selection of fresh baked bread, cheeses, and prepared meals perfect for preparing a snack, light lunch, or picnic. **T**:(450) 883-5544 $ and $$

Au Parfum de la Nature (6703 Chemin Pontbriand, Rawdon) Sample the tastes of the region, from duck and pheasant to buffalo and venison, served as three-, five-, or seven-course meals. Reservations required. **T**:(450) 834-4547. $$$ and $$$+

SUGGESTED TOUR:

Circled numbers correspond to numbers on the map.

Begin at **Terrebonne** ①. This town, with a quaint old center, rests on the shore of the Rivière Mille-Îles at the foot of the Saint Jean Rapids. In the 18th and early 19th centuries, businessmen and landowners harnessed the powers of the river for flourmills and saw mills. A successful bakery was established, supplying fur traders with biscuits. An imposing **church** presides over the old center of Terrebonne, on Rue Saint-Louis.

Note the impressive old stone houses along **Boulevard des Braves**. The buildings, once impressive residences, now house cafés, boutiques, and galleries.

ÎLE des MOULINS ②, off Boulevard des Braves, **T**:(450) 471-0619. *Open late June to Labor Day, daily 1–9. Guided tours and historical shows run Wed.–Sun. 1–9. Admission to the site is free, shows are $3 for adults, children under 12 are free.*

This is the largest preserved 19th-century pre-industrial site in Québec. A number of old mill buildings have been meticulously restored and put to use. A rough wood bridge gives access to the island that houses this picturesque and historical park. Thematic exhibitions and guided tours illustrate the history of the site and town.

Rawdon ③ was originally settled by Irish squatters who claimed the land. They were soon followed by Scottish, English, and French Canadian settlers. In the 1920s ethnically Slavic immigrants from Russia, Poland, and the Ukraine settled in the area, giving the town a unique and culturally diverse atmosphere.

PARC de la CHUTES de DORWIN ④, Route 337, **T**:(450) 834-2282. *Open year-round, daily 9–7.*

Legend has it that the evil witch Nipissingue pushed the Amerindian maiden Hiawitha into the gorge. It is said that a loud thunderclap turned him into

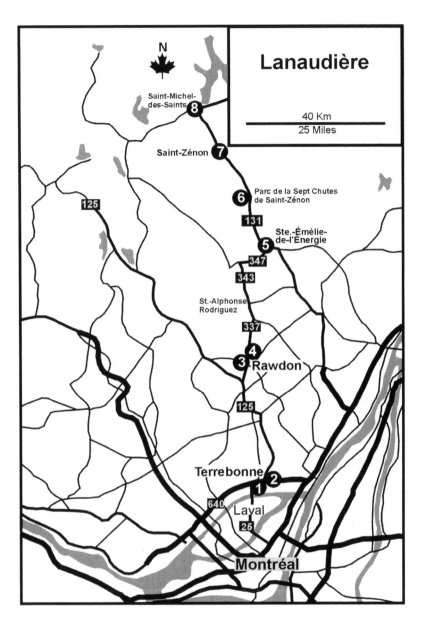

N

Lanaudière

40 Km
25 Miles

Saint-Michel-des-Saints **8**

Saint-Zénon **7**

6 Parc de la Sept Chutes de Saint-Zénon

131

Ste.-Émélie-de-l'Énergie **5**

347

343

St.-Alphonse Rodriguez

337

4
3 Rawdon

125

Terrebonne **2**
1

640 Laval
25

Montréal

rock at the bottom of the gorge, while Hiawitha became the beautiful and powerful waterfall.

Pleasant hiking trails lead to these spectacular waterfalls. The Rivière Ouareau drops dramatically through a rugged narrow gorge where several vantage points provide spectacular views of the falls. It is said that in the summer time the head of the witch Nipissingue can be seen in the rocks. The falls are also a spectacular site in the winter with plates of snow and ice rolling through the gorge.

The drive along this part of the trip affords sweeping views of lush fertile farmlands and glimpses of the rams that have long inhabited the area.

You will pass through **Saint-Alphonse-Rodriguez**, a cute village that is rapidly expanding and gaining in popularity.

Saint-Émélie-de-l'Énergie ⑤ is a charming, flower-filled, village at the entrance of a narrow valley created during the glacial era, with the rugged Rivière Noire running through it. A **commemorative park** in the town center recalls local and regional history.

The **Hôtel de Ville** has an interesting exhibit of old photographs depicting the history of the region, and a herbarium.

Stop at the **Musée de Vieux-Moulin** for a look at the history of the local logging and forestry history.

The **Parc de la Vieux-Moulin** has a number of hiking trails that bring visitors close to the natural beauty of the Noire River. Check out the **Sept-Chutes de la Rivière-Noire**, the **Sentier de la Matawinie** hiking trail, or the **Forest Interpretation Trail** off Rue Paradis.

PARC de la SEPT CHUTES de SAINT-ZÉNON ⑥, Route 131, **T**:(450) 884-0484. *Open May–Sept. daily 9–5. Small admission fee for adults, children under 12 are free.*

The welcome center and starting point for several spectacular hiking trails is located beside the road, at the base of a steep mountainside. The trails have a number of scenic viewpoints affording panoramic views of the surrounding forests, mountains, valleys, and villages. The first falls are reachable via a 1½ hour round-trip hike.

Continue on to **Saint-Zénon** ⑦. Founded in 1866, this village perched up on a mountain peak has perhaps the highest altitude in Québec — or close to it. The village was established, and flourished, on the wealth of the forests that surround it. Today, however, the forests are preserved and tourism drives the economy.

Drive behind the **church** for an incredible panoramic view of the Nymphes Valley.

End your trip at **Saint-Michel-des-Saints** ⑧. Established in 1863 on the banks of Lac Taureau, this beautiful northern village has thrived on both industry and tourism. Resorts, beaches, islands, and pure dark waters attracted visitors for near and far.

Section VIII

DAYTRIPS IN
MONTRÉAL

The largest city in Québec Province and the second largest in Canada, Montréal is one of the world's most spectacular cities. With the largest francophone population outside of Paris, the city has a distinctly European and French character. Its many varied cultures and ethnic neighborhoods make it a truly international destination.

Resting solidly in the powerful Saint Lawrence River between Québec City and Toronto, about 1,600 km (1,000 miles) from the Atlantic Ocean, the Island of Montréal is a cultural, commercial and industrial center. It is connected to the mainland by one tunnel and fifteen bridges, and is made up of twenty-nine independent municipalities, including the City of Montréal.

Searching for gold and a route to the Orient in 1535, Jacques Cartier landed on the island, where the Mohawk village *Hochelaga* was nestled at the bottom of the mountain. In the 17th century, the French decided to build a mission on Montréal Island in the name of colonization and the further proliferation of the Catholic faith. They sent Sieur de Maisonneuve to lead the mission that they named Ville Marie. It wasn't until the beginning of the 18th century that peace was found with the natives and the city began to prosper and grow. The city continued to develop and expand with the thriving fur trade of the 19th century, the influx of the British, and the growth of commerce and industry in the 20th century.

Finally recognized as one of the world's great cities, Montréal was host to the 1967 World Fair (Expo '67) and the 1976 Summer Olympic Games.

A large pedestrian zone, known commonly as the "Underground City," bustles beneath the streets. Covering about 29 km (18 miles) and connecting 60 of the city's major buildings and Métro stops, the network of corridors provides endless opportunity for exploration, eating and shopping. Built beginning in the 1960s, the Underground City houses a vast array of boutiques, department stores, exhibition halls, restaurants, cinemas and theaters.

For those visiting during the winter months, the Underground City not only provides activities and entertainment, but also a way to traverse the city that is protected from the elements.

Now nearing its 360th anniversary, Montréal is a place not to be missed. Visitors will lose themselves in its friendliness, history and culture.

Pointe à Callière Obelisk, Old Montréal

Trip 27
Montréal
Old Montréal

In the 18th century a massive stone wall (5.4 meters [18 feet] high and a meter [3 feet] thick) was built around the perimeter of Montréal to protect the city from those who would conquer it. As it grew, neighborhoods and businesses sprung up outside the walls. In the early 19th century the fortifications were torn down, uniting the Old City with the new. Interest in the original city was revived in the 1960s, breathing new life into Old Montréal. Wandering the narrow roads today, visitors experience centuries of change melding together, from a fortified city with French and British influences, to the 19th-century hub of Canadian politics, to the Victorian architecture of the Industrial Revolution.

Teeming with history and culture, Old Montréal and the Old Port offer an almost overwhelming number of sites, activities, diversions, and delicacies.

GETTING THERE:
By Car, Place d'Armes, the beginning point for this walking tour, can be reach via **Rue Saint Urbain,** which intersects Rue Sherbrooke, Rue Sainte Catherine, and Boulevard René Lévesque.

By Métro, take the **Orange** line to the **Place d'Armes** station.

PRACTICALITIES:
The **Tourist Information Centre**, 174 Rue Notre Dame East, **T**:(514) 844-5400 or **W**: tourism-montreal.org and **W**: oldportofmontreal.com, is located at the west corner of Place Jacques-Cartier and Rue Notre-Dame. *Open late Mar. to mid-June, daily 9–5; late June to Labor Day, daily 9–7; Labor Day to late Mar., Tues.–Sun. 9–5.* The building was previously the Silver Dollar Saloon, named for the 300 American silver dollars imbedded in the floor.

Horse-drawn carriages, called *calèches,* offer a pleasant, relaxing and nostalgic visit through Old Montréal. Carriages can be hired from Rue Notre-Dame, Place d'Armes, Rue de la Commune and Place Jacques-Cartier.

Old Montréal is brimming with activities, sites, and attractions. Visitors may want to spend more than one day exploring and enjoying all of the bounties of the area, or explore the Old Port on a separate day.

FOOD AND DRINK:

Restaurant Café BioTrain (20 Rue Notre Dame East) Vegetarian dishes in a casual and eclectic setting. **T**:(514) 398-0942. $

Claude Postel (75 Notre-Dame West) Perfect for luxurious and decadent pastries, chocolates and snacks from a fourth-generation French chef. **T**:(514) 844-8750. $ and $$

Le Jardin Nelson (407 Place Jacques Cartier) Pizza, crêpes, and light meals, accompanied by live jazz. **T**:(514) 861-5731, **W**: jardinnelson.com. $$

Le Fripon Restaurant Français (436 Place Jacques Cartier) Enjoy gourmet French cuisine and seafood in the dining room or on the terrace in this historic setting. **T**:(514) 861-1386. $$$

SUGGESTED TOUR:

Circled numbers correspond to numbers on the map.

In 1670, Dollier de Casson drafted a new plan for the city of Montréal, with a large open square at its center. **Place d'Armes** ① was used by military troops to run drills, and it was in this square that troops presented arms to the sovereign. A **statue** of Montréal's founder, Sieur de Maisonneuve, resides in the square.

NOTRE-DAME BASILICA ②, Place d'Armes, **T**:(514) 842-2925. *Open daily; Sept. 5 to June 23, 7–6; June 24 to Sept. 4, 7–8; Guided tours in English and French from 8–closing; 20-minute tour is $4; two-hour tour and lecture (by reservation) is $12; partially handicap accessible.*

Built between 1824 and 1829, this Gothic Revival basilica was designed by James O'Donnell (1774–1829), an Irish architect from New York. O'Donnell, who supervised the construction, is buried in its basement crypt. This church was the center of Montréal's religious life for nearly three centuries.

The twin towers of Notre-Dame, which are over 226 feet tall, stand majestically on the southern edge of Place d'Armes. Temperance, as the east tower is known, contains a ten-bell carillon. Perseverance, the west tower, is home to a 23,030-pound bell named Jean-Baptiste, which is rung only on special occasions.

The opulent interior boasts hand-carved, painted and gilded wood, exceptional stained-glass windows, and one of the world's largest organs. The religious works of art housed in the basilica illustrate passages from the Bible, as well as three-and-a-half centuries of parish history.

Behind the choir is the entrance to the **Sacred Heart Chapel**, also known as the Wedding Chapel. The original chapel was destroyed by fire in 1978. The new chapel, consecrated in 1982, was built using elements of the original chapel, blended with contemporary changes.

THE OLD SULPICIAN SEMINARY ③, 130 Notre-Dame Street West.

The Saint-Sulpice Seminary, built in 1685, is the oldest building in Montréal and reflects the architectural style common in 17th-century France. It was

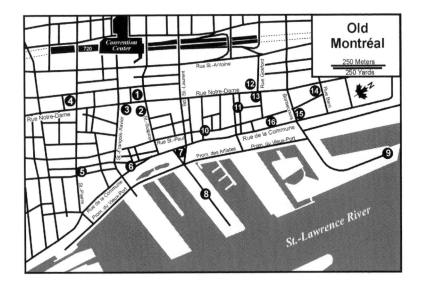

used as a residence and training center for the Messieurs de Saint-Sulpice, who ran Notre-Dame and were seigneurs of Montréal for two centuries. The **clock face**, made in Paris and erected in 1701, is the oldest public clock in North America.

Walk across Place d'Armes to the Eastern edge. The **New York Life Building**, 511 Place d'Armes, is an eight-story, red sandstone building with corner towers and arched windows. Built in 1888, this was Montréal's first skyscraper.

Continue walking around Place d'Armes to the north side. The main branch of Canada's oldest bank, **Bank of Montréal**, 119 Rue Saint-Jacques, dates from 1847. Its extravagant interior, redecorated in 1905, is worth a peek. Inside, there is a museum documenting the bank's history and displaying banking-related treasures. **T**:*(514) 877-6810. Open Mon.–Fri. 10–4; closed on major holidays.*

Walk west on **Rue Saint-Jacques**, Montréal's financial district. The grand 19th- and early 20th-century buildings are reminiscent of the city's earlier prosperity as the foremost metropolis of Canada. Before the 1970s, this was the financial heart of Canada.

Note the **Molson Bank**, 288 Rue Saint-Jacques, founded in 1854 by the ancestors of John Molson, famous for his brewery. Over the entrance are sandstone carvings of William Molson and two of his children. In the 19th century this bank, like others of the time, printed its own paper money.

ROYAL BANK of CANADA ④, 360 Rue Saint-Jacques, **T**:(514) 874-2959. *Open Mon.–Fri. 9:30–4; closed on major holidays.*

At the time of its construction in 1928, this twenty-story building was the largest in the British Empire. The ornate interior is worth a quick look with its bronze doors, marble staircase, vaulted ceilings, and lavish ornaments.

Make your way south one block on Rue Saint-Pierre. Turn right onto Rue des Recollets and left onto Rue Sainte-Helene. Strolling in this neighborhood, visitors are transported back in time to the 1870s, with majestic 19th-century buildings and gas-powered street lamps. At the end of Rue Sainte-Helene, turn left onto Rue Le Moyne and then right, back onto Rue Saint-Pierre.

Much of the city's history happened at the spot that is now **Place d'Youville** ⑤, recently converted to a quiet green park. Note the buildings that run on either side of the park; some of the oldest in the city.

Housed in a former fire station, the **Center d'Histoire de Montréal**, 335 Place d'Youville, is an interesting little museum with interactive exhibits illustrating critical events in the history of the city dating as far back as 1535, and shows how Montrealers, past and present, lived. **T**:*(514) 872-3207,* **W***: www2.ville.montreal.qc.ca/chm/engl/accueila.shtm. Open Tues.–Sun. 10–5, daily in summer. Admission $5 for adults, $3.50 for children, children 5 and under are free.*

Continue walking down Rue Saint-Pierre, past **Maison Mère d'Youville**, built in 1693, where a small park and outside exhibit honors Marguerite d'Youville, founder of the Grey Nuns.

Walk up **Rue de la Commune**, which stretches along the city's Old Port, providing a magnificent waterfront skyline. The buildings were erected in the 19th century atop the stone walls that once circled the city.

Pointe-à-Callière ⑥ is where the city started in May 1642. This small piece of land, where the St. Lawrence River is joined by the St. Pierre River, is the city's birthplace. Samuel de Champlain, believing the spot was a perfect location for a harbor, cleared the land in 1611. It wasn't until thirty-one years later that Maisonneuve built the settlement of Ville-Marie on the spot. In 1893, an **obelisk** was erected on the site to commemorate Maisonneuve's landing.

The ***Montréal Museum of Archaeology and History**, 350 Place Royale, has a fascinating multimedia presentation depicting the history of the city. A tunnel brings visitors to the **archaeological crypt** where they can see artifacts from the centuries of Montréal's development, including the remains of some of the city's original architecture. Scale models show the city's development at various stages throughout history. A self-guided tour will bring you through the museum and into the **Old Customs House**, 150 Rue Saint Paul West, built from 1836 to 1838 during the British occupation of the city. **T**:*(514) 872-9150,* **W***: pacmuseum.qc.ca. Open July–Aug., Mon.–Fri. 10–6, Sat. & Sun. 11–6; Sept.– June, Tues.–Fri. 10–5, Sat. & Sun. 11–5. Admission $11 for adults, $4 for* *children 6–12, children 5 and under are free.*

Originally the location where Native Americans landed with canoes full of furs to trade, and British and French boats arrived with supplies and settlers, the **Old Port** ⑦ is still alive and bustling. Today, barrels and bales have been replaced by tourists, activities, and entertainment. **T**:*(514) 496-7678,* **W**: *oldportofmontreal.com.* Take a ride on **La Balade du Vieux Port**, a shuttle and 50-minute guided tour of the Old Port that departs from Quai Jacques Cartier. **T**:*(514) 496-PORT. Scheduled mid-May through Aug. daily; early May and late Sept. weekends. First departure is at 11. Rates $4.50 for adults, $3.50 for seniors and students, $3 for children 12 and under.*

The Montréal Science Center ⑧, located on the King Edward Pier, is a new science and technology center with a number of unique activities that entertain as well as educate visitors. Different sectors introduce a wide range of scientific topics including life, matter, computers, electricity, and transportation. Nine self-guided tours assist visitors in finding their way through the museum and getting the most enjoyment from their visit. In addition to interactive science exhibits, you will find an IMAX theater and the IMMERSION Movie Game — an interactive group video game on a large screen. **T**:*(514) 496-4724,* **W**: *isci.ca. Open year-round, daily 10–5, closed Mon. in winter and fall. Admission prices depend on activities, starting at $10 for adults and $7 for children. Children under 4 are free. Combination tickets are available at a discount.*

The **Clock Tower Pier** ⑨ holds several interesting attractions. Take a look at the old **Clock Tower**, at the end of the pier, which was built in 1922 to honor the men of the Merchant Fleet who were lost in World War I. **T**:*(514) 496-PORT.* The **Labyrinth**, located in Shed 16, is challenging and fun, rain or shine. As you move through the maze, pick up clues to solve the mysteries of Shed 16. **T**:*(514) 499-0099,* **W**: *labyrintheduhanger16.com. Open mid-May to mid-June, Sat.– Sun. 11:30–5:30; mid-June to mid-Aug., daily 11–9; mid-Aug. to Sept., Sat.–Sun. 11:30–5:30. Admission $12 for adults, $11 for children 13–17, $9.50 for children 4–12, children 3 and under are free.*

For the brave at heart, join the **Ghost Trail**, which has a number of lively ghost tours through Old Montréal. Performers bring the history and heritage of the city to life. Participants of the "New France Ghost Hunt" will track the ghosts of prominent Montréalers through the streets, while "Montréal's Historical Crimes Scenes" re-creates some of the most infamous and seedier points in the city's history. Tours begin at the Bonsecours Stage, accessed from Jacques Cartier Pier or the Clock Tower Pier. **T**:*(514) 868-0303,* **W**: *phvm.qc.ca. Tours run late Jun. Through Aug., Thurs.–Sat. 8:30; May–June and Sept. for groups, by reservation only. Rates $15 for adults, $12 for students and $7 for children under 12.*

A unique way to see the city and surrounding islands is to take a **scenic cruise** on the Saint Lawrence River. Many companies depart from the Jacques Cartier Pier. **La Bateau-Mouche** offers one-and-a-half-hour guided tours and three-and-a-half-hour dinner cruises catered by the Queen Elizabeth Hotel. **T**:*(514) 849-9952.* **Les Dauphins du Saint-Laurent** offers two-hour guided tours, as well as shuttle service to Trois-Rivières and Québec City. **T**:*(514) 288-4499.* **Saute Moutons sur les Rapides** offers jet and speed boating tours of the Saint Lawrence River as well as rafting on the rapids of the Saint Lawrence. **T**:*(514) 284-9607.*

For a land and water adventure, try the **Amphi Bus**, departing from Rue de la Commune near the King Edward Pier. This exciting guided tour will take you through the streets of Montréal and onto the Saint Lawrence River in a unique brightly-colored vehicle. **T**:*(514) 849-5181. Tours run May–Oct. hourly 10–midnight. Rates $23.75 for adults, $17.50 for children 12 and under.*

Walk up Boulevard Saint-Laurent and turn right onto ***Rue Saint Paul** ⑩, the oldest street in Montreal. Strolling slowly along the narrow, winding road you can imagine the horse-drawn carriages and settlers that once traveled this route. Beautiful old buildings are now home to cafés, boutiques, and art galleries.

Turn left and stroll up **Place Jacques-Cartier** ⑪, one of the busiest and most interesting streets in the city. Originally an outdoor marketplace, the street's flower market, Victorian lamps, and roving entertainers delight visitors. The street, lined by terraced restaurants, is filled with artists, performers, locals, and tourists.

Detour for a stroll down **Rue Sainte Amable**, a narrow street filled with artists selling their original paintings of the city.

From the top of Place Jacques-Cartier, turn and admire the view sloping down to the Old Port.

Back on Rue Notre-Dame, admire **City Hall** ⑫, 275 Rue Notre-Dame East. Built between 1872 and 1878, it survived a major fire in 1922. It was from this balcony that the French President, General de Gaulle, in 1967 spoke his infamous words "Vive le Québec libre!" (Long live free Québec). Try not to miss seeing the building at dusk when the exterior is alight and shimmering. **T**:*(514) 872-3355. Open for guided tours 8:30–4:30. Admission is free.*

Nearby, facing 85 Rue Notre-Dame is **Marguerite Bourgeoys Square**. The sculptures depict Marguerite Bourgeoys in her role as the first teacher of Ville-Marie. She was instrumental in the development and history of Montréal and founded the Congregation of Notre-Dame.

Walk through **Place Vauquelin**, beside City Hall, and admire the ornate fountain. At the back of the square, look down at the **Champs-de-Mars** where you can see some of the original fortification walls that once enclosed the city.

Continue up Rue Notre-Dame, past City Hall, to **Château Ramezay** ⑬, 280 Rue Notre-Dame. This house served as the Governor's residence, dating from the 18th century, during the French occupation of Montréal. In 1895 the manor house was turned into a museum, providing a view of Montréal's and Québec Province's history through a unique collection of artifacts. Each room has a themed exhibit, including the Victorian Era, New France, the Fur Trade, and Arts and Crafts. Behind the manor, enjoy the 18th-century-style garden and relax at the patio café. **T**:*(514) 861-3708*, **W**: *chateauramezay.qc.ca. Open June–Sept., daily 10–6; Oct.–May, Tues.–Sun. 10–4:30. Admission $7 for adults, $4 for children under 18.*

Continue on Rue Notre-Dame to **Sir George-Étienne Cartier National Historic Site** ⑭, 458 Rue Notre Dame. This unique interactive museum transports visitors to the Victorian era through costumed guides and thematic exhibitions. Interpretive activities explain the life of Sir George-Étienne Cartier. **T**:*(514) 283-2282. Open June–Aug., daily 10–6; Sept.–Dec. and Apr.–May, Wed.–Sun. 10–12 and 1–5. Closed Jan.–Mar. Admission $6.25 for adults, $4.25 for children 6–16, children 5 and under are free.*

Walk back on Rue Notre-Dame one block and turn left onto **Rue Bonsecours**. Take a moment to appreciate the view from the top of the street. Note the **Pierre du Calvet House**, 401 Rue Bonsecours, a charming 18th-century structure and a beautiful example of the urban architecture commonly used to develop New France. Pierre du Calvet held meetings here with Benjamin Franklin in support of the American Revolution.

*CHAPELLE NOTRE-DAME de BON SECOURS and MUSÉE MARGUERITE BOURGEOYS ⑮, 400 Rue Saint Paul East. **T**:(514) 282-8670. *Open Tues.–Sun. May–Oct. 10–5; Nov. to mid-Jan. and mid-Mar. through Apr. 11–3:30. Closed mid-Jan. to mid-Mar. Admission $6 for adults, $3 for children 6–12, children 5 and under are free.*

Resting at the end of Montréal's oldest street, this chapel and museum are among the most important historical sites in the city. Montréal's first stone church, founded by Marguerite Bourgeoys, was begun in 1655. The church and museum display objects from the city's earliest days, prehistoric artifacts, and an archeological site. The museum exhibits also depict the life of Marguerite Bourgeoys, a courageous woman who helped to shape the history of the city. The tower offers a panoramic view of the city and old port.

MARCHÉ BONSECOURS ⑯, 350 Rue Saint Paul East, **T**:(514) 872-7730, **W**: marchebonsecours.qc.ca. *Open late June through Aug., daily 10–9; Sept. to late June, Sat.–Wed. 10–6, Thurs.–Fri. 10–9.*

Commonly recognized as the symbol of Old Montréal, the stunning silver dome of the market can be seen from several blocks away. At this, the first public market in Montréal, farmers and vendors proudly displayed their goods along Rue de la Commune. Since being build in 1844, the building has functioned as a public market, concert hall, meeting hall, the United Canada House of Parliament, and city hall from 1852–78. Today the market is home to cafés, art galleries, and high-end boutiques selling fashion, furniture, jewelry and much more.

Downtown Montréal

Modern-day skyscrapers and international flare meld together making the downtown area a critical part of Montréal's commercial and cultural persona. Office buildings and parks, boutiques and malls, cafés and discos cluster together at the base of Mont Royal providing a diverse and busy neighborhood, day and night.

GETTING THERE:

By Car, take **Rue Sherbrooke** to McGill University. There are metered parking spots along the streets.

By Métro, take the **Green** line to **McGill** stop. Walk up **Rue University** to **Rue Sherbrooke**.

PRACTICALITIES:

The **Tourist Information Office**, Rue du Square Dorchester, offers a vast amount of information for Montréal and Québec Province. **T**:(514) 873-2015, **W**: bonjourquebec.com or **W**: tourism-montreal.org. Open June–Sept., daily 7–8; Sept.–May, daily 9–6. Closed Christmas and New Year's.

FOOD AND DRINK:

Resto Bistro Bar Robert et Compagnie (2095 McGill College Road) European-style, light, gourmet and French cuisine. This sprawling restaurant has a festive and comfortable atmosphere. Blues and jazz music is on for Happy Hour. **T**:(514) 849-2742. $$

Restaurant Focaccia di Carpaccio (2075 Rue University) Fine Italian cuisine and a wine bar in a contemporary setting. **T**:(514) 284-1115. $$

Le Parchemin (1333 Rue University) This beautifully decorated restaurant is located in a former church, the perfect setting for gourmet French food. **T**:(514) 844-1619. $$$ and $$$+

Funky Town (1454 Rue Peel) The 1970s-era disco has a permanent home in Montréal, commanding long lines and international acclaim. **T**:(514) 282-8387. $$

ATTRACTIONS:
Circled numbers correspond to numbers on the map.

MUSÉE McCORD d'HISTOIRE ①, 690 Rue Sherbrooke West, **T**:(514) 398-7100, **W**: mccord-museum.qc.ca. *Open Tues.–Fri. 10–6, Sat.–Sun. 10–5. Admission $10 for adults, $3 for children 7-12, children 6 and under are free. Free on Saturdays 10–12.*

A family of distinguished merchants and lawyers, the McCords settled in Canada in the late 18th century. David Ross McCord was committed to collecting and preserving objects related to the history of Canada, and in 1919 he donated his collection to McGill University to start a museum of Canadian History. Later the museum relocated across the street to the former McGill Student Union building.

One of North America's most significant historical collections with more than 100,000 artifacts and 750,000 historical photos, the museum brings Canadian history to life through innovative, imaginative, and interactive exhibits. Objects on display range from toys to costumes, artwork, and photography. The First Nations collection displays items from Amerindians and Inuits.

UNIVERSITÉ McGILL ②, 805 Rue Sherbrooke, **T**:(514) 398-4455, **W**: mcgill.ca

Pass through the Greek Revival **Roddick Gate**, erected in 1924 in honor of Sir Thomas Roddick, Dean of the Medical School. A clock is imbedded in the gate, donated by Lady Roddick to honor her husband's uncompromising punctuality. Situated on 80 acres of land in the city's downtown area, the campus is made up of more than 80 buildings, representing a vast array of architectural styles — from towers and turrets to ornate carved façades. Stroll the lush green areas and admire the impressive campus of Montréal's oldest university.

In 1821, following a bequest from Montréal fur trader James McGill, the university was founded on a charter from King George IV. The first classes, in medicine, were held in 1829. Note the **Arts Building** at the end of the main avenue. The campus' oldest building offers a beautiful view of the downtown area from the front steps. The tomb of James McGill is in the front of the building.

The **Redpath Museum of Natural History** has a collection of modern and pre-historic animals. Objects in the collection include rare minerals, Egyptian mummies, African masks, dinosaur bones, fossils, and musical instruments from around the world. Visitors will also get a look at daily life in ancient cultures. **T**:*(514) 398-4086. Open July–Aug., Mon.–Thurs. 9–5, Sun. 1–5; Sept.–June, Mon.–Fri. 9–5, Sun. 1–5. Admission is free.*

Walk down the beautiful **McGill College Avenue** ③, a beautiful tree-lined street with spectacular buildings, sculptures, and gathering places for the local business people and visitors alike.

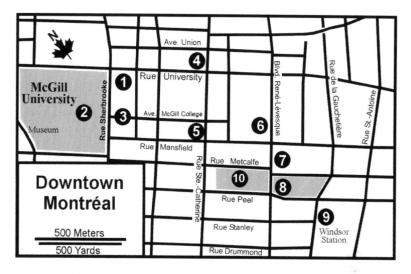

Downtown Montréal

500 Meters

500 Yards

The **National Bank of Paris** is an impressive building with walls of tinted blue glass. In front of the building, don't miss the amusing **sculpture** "Illuminated Crowd," by Raymond Mason. Stroll around the sculpted group of people to get a good look at the varied persons, expressions, and circumstances.

CHRIST CHURCH CATHEDRAL ④, 635 Rue Sainte-Catherine West, **T**:(514) 843-6577, **W**: montreal.anglican.org/cathedral. *Open year-round, daily 8–6.*

Built between 1857 and 1859, this Neo-Gothic church is charming. The original Christ Church was destroyed in a fire in 1856. The only object saved was a painting of the Last Supper, which can now be seen above the Canons' stalls in the present church. The square around and behind the cathedral is a great place to relax. It is dedicated to Raoul Wallenberg, "hero of humanity," who saved thousands of Jews from Hitler's concentration camps during World War II.

Part of the Underground City known as **Les Promenades de la Cathédrale** runs under the park and cathedral. The modern building at the opposite end of the square, **La Place de la Cathédrale**, was designed to evoke the features of a cathedral.

PLACE MONTRÉAL TRUST ⑤, 1500 Avenue McGill College, **T**:(514) 843-8000, **W**: placemontrealtrust.shopping.ca. *Open year-round, Mon.–Tues. 10–6, Wed.–Fri. 10–9, Sat. 9–5, Sun. 10–5.*

This beautiful and impressive skyscraper stretches for a full block between Rue Sainte Catherine and Boulevard de Maisonneuve. Take a few steps back to note its shape, colors and textures, designed as a blue glass cylinder within a rose marble square.

The five-story glass **atrium**, with its bronze tiered fountain, boutiques, and international food vendors is a popular meeting and resting-place for locals and visitors. Ride the panoramic elevator up for an absorbing view of the atrium and fountain.

Place Ville Marie ⑥, is a beautiful concrete commons, with a sweeping view of Avenue McGill College. The park was originally planned in 1930, inspired by New York City's Rockefeller Center, in order to fill a pit caused by the building of a pre-World War I railway tunnel under Mont Royal. The construction, starting in 1959, was the starting place for the "Underground City." The square offers a beautiful view of Avenue McGill College and the downtown area. Cross through the square and turn right on **Boulevard René-Lévesque**.

*BASILIQUE-CATHÉDRALE MARIE REINE du MONDE ⑦, on the corner of Boulevard René-Lévesque and Rue Mansfield, **T**:(514) 866-1661. *Open daily 8–5.*
This minor basilica, built at the end of the 19th century, is a scale replica of St. Peter's in Rome, at one-third the size. The structure, with its Greek columns, ornate decorations, and row of statues lining the cornice, makes a striking impression as you approach. The figures perched across the top represent patron saints from the different parishes that make up the Montréal Parish. Upon entering the church, visitors are greeted by portraits of all the bishops of Montréal. Inside, admire the large paintings that represent different episodes of Canada's history.
The **Mortuary Chapel**, to the left of the nave, houses the tombs of several bishops and archbishops. Note the walls and floors made from Italian marble and detailed with mosaics.

Just past the cathedral is **Place du Canada** ⑧, an oasis of peace and nature in the heart of the city. Note the **Château Champlain Hotel**, on the south side of the park, which looks remarkably like a cheese grater.
At the southeast corner of the park, note **Le 1000 de la Gauchetière**. This striking 51-floor building exemplified the new architectural design in the city. The indoor ice-skating rink, open year-round, is in a spectacular domed sky-lit hall. The stately copper-covered point atop the building makes it the tallest building in Montréal, the maximum height allowed in the city, whose ordinances require that no structure surpass Mont Royal. **T**:*(514) 395-0555,* **W**: *le1000.com. Skating admission $5.50 for adults, $3.50 for children. Equipment rental is available.*

WINDSOR STATION ⑨, on the corner of Rue Peel and Rue de la Gauchetière.
Designed by architect Bruce Price, who also designed Québec's Château Frontenac, this Romanesque Revival station was once the hub of Canada's

transcontinental railway system. The ornate structure has two towers, turrets, and arches. Alas, it was later abandoned in favor of newer stations and used only for urban commuter traffic.

Across from Windsor Station is **Saint George's Anglican Church**, on the corner of Rue Peel and Rue de la Gauchetière. This neo-Gothic church, built in 1870, is the oldest building along Place du Canada. The dark carved-wood interior boasts a tapestry from Westminster Abbey used in the coronation of Queen Elizabeth II. **T**:*(514) 866-7113,* **W***: st-georges.org. Open year-round, Tues.–Sun. 8:30–4:30.*

Between 1799 and 1854, **Dorchester Square** ⑩ was once the site of the Montréal Catholic Cemetery, used especially for the victims of the cholera epidemic of 1832. It was eventually moved to Mont Royal. The sister park to Place du Canada, the square is now a popular spot for local business people to relax and tourists to congregate.

This beautiful and busy park has a number of statues and memorials that are worth a look. A majestic lion commemorates **Queen Victoria's Jubilee.** Devotees of his work erected a statue of poet Robert Burns. There is also a statue of **Sir Wilfrid Laurier**, the first French-Canadian Prime Minister of Canada.

Notable as the building with the first wooden escalators in Montréal, the **Dominion Square Building**, on the northern edge of the park, built in 1929, is reminiscent of 15th-century grandeur. At the time of its construction the building was reported to be the largest and most modern building in Canada. In addition to the escalators, the building boasted an underground parking lot and a two-level shopping mall.

The **Sun Life Building**, 1155 Rue Metcalfe, spans the eastern edge of the park. When built in 1913, it was considered to be the tallest building in the British Empire. Now the headquarters of the Sun Life Insurance Company, during World War II the British government stored its Treasury bonds and gold reserves here.

Bus tours of the city depart from the square throughout the day. Tours give visitors a comprehensive overview of the city, as well as an informative and often entertaining look at its history. **Gray Line de Montréal**, **T**:(514) 934-1222, and **Autocar Impérial**, **T**:(514) 871-4733, both offer frequent and comprehensive tours.

Trip 29
Montréal

Place des Arts
and Chinatown

The leaders and people of Montréal had long neglected this French sector of the city. In the 1960s, after the French counterculture movement known as the Quiet Revolution, the government built Place des Arts. The modern cultural center inspired other modern complexes in the area, sparking new life to this part of the city.

Nestled beside the large, modern complexes and wide pedestrian squares are the narrow, exotic streets of Chinatown. The busy streets thrive with families and visitors enjoying the traditional and authentic flavor of the neighborhood. Oriental ornamentation adorns buildings, and large gates mark the entryways adding to the Asian feel of the area.

GETTING THERE:
By Car, you can reach Place des Arts by either **Boulevard de Maisonneuve** or **Rue Sainte-Catherine**.

By Métro, take the **Green** line to the **Place des Arts** station.

PRACTICALITIES:
Most of the concerts and shows at Place des Arts are scheduled at night. If there is a particular show you are interested in seeing, you may want to plan your tour of the area accordingly. Also check the schedule for festivals you may not want to miss, such as the annual Jazz Festival. See page 167 for local tourist information.

FOOD AND DRINK:
La Rotonde (At the Montréal Contemporary Art Museum) Provençale cuisine, elegantly displayed, in a beautiful, serene environment surrounded by art. **T**:(514) 847-6900. $$$

Chez Gauthier (3487 Avenue du Parc) Excellent French food in a nice setting. **T**:(514) 845-2992. $$$

Le Pavillon Nanpic (75A Rue de la Gauchetière West) This is a popular spot for Chinese food, specializing in Peking Duck. **T**:(514) 395-8106. $$

Grillades Thai (5101 Rue Saint-Laurent) Authentic Thai cuisine and an equally authentic atmosphere. **T**:(514) 270-5566. $$

ATTRACTIONS:
Circled numbers correspond to numbers on the map.

PLACE des ARTS ①, on the corner of Rue Sainte-Catherine West and Rue Jeanne Mance, **T**:(514) 842-2112. *The schedule of concerts and shows is available on the Internet. Times and prices vary with the show. Tickets can be purchased in advance from the website:* **W**: *pda.qc.ca*

This is the soul of Montréal's cultural life. Join Montrealers for a rest beside one of the peaceful fountains and pools. The large esplanade in the center of the complex is a popular meeting and gathering place.

The centerpiece of the complex is the massive concert hall, the **Wilfred Pelletier Auditorium**, which fans out across the top of the park as though it is holding court. This is home for the Montréal Symphony Orchestra, the Montréal Opera, and the Canadian Grand Ballet. The interior is decorated with a fine collection of paintings, sculptures, tapestries, and ceramics.

Don't miss the **Jazz Festival**, held annually at the beginning of July. Featuring Jazz musicians from around the globe, this popular festival fills Place des Arts and the surrounding streets each year.

To one side of the concert hall is the **Theater Building**, housing three state-of-the-art theaters. Two of the theaters, the Jean Duceppe and the Maisonneuve, are stacked one above the other, separated by a system of springs. The soundproofing system enables separate productions to take place simultaneously in the two theaters. The third theater, the Maurier Ltée, is an intimate studio theater.

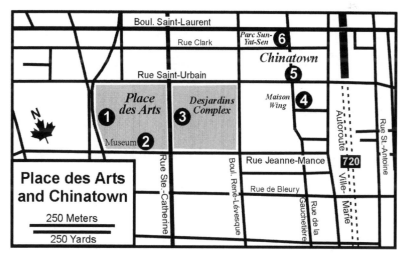

Opposite the theater building, across the esplanade, is the Contemporary Art Museum.

MONTRÉAL CONTEMPORARY ART MUSEUM ②, 185 Rue Sainte-Catherine West, **T**:(514) 847-6212, **W**: macm.org. *Open Tues.–Sun. 11–6, Wed. 11–9. Guided tours are held Wed. at 6:30, Sat. and Sun. at 1 and 3. The sculpture garden is closed in winter. Admission $6 for adults, $3 for students, children under 12 are free. Free admission on Wed. 6–9.*

This is the only museum in Canada devoted exclusively to contemporary art. The museum's permanent collection consists of nearly 6,000 works dating back as far as 1939, more than half of which are by Québec artists. Exhibit galleries include video screening rooms and areas for multimedia events, while a peaceful garden features contemporary sculptures. Temporary exhibits are often themed, addressing modern topics such as body image and cloning.

Cross to the Desjardins Complex, either via the tunnel, part of the Underground City, from the Contemporary Art Museum or across Rue Sainte-Catherine.

Walk through the **Desjardins Complex** ③, 150 Rue Sainte-Catherine, a large modern building with shops, entertainment, and restaurants. The complex consists of four towers connected by an atrium, which is used for hundreds of events, free to the public, each year. **T**:*(514) 845-4636.*

Turn left onto Rue René-Lévesque and then right onto Rue Saint-Urbain. Just past Complex Guy Favreau turn right onto Rue de la Gauchetière.

Maison Wing ④, on the corner of Rue de la Gauchetière and Rue Côté, built in 1826, is one of the oldest houses in the neighborhood. It is now a fortune cookie manufacturer.

Across the square, check out the **Holy Spirit Chinese Catholic Mission**, 205 Rue de La Gauchetière West. Inside is an amazing Oriental painting illustrating the Stations of the Cross.

Return back along Rue de la Gauchetière and cross Rue Saint-Urbain.

Chinatown ⑤ dates back to the 1860s when Chinese immigrants worked the mines and railroads. The immigrants settled downtown, forming a tight-knit community. Today the area is more commercial than residential, but it has retained its Asian flavor. Montréal's Chinese community continues to shop and gather here to celebrate traditional festivals. The narrow streets, designed for pedestrian traffic, are home to shops selling oriental crafts, imports, exotic foods, herbs, teas, and natural medicines.

Large arches, replicas of Chinese Imperial gates, welcome visitors to the neighborhood, transporting them into a truly exotic and flavorful community.

Parc Sun-Yat-Sen ⑥, on the corner of Rue de la Gauchetière and Rue Clark, built in honor of the "Father of modern China," welcomes community members and visitors alike. Take a rest and watch the constantly bustling streets.

Museum District

This neighborhood is the heart of Montréal's cultural and social life. Here, tourists and visitors gather at intriguing museums, fabulous cafés, and high-end boutiques to live fully. The history of the neighborhood is evident in the architecture. This was once called the "Golden Square Mile." Under the protective shadow of Mont Royal, it was formerly home to Montréal's wealthy elite. Magnificent homes and estates, at one time belonging to the city's richest few, now house galleries and upscale shops. It is obvious to all who meander these streets why the Museum District is synonymous with the art of living.

GETTING THERE:

By Car, the Museum District can be reached via **Rue Sherbrooke**.

By Métro, take the **Green** line to the **Peel** Métro stop.

PRACTICALITIES:

The Museum of Fine Arts holds phenomenal temporary exhibits, so art lovers may want to check the schedule of exhibits before planning your trip. See page 160 for tourist information.

FOOD AND DRINK:

Les Jardins du Ritz (1228 Rue Sherbrooke West) Treat yourself to an elegant, gourmet meal or try their traditional British-style high tea. **T**:(514) 842-4212, **W**: ritzcarlton.com. $$$ and $$$+

Bleu Marin (1437A Rue Crescent) Fresh seafood prepared by server and a well-stocked antipasto bar will be thoroughly enjoyed in the bright stone and yellow dining room. **T**:(514) 847-1123. $$$

Colazione Pino (1471 Rue Crescent) Fresh and delicious Italian food in a very festive atmosphere. **T**:(514) 289-1930. $$

Sir Winston Churchill Pub (1455 Rue Crescent) Popular with Montrealers and visitors for more than 25 years, the pub offers good food and great dancing. **T**:(514) 288-0623. $$

AREA ATTRACTIONS:

Circled numbers correspond to numbers on the map.

Stroll up elegant Rue Peel, named for Sir Robert Peel, founder of the London Police force.

CANADIAN GUILD of CRAFTS ①, 2025 Rue Peel, **T**:(514) 849-6091. *Open June–Sept., Mon. and Sat. 10–5, Tues.–Fri. 9–5:30; Oct.–May, Tues.–Fri. 9–5:30, Sat. 10–5.*

This beautiful gallery and shop features Amerindian and Inuit art. Special exhibits focus on ceramics, wood, and glass.

Continue up Rue Peel and turn left onto **Rue Sherbrooke West**, once known as Montréal's Golden Square Mile. The area was occupied by wealthy landowners who built sprawling estates at the base of Mont Royal.

Note the **Ritz Carlton Hotel** ②, 1228 Rue Sherbrooke West, Montréal's last remaining old hotel, built in 1912. The grand limestone façade and lavish lobby, decorated with marble, leather, and bronze, are reminiscent of by-gone days. Elizabeth Taylor and Richard Burton were married here.

Across the street, the **Château**, with its façade of limestone, looks like a medieval castle, transported in time and space. This immense apartment complex was built in 1925 for Pamphile du Tremblay, then owner of the French-language *La Presse* paper.

The **Erskine and American United Church** ③, 1339 Rue Sherbrooke West, built in 1894, has united the Erskine Church and American Presbyterian Church since 1934. The church is noteworthy for its Neo-Roman architecture with windows of varying shape, towers and gables. Inside, magnificent Tiffany stained-glass windows depict stories and themes from the Bible. The church is a prime example of the opulence of Montréal's Scottish-origin Protestant elite at the turn of the century.

Turn left onto **Rue Crescent** ④, one of Montréal's most popular streets, pulsating with activity. The street is home to many specialty shops, boutiques, and restaurants situated in the incredible Victorian architecture that has been well maintained. Haute-couture showrooms, luxury boutiques, and art galleries add a touch of class, while nightclubs, pubs, and outdoor cafés add life and laughter.

MONTRÉAL MUSEUM of DECORATIVE ARTS ⑤, 2200 Rue Crescent, **T**:(514) 284-1252. *Open year-round, Tues.–Sun. 11–6, Wed. 11–9. Admission is free.*

Items on display here illustrate the trends in decorative arts throughout the 20th century, from Art Nouveau to Postmodernism. The more than 4,000 objects in this impressive collection include furniture, sculptures, ceramics, jewelry, and textiles. The building was designed by architect Frank Gehry, who also did the

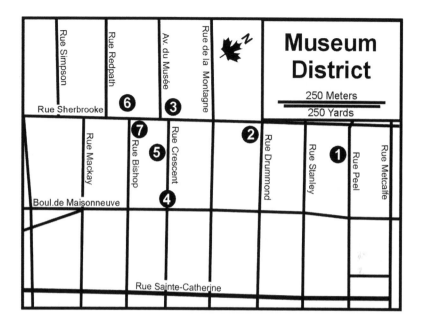

Guggenheim Museum in Bilbao, Spain.

Turn right and stroll up **Rue Sainte Catherine**. Turn right and walk up **Rue Mackay**.

Take a peek at the **Saint-James the Apostle Anglican Church** on Rue Sainte-Catherine, before continuing up Rue Mackay to Rue Sherbrooke West.

CHURCH of SAINT-ANDREW and SAINT-PAUL ⑥, corner of Rue Sherbrooke West and Rue Bishop, **T**:(514) 842-3431, **W**: standrewstpaul.com

One of the most significant institutions of Montréal's Scottish community, the Presbyterian church was built in 1932. Statues of the patron saints stand at either side of the Rue Sherbrooke entryway. The church is home to the Scottish-Canadian Black Watch or Royal Highland Regiment, which has been affiliated with this Presbyterian community since it was founded in 1862.

The stone interior is beautiful. A stained-glass window, overlooking the central altar, commemorates soldiers killed in World War I. Pause in the central aisle, turn and look at the stained-glass window towering above the gallery. This was first installed in the original Saint-Paul church in 1900 and later moved when the new church was built.

The 1932 Casavant organ, rebuilt in 1992, is the largest in Montréal. Organ recitals are held on Thursdays during July and August, at 12:15.

Leave the church through the Porte Cochère and look up in the tower. You may be able to spot the images of frogs high in the shadows of the tower. Frogs are medieval symbols of the spirit of evil being driven out of a sacred place.

MONTRÉAL MUSEUM of FINE ARTS ⑦, 1379-1380 Rue Sherbrooke West, **T**:(514) 285-2000, **W**: mbam.qc.ca. *Open year-round Tues.–Sun., and holiday Mondays, 11–5. Temporary exhibits are open the same hours as the permanent collection and Wednesdays 11–9. Admission $15 for the temporary exhibits, half-price Wed. 5:30–9. Admission to permanent collection is free. Handicap accessible.*

One of Canada's oldest and largest art museums, the Montréal Museum of Fine Arts opened in 1860. Today it is known as one of the country's most important art institutions. The permanent collection proudly displays work representing all forms of art throughout the ages. A packed and impressive schedule of temporary exhibits also continues to greatly add to the museum's reputation.

The museum spans two buildings, on opposite sides of Rue Sherbrooke. The **North Pavilion**, or Benaiah Gibb Pavilion, housed the museum's modest collection in the late 19th century. As the collection grew with acquisitions of work from around the world and across Canada, from Old Masters to contemporary, the building had to be expanded. This beautiful building boasts white Vermont marble, imposing columns, and massive doors. Its three floors are dedicated to the exhibition of art from the Americas.

Another expansion brought the museum across Rue Sherbrooke, into the **South Pavilion**, or Jean Noël Desmarais Pavilion. An enormous open lobby, large windows, and skylights give the museum a bright and warm atmosphere. A series of large vaulted galleries are dedicated to temporary exhibits. European art dating back to the Middle Ages, housed on the fourth floor, features frescos, stained glass, Flemish art, and Rembrandt. An impressive collection of International and Canadian 20th-century art is displayed on several floors.

The two pavilion buildings are connected by a series of underground galleries. The **Galleries of Ancient Cultures** display Egyptian, Greek, Roman, African, and Asian art. Visitors can admire art, ceramics, and ritualistic objects from around the world, some as old as known civilization.

Mont Royal

According to legend, Jacques Cartier climbed the mountain in 1535, declaring "c'est un mont réal" — it's a royal mountain — thus naming the mountain Mont Royal. It is from this mountain that the city's name, Montréal, was derived.

The mountain raises 230 meters (764 feet) above the center of downtown Montréal, majestic and protective. The highest of the mountain's three peaks has become a popular spot for leisure and recreation, providing peace and nature with sweeping views of the city below. The spectacular park was opened to the public in 1876 and draws visitors year-round.

Skirting the mountain to the north is the Outremont neighborhood — a place of traditional French residential streets, fine restaurants, and local commerce. West of the mountain, history and education come together at the University of Montréal and Saint-Joseph's Oratory.

GETTING THERE:

By Car, take **Rue Sherbrooke West** to **Chemin de la Côte-des-Neiges**. Turn left onto **Chemin Queen Mary** for the Oratoire Saint-Joseph.

By Métro, take the **Blue** line to the **Côte-des-Neiges** stop for the Oratoire Saint-Joseph and to the **Université de Montréal** stop for the University of Montréal. Take the **Orange** line to the **Mont-Royal** stop for Mont Royal Park.

PRACTICALITIES:

Mont-Royal Park offers a variety of sporting activities for each season. Plan your visit to the park for the season that best suites the activities you enjoy. The University of Montréal is at its most exciting during the school year when the campus is busy. See page 167 for tourist information.

FOOD AND DRINK:

Chez Lévéque (1030 Rue Laurier West) Quaint French *brasserie* with delicious food and a nice neighborhood atmosphere. T:(514) 279-7355. $$

Moishes (3961 rue Saint-Laurent) Founded in 1938, Moishes has become a Canadian institution. Well known for its high-quality steak and unique house specialties, such as pickled salmon and broiled peppers. **T**:(514) 845-1696. $$

Restaurant Thai Grill (5101 rue Saint-Laurent) Authentic, excellent Thai food and Montréal's first Thai Sunday Brunch. **T**: (514) 270-5566. $$ and $$$

Milos (5357 Avenue du Parc) Open kitchen and displays of fresh produce provide the perfect atmosphere for seafood with Mediterranean flare. **T**:(514) 272-3522. $$$

Mythos Ouzeri (5318 Avenue du Parc) Traditional Greek cuisine in an authentic atmosphere with stone walls, *ouzo* and live music. **T**:(514) 270-0235. $$$

LOCAL ATTRACTIONS:

Circled numbers correspond to numbers on the map.

ORATOIRE SAINT-JOSEPH ①, 3800 Chemin Queen Mary, **T**:(514) 733-8211, **W**: saint-joseph.org. *Open year-round, daily 9–5. Admission is free. Handicap accessible.*

This spectacular basilica is one of the world's most visited shrines. The copper-covered dome can be seen at great distances across the city and while approaching the city. Pick up a brochure for the numbered self-guided tour, which brings you through a primitive chapel, a votive chapel, a crypt, and a large basilica. Terraces offer breathtaking views of the surrounding cityscape of northern Montréal and the Laurentian Mountains. Behind the Oratory, the quaint Brother André's Chapel looks like a dollhouse version of a chapel. In the chapel loft, see the humble quarters where Brother André lived, with a small oil-burning stove, straight-backed chair and narrow bed. A prayer garden climbs the hilly ground beside the oratory, filled with beautiful statues representing the Stations of the Cross. The incredible Beckerath-style organ can be heard Wednesday evenings during the summer. The chimes beside the oratory were originally intended for the Eiffel Tower in Paris.

Alfred Besette took the name of **Brother André** when he entered the Congregation of Holy Cross in 1870. A doorkeeper at Notre-Dame College for forty years, he preached the healing powers of Saint Joseph to all that passed by. In 1904 he built a small chapel along the path that led from Notre-Dame College to Mont Royal. People who came to pray with him, crippled and ill, left the chapel healed and whole. By the 20th century the throngs of pilgrims that came to see Brother André were so vast that plans began for the large-scale shrine that became the oratory.

Building of the oratory began in 1924 but was suspended by economic and technical difficulties. It wasn't until 1936 that Benedictine monk-architect Dom Paul Bellot was called upon to finish designing and building the oratory. The

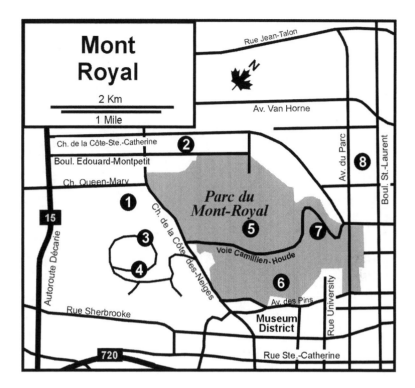

building was finally completed in 1967. Today the oratory is visited by millions of Roman Catholic pilgrims each year.

Religious artwork fills the oratory, including the carved-stone main altar and wooden carvings of the apostles. Note the impressive mosaic illustrating the life of Saint Joseph.

Leaving the oratory, turn right onto Chemin Queen Mary. Turn left on Avenue Decelles and then right onto Boulevard Édouard Montpetit.

UNIVERSITÉ de MONTRÉAL ②, 2900 Boulevard Édouard Montpetit, **T**:(514) 343-6111.

Originally a part of Laval University, which was founded by the Québec seminary, it became an autonomous university in 1919. Today it is Québec's largest university, with over 50,000 students, and one of the best-regarded research universities in North America. Check out the Art Deco-style Main Building created by architect Ernest Cormier.

Centre d'Exposition de l'Université de Montréal, 2940 Rue Côte Sainte-Catherine, hosts a vast array of temporary exhibits that range in theme from sciences to arts. *T*:*(514) 343-6111 ext. 4694,* **W**: *expo.umontreal.ca. Open Tues.–Thurs. and Sun. 12–6.*

MONT ROYAL   181

Montréal from Mont Royal

Return to Avenue Decelles and merge left onto Chemin de la Côte des Neiges. On the right, follow **Summit Circle** ③, which is a scenic loop around Summit Park. Stop at **Belvédère de Westmount** ④, between numbers 18 and 36 Summit Circle, for a view of Mount Royal Park and the Westmont area of Montréal.

PARC du MONT ROYAL ⑤, **T**:(514) 872-6559, **W**: lemontroyal.com. *Open year-round, daily 6–midnight.*

This beautiful mountainside park, planned by landscape architect Frederick Law Olmsted, who also designed New York's Central Park, has a wide variety of diversions and activities to offer. The park is criss-crossed with trails, perfect for walking, biking, or cross-country skiing. The pond provides a refreshing swim in the summer and exhilarating ice-skating in the winter. There are two breath-taking vista points on the mountain offering sweeping views of the city below. Vast green patches and sculpture gardens entice visitors to relax and take in the beautiful natural surroundings.

At the peak of the mountain, park and follow the footpath to the **Chalet Welcome Center**. During the 1930's and 40's, big bands gave public concerts by moonlight on the chalet steps. **T**:*(514) 844-4928. Open year-round, Mon.– Fri. 9:30–8.*

Belvédère du Chalet ⑥ is the sweeping patio that fans out in front of the Chalet offering views of the downtown area. Directly below, at the foot of the mountain, lays the campus of McGill University with its cylindrical McIntyre

MONT ROYAL   182

Medical Sciences Building. The Saint Lawrence River is visible as it loops around the city. Hike to the summit to see the **cross** that stands high above the city. Erected in 1924, it commemorates the promise made by Montréal's founder January 6, 1643 to carry a wooden cross on Mount Royal if the colony survived the threat of flooding. When lit, the 30-meter (98-foot) cross can be seen from miles away.

Belvédère Camillien-Houde ⑦, popular with local couples, is accessible off Voie Camillien Houde as you make your way down the other side of the mountain. From this vista point you can get a far-reaching view of eastern Montréal, dominated by the imposing futuristic structure of the Olympic Stadium. The Laurentian Mountains can be seen rising out of the north.

Leaving the park, visitors can explore the several interesting and authentic Montréal **neighborhoods** ⑧ of Outremont.

Turn left onto **Avenue du Parc**, a busy commercial street that was once one of the city's more elegant residential areas. In the 1950s the area became a lively Greek community with shops, restaurants, and pastry cafés. Note the Art Deco-style Rialto movie theater.

Avenue Laurier, which crosses Avenue du Parc, is an authentic French commercial street. Cafés and bakeries fill it with the aroma of pastries, fresh bread, and coffee. Bistros offer international dining while boutiques sell designer wear and home furnishings.

Several blocks farther along Avenue du Parc is **Avenue Bernard**, a charming neighborhood with residential and commercial buildings mingling and coexisting in harmony.

Trip 32
Montréal

*Olympic Park and the Botanical Gardens

Montréal's Olympic Park, built for the 1976 Summer Olympic Games, is internationally acclaimed. Excavation began in 1973, but only the stadium, velodrome, aquatic complex, and village were completed on schedule for the Olympics. In 1979 it was discovered that the tower, as planned, would be too heavy. The tower and stadium roof were not completed until 1987. Work continued on the park, with the intent of turning the expensive sports complex into a profit-generating attraction.

GETTING THERE:

By Car, follow **Rue Sherbrooke East** to **Boulevard Viau**. Parking is available at 3200 Boulevard Viau for $10.

By Métro, take the **Green** line to the **Viau** station.

PRACTICALITIES:

Packages are available to include several combinations, or all, of these attractions at a very attractive price. If you plan to spend the day, pick up the "Get an Eyeful" ticket which gives you access to the Olympic Park, Biodôme, Botanical Gardens, and Insectarium for $28.50 for adults and $14.25 for children 5–17. Children under 5 are free.

A free shuttle is available between Olympic Park and the Botanical Gardens. Look for the blue-and-black Nevette signs. The stops are located by the Biodôme and near the Insectarium at the Botanical Gardens. You can also walk easily between the parks by following the service road that runs behind the stadium and safely under Rue Sherbrooke.

See page 167 for tourist information.

FOOD AND DRINK:

At the Biodôme, **La Mousson Restaurant** offers an à la carte menu with hearty food and daily specials. **La Brise Cafeteria** is a self-service café with a wide variety of meals, pizza and sandwiches. **T**:(514) 868-3099. $$

At the Botanical Gardens, the **Fuji Pavilion** offers snacks, sandwiches, and salads in a beautiful outdoor setting. The **restaurant**, beside the main greenhouses, serves hot meals, grill foods, sandwiches, and snacks with both inside and outside seating. **T**:(514) 872-1400. $$

ATTRACTIONS:
Circled numbers correspond to numbers on the map.

OLYMPIC PARK ①, 4141 Avenue Pierre De Coubertin, **T**:(514) 252-8687, **W**:rio.gouv.qc.ca

The vast complex, comprised of a sports stadium, tower, six pools, and the velodrome building, is gathered around a large concrete esplanade:

OLYMPIC STADIUM ②. *Guided tours year-round daily at 11 and 2 in French, 12:40 and 3:40 in English. Closed Jan. to early Feb.*

Looking like a flying saucer or upside-down frying pan on the horizon, it is widely considered a marvel of modern architecture. Costing more than a billion dollars, the stadium is the masterpiece of architect Roger Tailibert, who also designed the Parc des Princes stadium in Paris.

The stadium has the capacity to hold nearly 56,000 spectators in unobstructed seats. Every year since the Olympics, the stadium is host to sports events, rock concerts, and trade shows.

Twenty-six suspension cables span from the top of the tower to the Kevlar roof of the stadium. The cables could be retracted, lifting the roof into a niche in the base of the tower. The roof could then be re-deployed, like a parachute, over the stadium.

The stadium was used for the services held by Pope John Paul II during his 1984 visit to Montréal.

A 574-foot **Tower** ③ rises high above the stadium. It is the largest leaning tower structure in the world, at an angle nine times greater than the Leaning Tower of Pisa, with its steel upper section leaning over the stadium roof at a 45° angle. Visitors can ride the cable car to the observatory at the top of the tower for a dizzying ride and breathtaking view of the city. From the observatory the Saint Lawrence River, downtown Montréal and Mont Royal can be seen. Large photographs identify the various buildings and sites that can be seen in each direction. **T**:*(514) 252-8687. Open Mon. noon–9, Tues.–Thurs. 10 a.m.–9 p.m., Fri.–Sun. 10 a.m.–11 p.m.*

The ultra-modern, pyramid-shaped **Olympic Village** ④ juts up nearby on Rue Sherbrooke. Built as housing for the athletes of the 1976 Olympic Games, the two 20-floor buildings are now residential apartments.

BIODÔME ⑤, 4777 Avenue Pierre De Coubertin, **T**:(514) 868-3000, **W**:

ville.montreal.qc.ca/biodome. *Open daily 9–5, during summer 9–6.*

Once the indoor cycling track of the 1976 Olympic Games, the building is now home to thousands of interesting and exotic plants and animals. Stroll through a rainforest while monkeys swing above, walk through a cave teaming with bats in flight, and watch penguins playfully slide down hills of snow and ice. Visitors will walk through a variety of authentically re-created ecosystems to discover flora, fauna, and climate from around the globe. Films and discussions on topics of nature and environment are held regularly in the amphitheater. **Naturalia**, on the lower level of the building, is a hands-on exploration center for all ages. Shells, eggs, feathers, and mounted animals are available to touch and investigate.

MONTRÉAL BOTANICAL GARDENS ⑥, 4101 rue Sherbrooke East, **T**:(514) 872-1400, **W**: ville.montreal.qc.ca/jardin. *Open Sept.–May daily 9–5; June–Aug. daily 9–7. Handicap accessible.*

These magnificent gardens cover acres, displaying more than 21,000 species of plants, flowers, and trees. Visitors will be tempted to spend the day here, strolling among rose gardens and orchards, marveling at the experimental garden or meandering through the diverse exhibits in the greenhouses. **"Salle Chlorophylle"** is a wonderful interactive center, located behind the hospitality greenhouse, where children of all ages can learn about plants, flowers, and other garden inhabitants from the inside out.

The beautiful and peaceful **Chinese Garden** ⑦, a replica of a typical Ming dynasty (14th–17th century) garden from southern China, is the largest of its kind outside of Asia. The landscape incorporates two essential elements of Chinese gardens, mountains and water. Seven pavilions, prefabricated in Shanghai, are nestled amongst the flora and water. The Friendship Pavilion, the largest in the garden, houses temporary exhibits. Climb the stone mountain, around jagged edges, past caves, and behind the waterfall for a view of the full garden.

The **Japanese Garden** ⑧ presents a harmonious landscape of water, boulders, and gardens. Sit on the wood walkway and watch the giant *kaoi* or meditate in the Zen garden.

The "Tree House" exhibit hall introduces visitors to the life of a tree. The First Nations garden, new in the summer of 2001, illustrates the link and dependency between the Amerindian and Intuit nations with the natural world. Ten exhibition gardens display and explain plants in themed groupings.

Not for the squeamish, the **Insectarium** ⑨ is a museum devoted completely to insects with more than 150,000 live and mounted specimens. Visitors will experience a whole universe that exists around us but that we rarely notice. In the summer, the butterfly house is alive with colorful butterflies, which soar freely among spectators. **W**: *ville.montreal.qc.ca/insectarium*

CHÂTEAU DUFRESNE ⑩, 2929 Avenue Jeanne d'Arc, **T**:(514) 259-9201. *Open year-round Thurs.–Sun. 10–5. Admission $6 for adults, $2.50 for children 6–12, children 5 and under are free. Handicap accessible.*

Inspired by the Petit Trianon Palace in Versailles, this striking mansion was built in 1916 by Dufresne brothers, influential people in this area of Montréal. With its stone exterior, forty-four rooms, lavish décor, and interior murals the château cost more than a million dollars to build! The former residence now exhibits the original furnishings and other objects from the early 20th century.

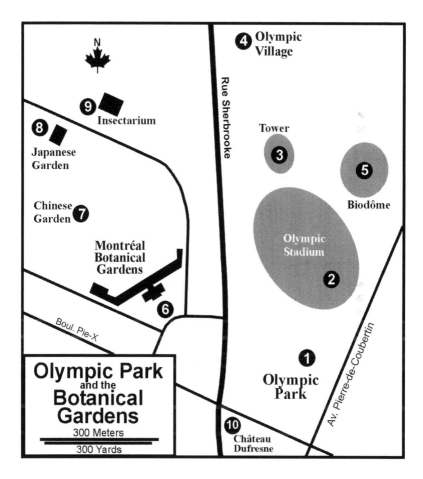

Trip 33
Montréal

Notre Dame and
Sainte Helen's Islands

In 1611, when Samuel de Champlain reached the island of Montréal, he found a string of small rocky islands located in the channel, just east of the city. He named the largest of the islands after his wife, Hélène Boulé. The island was recognized for its strategic importance by the French troops struggling to hold onto New France and the British invaders who built a fort there. It was turned into a park in the late 19th century.

In 1964, during preparation for the 1967 World's Fair, Montréal enlarged the natural island of Île Sainte-Hélène and created Île Notre-Dame beside it. In ten months of construction, the island was formed with soil and rock dug up during the construction of Montréal's Métro system.

These small islands, which welcome visitors to escape the urban bustle of the city for a peaceful, relaxing day amongst water and greenery, stretch lazily in the middle of the Saint Lawrence River.

GETTING THERE:

By Car, Cité de Havre and both islands can be accessed by following **Avenue Pierre Dupuy** to the **Concord Bridge**. Île Sainte-Hélène can also be accessed from **Pont Jacque-Cartier**. Look for the somewhat narrow exit about midway over the bridge.

By Métro, take the **Yellow** line to **Jean Drapeau** (formerly Île Sainte-Hélène).

By Ferry, seasonally, from the Jacques Cartier Pier in Old Montréal directly to Île Sainte-Hélène. *Navettes Maritimes du Saint-Laurent,* **T**:*(514) 281-8000.*

PRACTICALITIES:

Tourist Information is available on Île Sainte-Hélène, in the Parterre, near the Métro station. **W**: *parcjeandrapeau.com*

Parking on Île Sainte-Hélène is $10 (per parking lot) and it is $10 to access Île Notre-Dame. The best approach is to decide on one location to park your car for the day and tour the two islands by foot, bike, roller blades, or "dragon boat."

FOOD AND DRINK:

Hélène de Champlain (200 Tour de l'Isle, Île Sainte-Hélène) This elegant and stylish restaurant serves creative gourmet meals from master chefs. Enjoy a Trilogy of Mushrooms cooked in Chablis, or Chicken Grand Marnier. Open weekdays for lunch and daily for dinner. **T**:(514) 395-2424. $$$ and $$$+

Via Fortuna (At the Casino, Île Notre-Dame) Fantastic Italian cuisine in a distinctly Venetian setting. **T**:(514) 392-2746. $$ and $$$

Le Bonne Carte (At the Casino, Île Notre-Dame) Savor an international menu or the ample buffet in a casual and festive atmosphere. **T**:(514) 392-2746. $$

Le Festin du Gouverneur (at the Old Fort, Île Sainte Hélène) Enjoy an evening of comedy and song, with seasoned performers and traditional Québec cuisine. The show is bilingual and appropriate for all ages. **T**:(514) 879-1141. $$$

ATTRACTIONS:

Circled numbers correspond to numbers on the map.

Poking out from the land like a protective arm around the Old Port, **Cité du Havre** ① is a man-made, landfill jetty built to safeguard the harbor from the harsh currents of the Saint Lawrence.

Habitat '67 is an odd and intriguing site along the Cité de Havre and Saint Lawrence River. The apartment complex, designed by architect Moshe Safdie and built for the 1967 Worlds Fair, has the appearance of large concrete squares stacked haphazardly, dotted with occasional windows and doors.

The **Parc Jean Drapeau** stretches across both Île Sainte-Hélène and Île Notre-Dame, offering a wide variety of activities for visitors to enjoy.

OLD FORT and DAVID M. STEWART MUSEUM ②, Île Sainte-Hélène, **T**:(514) 861-6701, **W**: stewart-museum.org. *Open May–Sept. daily 10–6; Sept.– May Wed.–Mon. 10–5. Admission $10 for adults, $7 for children, children under 7 are free.*

Built by the British in 1820, the Old Fort on Île Sainte-Hélène has protected and served Montréal ever since. With vaults, arsenals, imposing walls, and carriage entrances the fort impresses and charms visitors. Costumed guides help to bring history alive as you travel through time to when the fort bustled with fur traders, blacksmiths, bakers, town criers, and carpenters. Visitors may play traditional games, listen to stories and legends, eat traditional foods, or be recruited into the King's Army. The sound of bagpipes and drums, played by the Olde 78th Fraser Highlanders, completes the authenticity of the atmosphere.

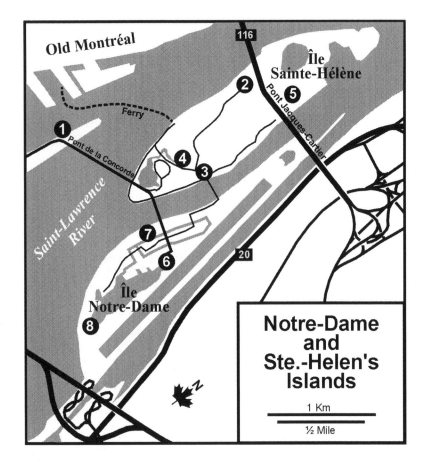

Notre-Dame and Ste.-Helen's Islands

The Stewart Museum depicts the history of Canada, from discovery through exploration and development. Collections are representative of North American history from the 16th through the 19th century. The museum addresses the themes of sociology, politics, military, science, and technology. The nearly 24,000 objects are grouped together into collections — history, household objects, antique arms, science and technology, and the library collection.

BIOSPHÈRE ③, 160 Chemin Tour de l'Île, Île Sainte-Hélène, **T**:(514) 283-5000, **W**: biosphere.ec.qc.ca/. *Open late June to Labor Day daily 10–6; Sept.–June Tues.–Sat. 10–4. Admission $9.78 for adults, $5.75 for children 7–17, children 6 and under are free.*

This, the largest building of its kind in the world, at more than 75% of a complete sphere, was designed by the visionary engineer Buckminster Fuller.

The Biosphère

As the United States pavilion during Expo 67, it was one of the biggest attractions at the fair.

Dedicated to the understanding and preservation of the ecosystems of the Saint Lawrence and Great Lakes network, the Biosphère is a center for environmental observation and public information. There are four large exhibit rooms, each focusing on a specific aspect of water. Exhibits and activities teach visitors about the state of the environment today, the relationship of water to all living creatures, and ecosystems.

NOTRE DAME & STE. HELEN'S ISLANDS   191

ÎLE SAINTE-HÉLÈNE POOL ④, located next to the Métro station. *Open late June to late Aug. daily 10–7. Admission $3.25 for 14 years and over, $1.75 for children 6–13, under 6 is free.*

This brand-new pool offers a long-awaited way to cool off and relax. It's a perfect way to escape the heat and hustle of the city.

LA RONDE ⑤, Île Notre Dame, **T**:(514) 397-2000, **W**: laronde.com. *Open mid-May to June 1, weekends 10–9; June 1 to mid-June daily 10–9; mid-June to Sept., daily 10:30–11. Admission is $35 for adults, $23 for children, children under 3 are free.*

This amusement park, part of the Six Flags chain, is the largest in Québec Province. With more than 35 thrilling rides, exciting shows, and spectacular views of the city, it's a hit with visitors of all ages. The park also hosts an international fireworks show each summer starting at 10 p.m. Pyrotechnique experts from around the world come to display their craft in bright colors and sonic booms across the Montréal sky.

MONTRÉAL CASINO ⑥, Île Notre-Dame, **T**:(514) 392-2746, **W**: casino-de-montreal.com. *Open 24 hours a day. Admission is restricted to 18 years and over.*

Originally the French and Québec pavilions at the Expo 67, the building opened as the Casino in 1993. With more than 3,000 slot machines, 120 gambling tables, the Cabaret, and four restaurants the casino offers world-class entertainment.

FLORAL GARDENS ⑦, **T**:(514) 872-0199 for information on boat rentals.

Acres of gardens meander across both islands, delighting visitors with flowers, trees, public artwork, wildlife, and views of the rivers and city. Cross the du Cosmos footbridge between the islands to take full advantage of all the gardens. Find the perfect spot of shade and grass for a picnic. Or, experience the gardens from the lagoons of Île Notre-Dame by renting a canoe, kayak or pedal boat.

Many sculptures are located throughout the gardens providing an open-air gallery for public viewing:

"Puerta de la Amistad" — Meaning "friendship gate," located on the Parterre, Île Sainte-Hélène, was a gift from Mexico for Montréal's 350th anniversary. Sebastian, Mexico, 1993.

"Ville Imaginaire" — A gift from Lisbon, Portugal, to celebrate the 30th anniversary of Montréal's Métro system, this sculpture is a reflection on how people create mythic spaces out of necessity. Charters de Almieda, Portugal, 1997.

"L'Homme" — On the belvedere, Île Sainte-Hélène, this sculpture was created to reflect the theme of Expo 67, "Man and His World." Alexander Calder, 1967.

"Le Phare du Cosmos" — On the southwest end of Île Sainte-Hélène, was designed to express the "language and cultural values of the new civilization of space and electronics." Yves Trudeau, Québec, 1967.

Kwakiutl Totem Pole — Near the Canadian Pavilion and Flower Gardens, Île Notre Dame. The totem pole is a remainder from the "Indians of Canada" pavilion of Expo 67. Henry and Tony Hunt, 1967.

"Acier" — Located in the water near the Casino de Montréal, Île Notre-Dame, this sculpture represents the three main themes of the Québec pavilion at Expo 67: challenge, combat and élan. The shapes are multiplied by their reflections in the water, giving a fascinating illusion of movement. Pierre Heyvaert, 1967.

Wallace Fountain — In the flower Garden, Île Notre-Dame, this neo-Renaissance-style fountain was a gift from the City of Paris. Based on a sculpture by Charles Auguste Lebourg, 1980.

"Obélisque Oblique" — Facing the main entrance to the Casino de Montréal, Île Notre-Dame, the obelisk was a gift from France during Expo 67. The sharp forms of the sculpture point in different directions, symbolizing the destiny of modern men and women who are called and pulled from all directions. Henry Georges Adam, 1962.

"Moai Head" — Located in the Flower Garden near the Pont de la Concorde, Île Notre-Dame, this replica is made from a mold taken from one of the original heads on Easter Island. 1970.

"Oh Homme!" — In the Rose Garden of the Hélène de Champlain Restaurant, Île Sainte-Hélène, this sculpture is part of a two-part piece titled "Oh Homme! Oh Femme!" presented at the 1971 man and His World Exhibition. Yvette Bisson, 1964.

"Girafes" — On Rue McDonald, Île Sainte-Hélène, this untitled black steel sculpture was given its nickname because of the resemblance to a group of giraffes. Robert Roussil, 1974.

ÎLE NOTRE-DAME BEACH and WATER SPORTS ⑧. *Open late June to late Aug., daily 10–7. Beach admission over 14 is $7.50, 13 and under is $3.75, children under 6 are free, $19 for family of 4. Rental prices for water sports is $9–$19 per hour.*

Possibly the cleanest and most beautiful beach in the Montréal area, this sandy beach promises fun and relaxation for everyone. The Water Sports Pavilion rents sailboats, windsurfers, canoes, kayaks, and pedal boats.

Section IX

DAYTRIPS AROUND
MONTRÉAL

Exploration of the areas surrounding Montréal treats visitors to a look at Québec Province, with past and present, nature and industry coexisting in harmony. Farms and battlefields have given way to suburbs and commuters. Rocky shorelines now hold inviting green parks, laced with paths for cycling and skating.

The regions around the city, to the south and east, are steeped in history, culture, and tradition. The Richelieu Valley, with its many forts and historical sites, whispers the secrets of the French struggle to maintain their seat in Québec. Laval and the West Island tell of the growth and development of Montréal, beyond the limits of the city, and the diversity of the community. The many lakes and rivers illustrate the importance, development, and history of water in the growth of the province.

Despite the influx of commuters and industries, Laval, the West Island, and Richelieu Valley have maintained large areas of natural splendor. With a bounty of lakes and rivers, aquatic preservation and appreciation are long-standing traditions.

Driving through the quaint old villages and natural strongholds, past rural splendors and historical interests, visitors can't help wondering — how much longer before it all gives way to the pressures of growth and modernity?

West Island

Benefiting greatly from its proximity to Montréal, its natural resources and industrial development, the West Island has become a prime destination for locals and visitors to work, live, and play. Bordered by the Saint Lawrence River, Lac Saint Louis, Lac des Deux Montagnes, and Rivière des Prairies the West Island is home to many parks and outdoor activities. Boating, rafting, and cycling are among the many popular activities in the area.

A shoreline drive, around the western end of Montréal Island, offers panoramic views of the Saint Lawrence River as it passes by beautiful green parks, impressive country homes, and quaint villages.

GETTING THERE:

By Car, take **Rte. 10** to **Rue Wellington** toward Verdun, just outside the city.

Turn left onto **Rue Dublin**, and follow that to **Place Dublin** for the Maison Saint Gabriel.

Continue on **Rue Wellington** and turn right onto **Boulevard LaSalle** and follow this road around the island. Boulevard LaSalle will change names several times as you pass from town to town.

From Saint-Laurent, take **Rte. 15** south back to Montréal.

PRACTICALITIES:

Tourist information about the West Island can be found at **T**:(514) 873-2015, **W**: tourism-montreal.org

Small, seasonal tourist information kiosks are set up along the route around the island and some information is available at the various museums and attractions.

FOOD AND DRINK:

Restaurant l'Habitant (5010 Boulevard Lalande, Pierrefonds) Situated in a historic house built in 1799, with a fireplace, this award-winning restaurant serves French and regional cuisine. **T**:(514) 684-4398. $$ and $$$

Restaurant Le Chandelier (825 Rue Côte-Vertu, Saint Laurent) This French restaurant, in a historical setting, is on Canada's "Best 100 Restaurants" list. **T**:(514) 748-5800. $$$

Le Bifthèque Restaurant (6705 Chemin Côte-de-Liesse, Saint Laurent) Steak and seafood in a friendly, comfortable atmosphere. **T**:(514) 739-6336 $$ and $$$

SUGGESTED TOUR:
Circled numbers correspond to numbers on the map.

MAISON SAINT-GABRIEL ①, 2146 Place Dublin, **T**:(514) 935-8136, **W**: maisonsaint-gabriel.qc.ca. *Open July–Aug., daily 11–5 with guided tours every hour; mid-Apr. through June and Sept. to mid-Dec., Tues.–Sat., guided tours at 1:30, 2:30 and 3:30, Sun. guided tours at 1, 2, 3, and 4. Admission is $8 for adults, $2 for children, children under 6 are free.*

This farmhouse, originally built in 1668 by Marguerite Bourgeoys, was a home for young orphan girls who were sent to New France to find a husband and populate the new colony. The first house was destroyed by fire in 1693 and rebuilt several years later. One of the oldest homes on Montréal Island, the building was restored in 1965 and opened as a museum. An exhibit tells visitors of the work of Marguerite Bourgeoy and her order of nuns. 18th-century furniture, tools and domestic equipment are also on display. The 19th-century stone barn on the property is also of interest.

Return to Rue Wellington, turn left, and continue to Boulevard LaSalle. Turning right here, the drive offers many beautiful views of the Saint Lawrence River.

In **LaSalle**, a long stretch of park on the river welcomes visitors to sit and relax, rollerblade, and cycle. Stop along the way to check out the **Rapides de Lachine** ②, low and choppy rapids at the mouth of the Saint Lawrence River. Walk across the old hydro-dam, constructed in 1895, for views of the river and Île aux Hérons, which has been designated a nature reserve to protect the herons.

Rafting is available on the Rapides de Lachine through **Les Descents sur le Saint-Laurent**, 8912 Boulevard LaSalle, Ville-LaSalle. Discover the Saint Lawrence River and Lachine Rapids by raft or hydro jet. **T**:*(514) 767-2230,* **W**: *raftingmontreal.com. Rates range from $23 to $48. Reservations are required.*

FLEMING MILL ③, 9675 Boulevard LaSalle, LaSalle, **T**:(514) 367-6439. *Open May–Aug., weekends 1–5.*

Unique in Québec, this is one of the few remaining windmills from the British occupation. Over 200 years of local cultural and economic history is depicted in exhibits and explained with guides and videos.

Continue on to **Lachine** ④. Robert Cavalier de La Salle, always looking for a passage to the East, was granted this piece of land on the Saint Lawrence River, west of the city, then called Ville-Marie. Locals nicknamed the land La Chine,

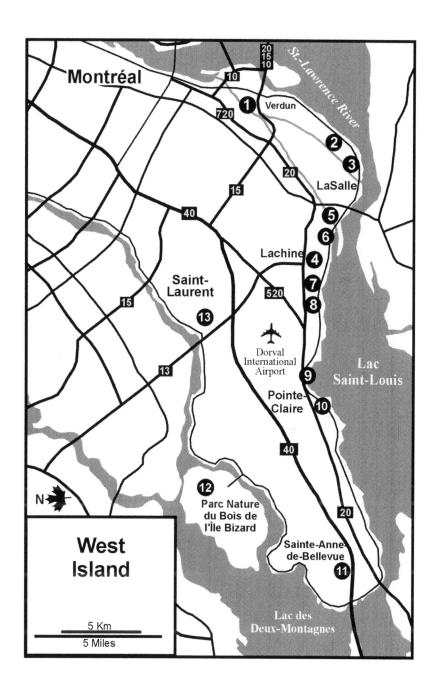

WEST ISLAND   197

meaning China. The town soon became an outpost of Ville-Marie.

On August 4, 1689 about 1,500 Iroquois attacked the town, burning the village to the ground and killing more than 200 people. Another 100 local people were taken prisoner by the Iroquois. It was thought that the attack was revenge for the execution of several Iroquois chiefs two years earlier.

Today this bustling, peaceful town is proud of the role it has played in the history of Montréal and Québec. Beautiful riverside parks, historical sites, and museums welcome visitors.

LE MUSÉE de la VILLE de LACHINE ⑤, 110 Chemin de LaSalle, Lachine, **T**:(514) 634-3471 ext. 346. *Open Apr.–Dec., Wed.–Sun. 11:30–4:30. Guided tours by reservation only on Thurs. and Fri. Admission is free.*

This expansive museum complex has many buildings and exhibits to interest visitors. The LeBer-LeMoyne House, built in 1669, exhibits object of local culture and heritage. The Dépendance and the Benoît-Verdickt Pavilion house contemporary art exhibits. The L'Entrepôt building has multidisciplinary and multicultural exhibits.

LACHINE OUTDOOR SCULPTURE PARK ⑥, Parc René-Lévesque, Lachine, **T**:(514) 634-3471 ext. 346. *Open year-round. Reservations are required for an audio-guide.*

This open-air museum is home to about 50 large sculptures, celebrating contemporary art and artists of Québec. The park occupies a peninsula, built from land reclaimed from the river to protect the Lacine Canal. Walking paths cross the park to the tip of the peninsula, offering views of the river and sculpture gardens.

CENTRE d'INTERPRÉTATION du CANAL de LACHINE ⑦, 711 Boulevard Saint-Joseph, **T**:(514) 283-6054. *Open mid-May to Labor Day, Mon. 1–6, Tues.–Sun. 10–6.*

The stone Pavilion Monk displays photographs and exhibits on the history and construction of the Lachine Canal, built from 1821 to 24 to enable safe passage of ships between Lac Saint-Louis and the Saint-Laurent River, avoiding the Lachine Rapids, and effectively linking Lac Saint-Louis with Montréal Old Port. During the 19th century, more than 15,000 ships a year traveled along this waterway.

FUR TRADE NATIONAL HISTORIC SITE ⑧, 1255 Boulevard Saint Joseph, Lachine, **T**:(514) 637-7433, **W**: pc.gc.ca/lhn-nhs/qc/lachine/index_e.asp. *Open Apr. to mid-Oct., daily 10–12:30 and 1–6, closed Mon. mornings; mid-Oct. to Nov., Wed.–Sun. 9:30–12:30 and 1–5. Admission $3.50 for adults, $1.75 for children 6–16, children under 6 are free.*

Entering the stone depot, built in 1803, visitors are transported back to the

19th century. The depot was used to hold goods, imported from England and made locally, that were intended for barter with fur traders. Touch pelts and bales of fur. Look over cases of goods and rations. Native trappers, French Canadians, and Scottish merchants come to life before visitors. Guided and self-guided tours are available to help visitors understand the fur trade and its importance to the growth of the colony.

The drive along the river, west of Lachine, passes through superb little villages, by beautiful, large country estates, yacht clubs, and parks.

Pointe-Claire, a beautiful, traditionally anglophone village, was named for the sweeping clear views it has of Lac Saint-Louis. **Stewart Hall** ⑨, Chemin Lakeshore, is a half-scale model of a castle in Mull Island, Scotland. The copper-roofed, stone mansion, built in 1915, was donated to the town of Pointe-Claire to be used as a cultural center. The building boasts a library and art gallery, and hosts concerts, plays and conferences. There is a beautiful garden, behind the hall, along the lake. T:*(514) 630-1220. Open Jun.–Aug., Mon.–Fri. 8–9, Sat. 9–5; Sept.–May., Mon.–Fri. 8:30–9, Sat. 9–5, Sun. 1–5. Hours may vary for the art gallery and library.*

La Pointe ⑩ is a small peninsula, jutting into Lac Saint-Louis. At the end is a **convent**, built in 1867, belonging to the Congregation of Our Lady. The stone **windmill** behind the convent dates back to 1709. Originally the part of the remote fortifications of Montréal, the building was used as a refuge in case of Amerindian attacks.

Nearby are the **Church of Saint-Joachim**, built in 1882, and the **presbytery**. The architecture and structures themselves are interesting, but the views they offer are spectacular.

The road continues through the peaceful and affluent towns of **Beaconsfield** and **Baie-d'Urfé**.

Sainte-Anne-de-Bellevue ⑪, located at the westernmost end of the West Island, is a quaint town and yachting center. The **promenade** of parks, terraced restaurants, and boutiques along the waterfront is great for strolling.

Learn about modern milk production at the **Macdonald Campus Farm**, 21111 Rue Lakeshore. Part of McGill University, this experimental farm, with its highly modernized and sophisticated barn, is open to the public. T:*(514) 398-7701. Open weekdays 11–3, weekends 11–1.*

The **Morgan Arboretum**, on the corner of Rue Sainte Marie and Rue des Pins, is a twelve-and-a-half acre park where visitors can take a peaceful stroll, appreciate the trees and watch the birds. In the winter, visitors enjoy the beautiful locale for cross-country skiing. T:*(514) 398-7811,* **W**: *morganarboretum.org. Open Mar.–Dec. daily 9–4. Admission is $5 for adults and $2 for children.*

The **Saint Lawrence Valley Ecomuseum**, 21125 Rue Sainte Marie, is a wildlife park featuring more than ninety animals from the Saint Lawrence Valley living in their natural settings. Education centers and an amphitheater provide information about the park, area wildlife, and conservation through discussions and videos. **T**:*(514) 457-9449,* **W***: ecomuseum.ca. Open year-round daily 9–5. Admission $7 for adults, $4 for children 4–14, children 3 and under are free.*

PARC NATURE du BOIS de l'ÎLE BIZARD ⑫, 2115 Rue Bord du Lac, l'Île Bizard, **T**:(514) 280-8517, **W**: services.ville.montreal.qc.ca/parcs-nature/

A large marsh, crossed by a .3-mile footbridge, is one of the many natural bounties offered in this park. Wooded areas, access to Lac des Deux Montagnes, a beach and paths for walking and cross-country skiing are among the others. A guest chalet provides a welcome respite.

SAINT-LAURENT ART MUSEUM ⑬, 615 Avenue Sainte-Croix, **T**:(514) 747-7367. *Open year-round Wed.–Sun. noon–5. Admission $4.*

This beautiful 19th-century church is home to a nice collection of religious art, folk ark, furnishings, textiles and tools. The exhibits illustrate the traditional arts and crafts of the region, while the replica of a silversmith's shop is interesting.

Trip 35
Laval

Île Jésus, just north of the island of Montréal, was at one time home to a number of small villages, each with their own personality. Saint-François-de-Salès, the first parish on the island, was formed in 1702. As the City of Montréal grew and expanded, people began to move out. With the influx of new residents, the space between the villages of this island began to develop, until it was difficult to decipher where one village ended and another began.

In 1965, Québec's Legislative Assembly passed a bill merging the communities of Île Jésus into a single municipality called Laval. Many of the neighborhoods around the now-bustling urban municipality still maintain the charm and personality of the old villages they once were.

Sitting solidly at Montréal's back door, Laval is the second-most populated city in Québec — second only to Montréal — with over 350,000 residents.

GETTING THERE:

By Car, Laval is only 11 km (7 miles) north of Montréal by **Rte. 15**, which crosses the western portion of the island. When you are done touring, return to **Rte. 15** south to Montréal.

PRACTICALITIES:

Laval is very tightly settled and very busy. As you drive around the island, keep an eye out for stop signs, which are frequent and not always obvious.

The **Maison du Tourisme** is located at 2900 Boulevard Saint Martin West. **T**:(450) 682-5522, **W**: tourismelaval.com or **W**: ville.laval.qc.ca. *Open June–Aug., Mon.–Fri. 8:30–7, Sat.–Sun. 8:30–4:30; Sept., Mon.–Fri. 9–5, Sat.–Sun. 8:30-4:30; Oct.–May, Mon.–Fri. 9–5.*

FOOD AND DRINK:

La Maison des Chavignol (3 Avenue de Terrasses, Sainte Rose) Classic French cuisine in a charming, old-town, atmosphere. T:(450) 628-0161. $$$

Les Menus Plaisirs (244 Boulevard Sainte Rose, Sainte Rose) Enjoy excellent regional dishes, local game, or fondue, on the terrace or in the dining room. Open for lunch and dinner. T:(450) 625-0976. $$$

Univers Café Resto Bar (3453 Boulevard Saint Martin West, Chomedey) Casual Italian cuisine and a friendly setting. Open for breakfast, lunch, and dinner. **T**:(450) 680-1691. $$

Tops de Laval (1545 Boulevard le Corbusier, Chomedey) A popular nightclub, known for its high level of energy, located in a building with a restaurant and recreational complex. Open Thurs.–Sat. 10pm–3am. **T**:(450) 973-8677. $$

ATTRACTIONS:
Circled numbers correspond to numbers on the map.

COSMODÔME ①, 2150 Autoroute des Laurentides, **T**:(450) 978-3600, **W**: cosmodome.org. *Open Jul.–Aug., daily 10–6; Sept.–Jun., Tues.–Sun. 10–6. Admission $11.50 for adults, $7.50 for children, children under 6 are free. Children under 6 are not admitted to the multimedia show.*

Here is a museum dedicated to the science and secrets of space. Interactive exhibits educate visitors on all aspects of space: travel, exploration, communications, solar systems. The museum is separated into three sections: "Time-Space" is dedicated to the history of space exploration. "Use of Space" explores the arena of space application and technology. "Exploration of Space" gives visitors a chance to walk through the solar system (well, a scale model of it) and brings the planets, sun, and moon to life.

A multimedia presentation, on a 360° screen, will leave you breathless. Visitors sit on a platform that moves in conjunction with the visual presentation. The show takes a look at the history of mankind's exploration of space.

The Cosmodôme holds a "space camp" for kids aged 9–15, during which attendees can experience firsthand some of the same training that NASA astronauts go through. Camp can be done, by reservation only, for a half-day, full day, three days, or six days.

MAISON des ARTS des LAVAL ②, 1395 Boulevard de la Concorde West. **T**:(450) 662-2040 or (450) 662-4440. *Alfred Pellan Hall is open Wed.–Thurs. 1–5, Fri. 1–9, Sat. 12–9, Sun. 12–5. Admission is free.*

The arts center, founded in 1986, is the city's arts and culture focal point, whose program features theater, visual arts, dance, music, literature, comedy, and family entertainment. The Alfred Pellan Hall is a multi-purpose exhibition hall.

CENTRALE de la RIVIÈRE des PRAIRIES ③, 3400 Rue du Barrage, **T**:1-800-365-5229. *Open mid-May to June, Mon.–Fri. 9, 10:30, 12, 1:30 and 3; July–Aug., Wed.–Sun. 9:30, 11, 12:30, 2 and 3:30. Admission is free.*

One of Canada's oldest hydroelectric plants still in operation, the plant was built between 1928 and 1930. Uncover the secrets to producing electricity from

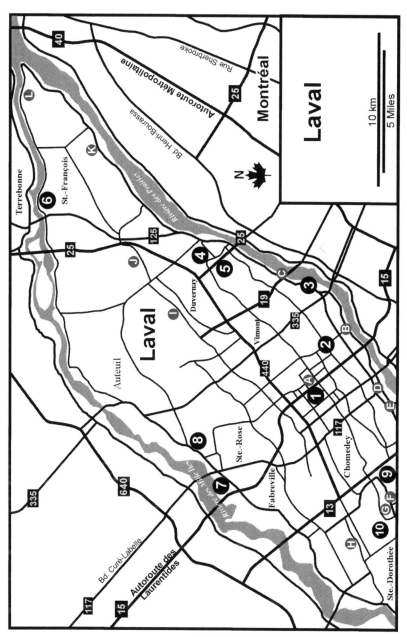

water as you walk through an "alternator-turbine group" and explore the interactive interpretation center.

Continue on to **Vieux Saint-Vincent-de-Paul** ④. This charming village center, built in 1740, is now home to restaurants, outdoor cafés, boutiques, and galleries. Beside the small town center is the beautiful **Saint Vincent de Paul Church**, built in 1853.

CENTRE de la NATURE ⑤, 901 Avenue du Parc, **T**:(450) 662-4942. *Open year round daily 8–10.*

This beautiful green park is home to a herd of Virginia deer, which can frequently be seen resting and grazing. Greenhouses and a farm introduce visitors to the local flora and fauna, while the nature center, with its observatory, brings the stars a bit closer to earth. The park provides outdoor sports such as canoeing, kayaking, hiking, rock climbing, and shuffleboard.

In winter the park is busy with cross-country skiers, ice skating, and sledding. Equipment rental and heated shelters are available.

L'EGLISE SAINT-FRANÇOIS de SALES ⑥, 7070 Boulevard des Milles-Îles, Saint François, **T**:(450) 666-3563.

This charming little Catholic Church, built in 1847, is the oldest in Laval. Peek inside at the beautiful pieces of religious art.

PARC de la RIVIÉRE des MILLE-ÎLES ⑦, 345 Boulevard Sainte Rose, **T**:(450) 622-1020, **W**: parc-mille-iles.qc.ca. *Park open mid-May through Sept. daily 9–6. The interpretation center is open July–Aug. daily 9–7. Admission is $5 for adults, children are free. Kayaks and canoes are available for rent by the hour or by the day.*

Situated in the middle of a wildlife sanctuary, this is the largest natural park in the Montréal area. Vast swamps and forests are home to birds, mammals, reptiles, and fish. With the calm river, natural beauty, and numerous islands just waiting to be explored, the park is a popular destination for people wanting to canoe and kayak. Or, take a ride in a "rabaska," a huge canoe used by native Indians. River excursions and ecological tours are available with a guide, upon reservation. The park also has watercraft available for rental.

Take a cruise with **Croisières dans les Îles**. Climb aboard the Blue Heron pontoon boat for a ride along the Riviére des Mille-Îles and through time. A nature specialist guides visitors on a tour of the history and ecology of the area. **T**:*(450) 622-1020. Tours run May, June, and Sept., Sat.–Sun. 1:30 and 3:30; July–Aug., daily 11, 1:30, 3:30, and 6:30. Admission $15 for adults, $8 for children 6–12, children 5 and under are free.*

Don't miss the **Théâtre l'Ollonois** for a truly unique and entertaining adventure. The theater group presents "The Adventures of Capitaine Dubord" — where spectators become crewmembers aboard Rabaska canoes and assist the captain in the search for treasure. The group meets up with characters from different eras and cultures, including natives and early settlers. The journey ends at sunset. **T**:*(514) 990-9398. Open June–Sept., Tues.–Sat. 7–9:30pm. Call for prices. Reservations are required.*

In winter the park is busy with cross-country skiers, ice skating, and sledding. Equipment rental and heated shelters are available.

Nearby is **Vieux Sainte-Rose** ⑧. Situated along the Mille-Îles River, the village was once a popular vacation spot for the wealthy. Explore the many local artisan and antique shops.

The **Church of Sainte-Rose of Lima**, 219 Boulevard Sainte Rose, was built between 1852 and 56. The impressive church, with its twin towers topped by steeples, has a beautiful interior. The church was acknowledged as a cultural asset in 1974. Visit the **Marina Venise**, 110 Rue Venise, to relax beside the river, cool off in the pool, or tour the Mille-Îles River by pontoon boat. Follow signs off Boulevard Sainte Rose to find your way to the marina.

Continue southwest to **Vieux Sainte-Dorothée** ⑨, a picturesque and historical district that is the flower-growing center of Québec. The beautiful public square, built in 1973, is the perfect place to people watch, chat with locals, or take a break.

Drive the spectacular **Route des Fleurs** to take in all the area has to offer. From Vieux Sainte Dorothée, turn right onto Rue Principale. At **Les Serres Sylvain Cléroux**, 1570 Rue Principale, you will be amazed by the sheer size of the place and awed by the number of flowers. Exhibition greenhouses display over 500 varieties of vegetables, arranged by season and theme. **T**:*(450) 627-2471. Open year round Mon.–Wed. 9–6, Thurs.–Fri. 9–9, Sat. 9–5, and Sun. 10–5. Admission is free.*

Turn left on Montée Champagne. Visit with flower merchants, horticulturists, and gardeners. Stop at **Paradis des Orchidées**, 1280 Montée Champagne, and marvel at the splendor of these greenhouses dedicated to orchids. **T**:*(450) 689-2244. Open year round Sat.–Sun. 10–5. Admission is free.*

Turn left onto Avenue des Bois and left again onto Route 148.

FLEURINEAU - L'ECONOMUSÉE de la FLEUR ⑩, 1270 Rue Principale, **T**:(450) 689-8414, **W**: economusees.com. *Open year round Mon.–Wed. 9–6, Thurs.–Fri. 9–9, Sat. 9–5, and Sun. 10–5. Admission is free.*

Learn about the production, history, and marketing of dried flowers from one of Québec's leading dried flower producers.

ROADSIDE CROSSES:

The island's connection to the church is long and strong, from the Jesuits who were granted possession of and named the island in 1636 to the Bishop of Laval, who obtained ownership of the island and granted it to the Québec Seminary in 1680. The Québec Seminary remained owner of the island until 1854 when the seigniorial regime was abolished.

Today the island is dotted with more than 25 roadside crosses, some more than twenty feet tall. The crosses are made of metal, wood, and granite. They come in different colors and with different symbolic adornments. Driving around the island the crosses can be seen in parks, alongside the river, in people's yards, and beside fields. They are testament to the deep faith that still prevails in Québec.

A more complete list of roadside crosses with a map of their locations is available at the tourist information office, however, it is only available in French. *Circled letters below refer to the map on page 203.*

Calvaire Labelle Ⓐ, at the intersection of Autoroute 15 and Boulevard Saint-Martin.

Croix Vanier Ⓑ, across from 387 Boulevard des Prairies.

Calvaire Desnoyers Ⓒ, on Boulevard Lévesque, beside Pont Papineau-Leblanc.

Croix Clairmont Ⓓ, at the corner of Rue 2nd and Avenue 80th.

Calvaire Édouard Lavoie Ⓔ, 5315 Boulevard Lévesque West.

Calvaire Sauriol Ⓕ, across from 341 Chemin du Bord-de-l'eau.

Calvaire Lacroix Ⓖ, 395 Rue Principale.

Croix Barbe Ⓗ, 418 Rang Saint-Antoine.

Croix Fortin Ⓘ, 4085 Boulevard Saint-Elzéar.

Croix Deguire Ⓙ, across from 5650 Chemin du Bas Saint- François.

Croix Paquette Ⓚ, 8230 Boulevard Lévesque.

Croix Tourville Ⓛ, across from 9860 Boulevard des Mille-Îles.

Croix Vanier

LAVAL 206

Southern Richelieu Valley

Connecting the Saint-Lawrence River with Lake Champlain, the Richelieu River has played an important role in Québec's history. Concerned with protecting the settlers from Indian attacks during the 18th century, the French built a series of forts along the Richelieu River. The region is commonly known as the Valley of Forts.

The threat of invasion over in the 19th century, Rivière Richelieu was no longer vital for the security of Canada. Emphasis shifted to commerce, and the river became an essential link in the communication and trade between Montréal and the United States. An extensive canal system was built along the river to facilitate the safe passage of ships around the many sets of falls.

GETTING THERE:

By Car, Hemmingford is about 80 km (50 miles) from Montréal. Take **Rte. 15** south from Montréal. Turn right onto **Rte. 202** west toward Hemmingford. Follow the signs to Parc Safari.

From Parc Safari, follow **Rte. 202** east. At the junction of **Rte. 221**, turn left toward Lacolle, and then turn right, staying on **Rte. 202**.

Turn right onto **Rte. 223**, following it along the Richelieu River to Chambly. Take **Rte. 10** west, returning to Montréal.

PRACTICALITIES:

Tourist Information Office, 1 Rue Principale, Saint-Paul, in the old blockhouse building. **T**:(450) 246-3227.

The **Office de Tourisme et des Congrès du Haut-Richelieu** is located at 31 Rue Frontenac, Saint-Jean-sur-Richelieu. **T**:(450) 542-9090, **W**: tourisme-monteregie.qc.ca

FOOD AND DRINK:

Restaurant Le Samuel II (291 Rue Richelieu, Saint-Jean-sur-Richelieu) French, local and regional dishes for lunch and dinner. **T**:(450) 347-4353. $$ and $$$

Le Manneken Pis (320 Rue Champlain, Saint-Jean-sur-Richelieu) Overlooking the marina and specializing in scrumptious Belgian waffles. $\mathbf{T}$:(450) 348-3254. $

Lacolle (7 Rue de l'Église, Lacolle) This delightful, authentic Greek restaurant is housed in an old church. $\mathbf{T}$:(450) 246-3897. $$

SUGGESTED TOUR:
Circled numbers correspond to numbers on the map.

*PARC SAFARI ①, 850 Route 202, Hemmingford, $\mathbf{T}$:(450) 247-2727 or 1-800-465-8724, $\mathbf{W}$: parcsafari.com. *Open mid-May to mid-Sept. daily at 10. Admission $29 for adults, $19 for children 11–17, $13 for children 3–10, children under 3 are free.*

This combination of zoo, wildlife reserve, and amusement park keeps visitors amazed and entertained for hours. Drive through wildlife habitats while animals from all over the globe walk around your car. Open your windows and they may just try to stick their heads in! You can feed and pet these animals, which include deer, elk, zebra, reindeer, and mountain goats — just to name a few.

When you've finished the safari drive, explore the rest of the park for more animals, rides, restaurants, and a water park. In the "Nairobi Park" play at being Tarzan on swinging vines or try your luck getting in and out of the labyrinth. The "Rhino-Rhino Club" is for kids only, with games, songs, and adventures led by a special guide.

In business for more than a quarter of a century, the park's mission is to preserve the animals' quality of life.

Continue on to the **Blockhaus de la Rivière Lacolle** ②, 1 Rue Principale, Saint-Paul, a quaint two-story, square wooden building. Erected in 1781, this is the only blockhouse remaining in Québec with its original structure. Holes made from musket-balls are still visible in the walls. An interpretation center illustrates the history of the area. $\mathbf{T}$:*(450) 246-3227. Open May–Labor Day daily 9:30–5:30.*

FORT LENNOX NATIONAL HISTORIC SITE ③, Île-aux-Noix, $\mathbf{T}$:(450) 291-5700. *Open mid-May to June, Mon.–Fri. 10–5, Sat.–Sun. 10–6; July–Aug., Mon.–Sun. 10–6; Sept. to early Oct. by reservation during the week, Sat.–Sun. 10–6. Admission $6.50 for adults, $3.25 children 6–13, children under 6 are free.*

Accessible by ferry from Avenue 61st, this magnificent fort sits solidly on the small Île-aux-Noix, in the middle of the Richelieu River. Surrounded by a beautiful grassy park, paths for walking, and the river, it is a peaceful place to have a picnic and relax.

This 19th-century British fort has been authentically restored and maintained. Guides in period costumes introduce visitors to the life of soldiers and their families living in the fort. Inside the walls of the fort, built from 1819 to

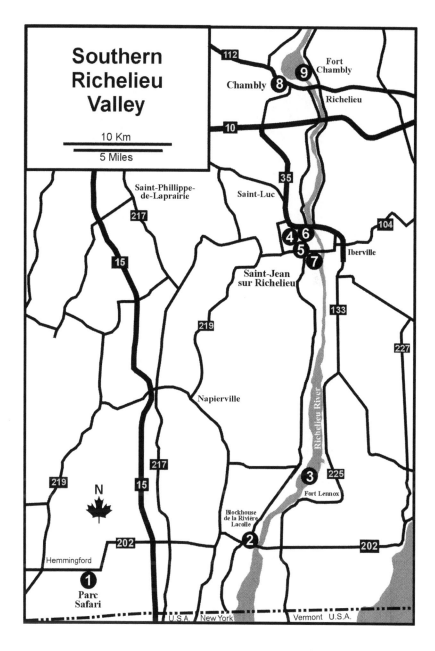

Southern Richelieu Valley

10 Km

5 Miles

1820, are large masonry buildings that look as though they are still in use by the soldiers.

SOUTHERN RICHELIEU VALLEY 209

Fort Lennox

Tour the barracks, guardroom, prison, and officers' quarters. A small museum displays artifacts and everyday objects from the era. The black-powder firing demonstrations with muskets and cannon firings are exciting.

Head north to **Saint-Jean-sur-Richelieu** ④. Owing to its location along the Richelieu River, between the Saint-Lawrence River and the United States, Saint-Jean has had an important role in the history and development of Canada. With the Canadian Railway in 1836 and the opening of the Chambly Canal in 1843, the city's importance grew.

Every August, Saint-Jean comes to life, the sky filling with brightly colored balloons during the **Saint-Jean-sur-Richelieu Hot-Air Balloon Festival**.

The **Musée du Haut Richelieu** ⑤, 182 Rue Jacque-Cartier North, addresses the role of the ceramics industry, old and new, in Québec's history. Located inside the former public market, large collections of pottery and dinnerware are on display. The museum also features exhibits on local history, the influence of the Amerindians in the area, and the importance of the military role in the "Valley of Forts." **T**:*(450) 347-0649. Open late June to Labor Day, Tues.–Sun. 9:30–5; Labor Day–June, Wed.–Sun. 9:30–5. Admission $4 for adults, $2 for children 6–17, children under six are free.*

Old Saint-Jean-sur-Richelieu has a number of interesting buildings, including the old **fire station**, built in 1877, with its small tower on top. The neighborhood boasts several Victorian-style homes as well.

Note **Saint-James' Anglican Church**, on the corner of Rue Jacque-Cartier and Rue Saint-George, built in 1816, which looks like it belongs in New England. The **Cathedral of Saint-John the Evangelist**, on Rue Longueuil, is also worth a look. This church, built between 1828 and 1853, has a beautiful interior.

SOUTHERN RICHELIEU VALLEY 210

The **Musée du Fort Saint-Jean** ⑥, Rue Jacque-Cartier North, on Fort Saint-Jean, is located in a former guardhouse, built in 1850. The museum traces more than 300 years of military history in Canada through exhibits of weapons, uniforms, and military artifacts. The remains of the fort's ramparts can be toured as well.

The fort, first built in 1666, was a wooden structure erected by the French to defend against the Iroquois. In 1748, it was replaced by a second fort to protect New France against the British forces. Fort Saint-Jean was burned to the ground, in 1759, by the French in order to avoid capture. The fort was rebuilt in 1775 and subsequently captured by the Americans after a 45-day siege. Having suffered severe fire damage during its capture, the fort was rebuilt again in 1837 after the Patriots' Rebellion.

LES CROISIÈRES RICHELIEU ⑦, 68 Saint-Maurice, offers cruises along the Richelieu River. **T**:(450) 346-2446 or 1-800-361-6420. *Tours run late June through Aug. daily. Fees are $18 for adults, $9 for children, children under 4 are free.*

Cruise this scenic river aboard the *Fort Saint-Jean II*. The trip offers views of beautiful summer homes, the Chambly Canal, and the Royal Military Academy.

Continuing your drive toward Chambly, the road seems to be playing hide-and-seek with the Chambly Canal and Richelieu River. The views are beautiful as you pass quaint cottages, over narrow bridges, and by long green spaces on your way north to **Chambly** ⑧. The Chambly Basin, formed by the widening of the Richelieu River after some major rapids, is the scenic backdrop for this suburb of Montréal. The town secured its place in the history and development of Montréal and Québec Province, first with the building of the fort. Then, in the 19th century, the rapids' strength was harnessed to power mills for the textile, lumber and grain industries. With the completion of the canal, the town became an important commercial spot for U.S. — Canada trade. With the growth of neighboring Montréal, Chambly also became an essential city for the support of Montréal and its many commuters.

The **Canal de Chambly**, 1840 Rue Bourgogne, has a long history and an important role in the area. Opened for operation in 1843, the canal enables vessels on the Richelieu River to bypass a series of rapids between Saint-Jean-sur-Richelieu and the Chambly Basin. At the turn of the century, about 4,000 boats traveled the canal annually. Today, the canal is used for recreational boating. Eight of the nine locks still have their original manual mechanisms. The former towpath, running alongside the canal, is now popular for cyclists and walkers. An interpretation center houses exhibits on the history of the area and the canals. **T**:*1-800-463-6769. Open mid-June to mid-Aug., daily 8:30–8; mid-May to mid-June and mid-Aug. to mid-Oct., hours vary. Admission is $1.50* *for adults and $1 for children.*

Parc des Rapides, along Rue Richelieu, was formerly the site of the wool factories and mills, which were powered by the rapids. Today, the park offers stunning views of the rapids and the Chambly Dam. Wooden homes still stand along the street, memories of Chambly's industrial heritage.

FORT CHAMBLY NATIONAL HISTORIC SITE ⑨, 2 Rue de Richelieu, Chambly, **T**:(450) 658-1585, **W**: pc.gc.ca/lhn-nhs/qc/fortchambly/index_e.asp. *Open Apr. to mid-May and Sept.-Nov., Wed.–Sun.; mid-May to Aug., daily. Admission $5.75 for adults, $3 children 6–16, $14.50 for families, children 5 and under are free.*

Fort Chambly is the only remaining fortified structure in Québec that dates back to the French Regime.

The first fort on this site was made of wood, built by Jacques de Chambly in 1665. The fort was erected to defend against Iroquois war parties in route to Montréal. Two more wood forts were built on the site before a stone fort was built in 1709.

The French colonials built this fortification at the foot of the Chambly Rapids in an attempt to keep the British from reaching Montréal. The fort was captured by the British army in September 1760.

High stone walls of the immense square fort rise sharply from a beautiful park, towering over the Chambly Basin and Richelieu River. An **interpretation center** inside the fort exhibits archaeological ruins and artifacts illustrating the history and culture of New France, and transports visitors to the daily lives of 18th-century French soldiers and colonists.

Also of note, a small **chapel** with a mansard roof faces the entrance of the fort. A **guardhouse**, 8 Rue Richelieu near the fort, was built by the British after the conquest, in 1814. The building contains exhibits on the military history of the area, the British occupation and the development of Chambly.

Northern Richelieu Valley

This part of the Richelieu Valley is commonly known as The Patriots' Road, because during the Patriots' Rebellion of 1837 a significant portion of the French Canadian population took up arms against the British government. Due to its military heritage and strategic location, the valley played an important role in the rebellion and in Canada's history. Battles took place at Saint-Denis, Saint-Charles, and Saint-Eustache, where the British finally squashed the Patriot's rebellion.

The Patriots' Road follows the Richelieu River through quaint old villages and natural parks. Throughout the year, artistic events, harvest celebrations, and historical festivals attract visitors from near and far.

GETTING THERE:

By Car, Richelieu, the starting point for this tour, is about 40 km (25 miles) from Montréal on **Rte. 10**.

Take **Rte. 133** north. Follow **Rte. 133** along the Richelieu River to Sorel, and continuing on to Sainte-Anne-de-Sorel.

Take **Rte. 30** south from Sorel to **Rte. 10**, then take **Rte. 10** west back to Montréal.

PRACTICALITIES:

The **Office de Tourisme du Bas-Richelieu**, 92 Chemin des Patriotes, Sorel, has maps and information about the Sorel-Tracy area and the Richelieu Valley. **T**:(450) 746-9441 or 1-800-474-9441, **W**: tourisme-monteregie.qc.ca

FOOD AND DRINK:

Bistro le Vieux Bourgogne (1718 Avenue Bourgogne) Cute bistro with fresh, light meals. **T**:(450) 447-9306. $ and $$

Les Chanterelles du Richelieu (611 Chemin des Patriotes, Saint-Denis-sur-Richelieu) Gourmet French cuisine in the beautiful dining room and on the terrace. **T**:(450) 787-1167. $$$

Chez Marc Beauchemin (124 Île d'Embarras, Sainte-Anne-de-Sorel) Fresh seafood, regional and local dishes. Try the "gibelotte et filets," a fish-and-vegetable soup with its origins in the area. **T**:(450) 743-6023. $$

LOCAL ATTRACTIONS:

Circled numbers correspond to numbers on the map.

Saint-Mathias ①, first settled in 1700 and originally an important port along the Richelieu River, is now home to large residences and marinas. During the American War for Independence, Ethan Allen and the Green Mountain Boys took over the village in an attempt to convince its residents to join the United States.

The **Church**, 279 Chemin des Patriots, is worth a look for its artistic interior. **T**:*(450) 658-1671. Open year round Sat. 3:30–4:30, Sun. 9:30–11:30, for guided tours only, Mon.–Fri. by reservation only.*

The picturesque town of **Mont Saint-Hilaire** ②, nestled between the Richelieu River and Mont Saint-Hilaire, has a rich history as the birthplace to several popular and successful Québec artists. The many orchards in the area make up a prosperous apple industry.

Note the **Rouville-Campbell Manor**, a large Tudor-style house, built in the 1850s, with tall brick chimneys. The mansion was built by Major Thomas Edmund Campbell, modeled after his ancestral home in Inverane, Scotland.

The area is renowned for its wealth of agro-tourism sites. The **Maison des Cultures Amérindiennes**, 510 Montée des Trente, is an urban sugar shack, featuring the traditional Amerindian way of harvesting maple sap. Learn about maple sugaring and enjoy trails with interpretation panels. **T**:*(450) 464-2500,* **W**: *maisonamerindienne.com. The public park is open year round daily. The sugar shack is open year round, Mon.–Fri. 10–5, Sat.–Sun. 1–5. Admission $6 for adults, $4 for children 6–17, children 5 and under are free.*

The **Cidrerie du Verger Gaston** is an organic apple orchard, cider factory and economuseum. Tours of the cider cellar and tasting are available. The small museum illustrates the history of the apple industry in Québec. **T**:*(450) 464-3455. Open May–Nov., daily 10–6; Dec.–Apr., Sat.–Sun. 11–5. Admission is free.*

MUSÉE d'ART de MONT SAINT-HILAIRE ③, 150 Rue du Centre-Civique, **T**:(450) 536-3033. *Open year round, Tues. 10–8:30, Wed.–Sat. 10–5, Sun. 1–5. Admission $2.50, children fifteen and under are free.*

This museum is dedicated to the exhibition of work by artists born in the Montérégie region of Québec. There are permanent and special exhibits, as well as guided tours.

CENTRE de la NATURE du MONT SAINT-HILAIRE ④, 422 Chemin des Moulins. **T**:(450) 467-1755, **W**: centrenature.qc.ca/en/index.html. *Open year round, daily 8–one hour before sunset. Admission $4 for adults, $2 for children, children under 6 are free.*

This is the first nature reserve in Canada. The mountainous park, with hiking trails and a lake, is home to more than 180 species of birds, as well as other creatures. In winter, the park is a popular destination for snow shoeing,

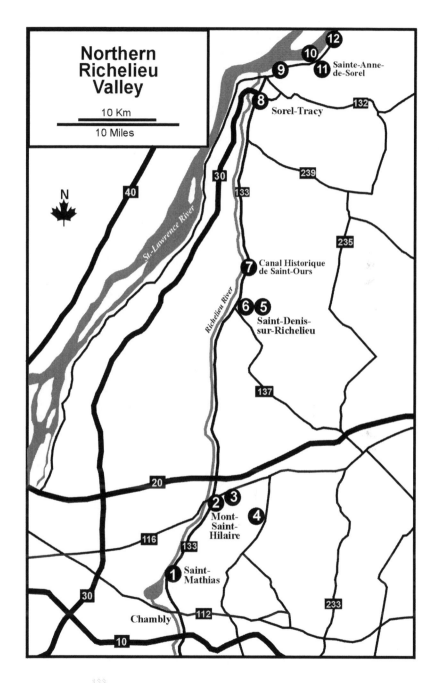

Northern Richelieu Valley

10 Km
10 Miles

N

Sainte-Anne-de-Sorel

Sorel-Tracy

St-Lawrence River

Canal Historique de Saint-Ours

Richelieu River

Saint-Denis-sur-Richelieu

Mont-Saint-Hilaire

Saint-Mathias

Chambly

cross-country and off-trail skiing. From the summit, drink in views of the Richelieu River, the Saint Lawrence Valley and the Olympic Tower in Montréal.

Continue north to **Saint-Denis-sur-Richelieu** ⑤. This picturesque and proud agricultural village was the site of a Patriot victory in November 1837. A nice square in the village center has a monument erected in 1987 at the 150th anniversary of the rebellion, to honor and memorialize the Patriots.

The **church**, near the town center, was the first two-story religious building in Québec. One of the twin copper towers houses the liberty bell that was used to call the Patriots to battle. Some of the impressive carved-wood interior dates as far back as 1810. **T**:*(450) 787-3623. Open June–Aug., Tues.–Sun. 11–6 for one-hour guided tour only. Reservations should be made two days in advance.*

MAISON NATIONALE des PATRIOTES ⑥, 610 Chemin des Patriots, **T**:(450) 787-3623. *Open May–Sept., Tues.–Sun. 10–5; Nov., Tues.–Fri. 10–5; Oct. and Dec. to Apr. by appointment only. Admission $4 for adults, $3 for students, $2 for children 6–12, children five and under are free. Displays and slide shows are in French only.*

This mansion, formerly the home of merchant Jean-Baptiste Mâsse, built in 1810, is dedicated to the Patriots of 1837. Exhibits illustrate the economic, social, and political environment of the time. A slide show recounts the history of the upraising and the events that led the Patriots in their long war for democracy.

CANAL HISTORIQUE de SAINT-OURS ⑦, 2930 Chemin des Patriots, **T**:(450) 447-4888, **W**: pc.gc.ca/lhn-nhs/qc/saintours/visit/index_e.asp. *Open late Jun. to Labor Day, daily 8:30–8; mid-May to mid-June and Sept. to mid-Oct., Mon.–Fri. 8:30–10:30 and 2:30–4, Sat.–Sun. 8:30–6. Admission $1.50 for adults, $1 for students, children under 6 are free.*

The Saint-Ours canal was opened in 1849 to allow passage between the Saint Lawrence River and Lake Champlain. The lock, built in 1933, is still used by pleasure boats traveling on the Richelieu River. A beautiful park with picnic areas now surrounds it.

Farther north is **Sorel-Tracy** ⑧. Situated where the Saint-Lawrence, Richelieu, and Yamaska Rivers meet, this small industrial city has a long history of shipping and navigation. The town is also known for Baron Von Riedesel, who in the 18th century was the first person in North America to decorate a Christmas Tree with candles.

Royal Square was created in 1791 as a parade ground for the military. Today, the square is a nice green park with criss-crossing paths that, from the air, take the shape of a British Flag.

Christ Church, on Rue Prince facing Royal Square, built in 1842, stands at the site of the oldest Anglican mission in Canada.

Rue du Roi, stretching from Royal Square to the waterfront, is home to many boutiques, restaurants, and cafés. The busy street leads to the **Old Market**, a yellow brick building erected in 1940.

CENTRE d'INTERPRÉTATION du PATRIMOINE de SOREL ⑨, **T**: (450) 780-5740 or 1-877-780-5740. *Open July–Aug., daily 10–7; Sept.–June, Wed.–Fri. 10–5, Sat.–Sun. 1–5. Admission $3 for adults, $1.50 for children.*
Permanent and seasonal interactive exhibits illustrate the history and culture of the area. Displays include a look at the importance and preservation of water and inventions that have come from the area.

Nearby is the **Lac Saint-Pierre World Biosphere Reserve** ⑩. Where the waterways and channels drift around islands and spill into Lac Saint Pierre, a natural wonderland thrives. More than 288 species of birds, twelve of which are endangered, use this reserve to nest and during migration. The waterways are home to nearly 80 types of fish, two of which are on the endangered list. 103 islands dot the waterways.
Lac Saint-Pierre is a popular location for water sports and fishing. Sport fishermen delight in the bounty of bass, pike, catfish, and sturgeon.
Ninety percent of the area has been successfully preserved in its natural state. This is not only a unique and heroic feat in-and-of-itself, but also in light of the international seaway which crosses the reserve, and the industrial development at the edges.
Around the area, look for houses that rest on top of stilts. These homeowners opt to live among the natural beauty and wonder of the area, despite the threat of flooding each spring.
Cruises are available on the Saint Lawrence River, around the islands and on Lac Saint Pierre. **Randonnèe et Coucher Nature des Îles** departs from the Marina de Saurel, twice a day, for a three-hour tour of Lac Saint Pierre and the channel islands. **T**:*(450) 780-5740 or 1-877-780-5740. Tours run June and Sept., Sat.–Sun.; July–Aug., daily at 11, 3 and 6:30.* **Croisière des Îles de Sorel** departs from the marina in Sainte Anne de Sorel. **T**:*(450) 346-2446 or 1-800-361-6420. Tours run late June through Aug., Tues.–Sun. 1:30 and 3:30.*
Arriving at **Sainte-Anne-de-Sorel** ⑪, stroll along the **quai**, watch the boats, and take in the sights of the river. This is also a great place for a picnic. Expeditions with **Canots Rabaskas Sorel/Sept Îles** depart from the quai for exciting canoe trips among the natural bounties of the area. **T**:*(450) 742-3080,* **W**: *expedition-canot.qc.ca*
Nearby is the **Sainte-Anne Church**, a historical monument, with fourteen splendid frescos inside by artist Suzor Côté.
The **Maison du Marais** ⑫, 3742 Chemin du Chenal du Moine, Sainte Anne de Sorel, has an interpretation center dedicated to educating visitors about the unique and wondrous environment found in the marshlands. Walking trails, an

observation tower, and a floating bridge enable exploration of the Baie Laval-lière. **Excursions dans les Marais** provides guided tours of the marsh in a motorized *rabaskas* canoe. **T**:*(450) 742-3113 or 1-877-742-3113. Tours run daily late June through Aug. Reservations are required for tours.*

Section X

DAYTRIPS IN THE LAURENTIANS

The Laurentians Mountains, also known as Laurentides, stretch across Québec north of Montréal. This region remained largely uninhabited until the 19th century, when Father Antoine Labelle began to persuade his fellow French Canadians to settle in the untouched wilderness. He handpicked locations for new settlements, traversing the region by canoe and on foot, and established more than twenty parishes in the mountains. Many of the towns still carry the names of their patron saints, particularly in the area of the Laurentians nicknamed "Valley of the Saints," that lays along Rivière Nord.

Despite Father Labelle's efforts to establish settlements in the rugged area, the villages struggled. Attempts at farming proved difficult and unsuccessful. However, in the 20th century, residents began to develop a new economic foundation with the influx of sports enthusiasts and vacationers from Montréal. The villages of the Laurentians quickly discovered their ability to flourish on the tourism trade.

Much of the mountainous region has remained pristine, protected by the people who live and play in the area. At the beginning of the 20th century, Lac Tremblant remained a logging area with no roads. Even today, the northern end of the lake is not accessible by road. Residents with houses on the north shore of the lake use boats in summer, and snowmobiles in winter, to reach their homes.

This natural wonderland has a magical quality with its dense forests, shimmering lakes, and fairy-tale villages. The region boasts the highest concentration of downhill ski resorts in North America. With abundant lakes and rivers, it is also popular for aquatic sports enthusiasts.

Saint-Jérôme
to Sainte-Adèle

The southern portion of the region, an easy drive from Montréal, is known as the Gateway to the Laurentians. It is here that the administrative and industrial center of the region can be found.

From the commercialized town of Saint-Jérôme, the drive along Rivière du Nord quickly leaves the city behind for steep hills, picturesque forests, and quaint ski villages. The area has a truly alpine atmosphere, with chalets tucked away on lush fields, and isolated lakes surrounded by tall pines.

GETTING THERE:

By Car, Saint-Jérôme is about 51 km (32 miles) from Montréal. Take **Rte. 15** north to exit 43.

From the center of Saint-Jérôme take **Rte. 117** north. Turn left onto **Rte. 364** to Saint-Sauveur-des-Monts.

Return to **Rte. 117**, turn left and continue north to Sainte-Adèle.

From the center of Sainte-Adèle, take **Rte. 370** to Sainte-Marguerite-du-Lac-Masson.

Follow **Rte. 370** back toward Sainte-Adèle and take **Rte. 15** south, returning to Montréal.

PRACTICALITIES:

If you're planning to enjoy some of the winter sports available in the area, you may want to stay overnight. The Laurentians are very popular and busy during the winter months, when Montrealers head north to ski, snowmobile, and snowshoe. If you decide to make it an overnight, make your reservations early.

The **Tourist Information Office** is located at 1490 Rue Saint-Joseph, Sainte-Adèle. **T**:(450) 229-3729 or 1-800-898-2127, **W**: laurentides.com.

FOOD AND DRINK:

Café Mondo (283 Saint-Georges, Saint-Jérôme) Light meals, coffees, and gourmet pastries in a comfortable and contemporary setting. **T**:(450) 660-6060. $$

Resto-Bistro Le Saint-So (129 Rue Principale, Saint Sauveur-des-Monts) Specializing in fondue, in many varieties, and situated in a comfortable, homey environment. **T**:(450) 227-3695. $$

Restaurant Aux Tourterelles (1141 Chemin Chantecler, Sainte-Adèle) Award-winning restaurant overlooking Lac Sainte-Adèle, featuring innovative French cuisine. **T**:(450) 229-8160. $$

Martin-Le-Pêcheur (275 Avenue Canadienne, Sainte-Adèle) Local fish and game served with fresh vegetables and edible flowers. **T**:(450) 229-7020. $$$

SUGGESTED TOUR:

Circled numbers correspond to numbers on the map.

Begin at **Saint-Jérôme** ①. This small city, commonly known as the "Gateway to the Laurentians," pulsates. Stroll around the downtown area to see the many **murals** covering the old buildings.

The nice **Park Labelle** rests in the city center, with several interesting sculptures, making it a popular place with the locals. Yellow signposts abound downtown, directing visitors to all of the sites.

The **Cathedral** dominating the city center, with its impressive twin spires, is worth a look. It was built between 1897 and 1900, although the antique altar dates from 1868.

From the park, walk toward the river (away from the cathedral). A wood **promenade** runs along the river, with interpretation panels describing the history of the city. This is a very pleasant stroll.

The **Roland Amphitheater** is near the park, in the center of town, rising high above Rivière du Nord. This beautiful outdoor concert hall is able to seat almost 500 spectators. Each summer it is home to **Festival d'Été Rivière-du-Nord** — an event-filled music festival featuring performances for all ages and all tastes. Sundays feature new talents, while Fridays offer shows and cinema for children and families.

Saint-Jérôme is "0 kilometer" for **Le P'tit Train Linear Park** ②. Extending along the former railway line that ran through the Laurentians, this beautiful recreational park provides a picturesque and safe place for walking, cycling, and in-line skating surrounded by nature's beauty. The 120-mile park stretches northwesterly through the Laurentians, connecting towns from Saint-Jérôme to Mont-Tremblant, and beyond. User services, facilities and information are available along the park. **T**:*(450) 436-8532 or 1-800-561-6673. User fees: bicycles, May–Oct. $5 for 18 and over, under 17 free; cross-country skiing, Dec. through mid-Apr. $7 for 18 and over, under 17 free.*

CENTRE d'EXPOSITION du VIEUX-PALAIS ③, 185 Rue du Palais, **T**:(450) 432-7171. *Open year-round Tues. noon-8, Wed.-Sun. noon-5. Admission is free.*

Saint-Jérôme
to
Sainte-Adèle

10 Km

5 Miles

This visual arts exhibition center has a variety of interesting and educational activities, informative exhibits, creativity workshops, presentations, and lectures. Exhibits cover art from classic to contemporary and artists from local to international.

Régie Intermunicipale du Parc Régional de la Rivière-du-Nord ④, 1051 Boulevard International, is a beautiful park with abundant natural wealth and historical significance. Within it visitors discover Wilson Falls, the ruins of a pulp mill, and an old hydroelectric dam. **T**:*(450) 431-1676. Open year-round, daily summer 9–7, winter 9–5. Admission $5 per car.*

Follow Route 117 north out of Saint-Jérôme. The road rises casually up into the Laurentian Mountains. Turn left onto Route 364, and follow the road steeply uphill to ***Saint-Sauveur-des-Monts*** ⑤. This fairytale village is tucked away between high sloping mountains. Visitors feel like they've just discovered a

Saint-Sauveur-des-Monts

buried treasure as they round the corner into a brightly colored, busy little town. The main street is alive with people mulling around and shopping in the boutiques, artist galleries, and handicraft shops. The many bistros, cafés, restaurants, and pubs feature gourmet cuisine from around the globe. Park and meander through this mountaintop paradise.

Check out the beautiful **church**, built in 1903, that dominates the center of the village.

In the summer months, take a refreshing break at **Parc Aquatique Mont Saint-Sauveur**, 350 Rue Saint-Denis. A variety of wave pools, rivers, slides, and activities provide an exhilarating and fun visit. **T**:*(450) 227-4671,* **W**: *montsaintsauveur.com. Open June and late Aug., daily 10–4; July to mid-Aug., daily 10–7. Admission $29 for adults, $25 for children, $14 for children 3–5, children under 3 are free.*

Les Excursions Rivière du Nord leads excursions, by canoe and bike, on Rivière du Nord and running along the "P'tit Train du Nord" linear park. Trips include all necessary equipment and shuttle services. **T**:*(450) 229-1889 or 1-866-342-2668,* **W**: *riviere-du-nord.ca/. Reservations are recommended. Rates are $39 for two-person canoe trip, $12 for additional persons; $13 per person for optional return bike trip; $56 for a family canoe package for 2 adults and 2 children.*

Take a left on Rue Saint-Denis to see the delightful **Saint-Francis of the Birds Anglican Church ⑥**. The church was built in 1951 using more than 600 pine logs from local forests in the Scandinavian tradition. Inside, the pulpit and lectern were made from solid oak. The statue adorning the lectern came from a British ship built in 1870. The impressive main window depicts Saint Francis

with 21 species of birds native to the Laurentians. Another impressive window represents the Holy Spirit, descending on Earth to restore order to the chaos of creation. The remaining windows represent night, day, and the four seasons. T:*(450) 227-2180.*

Return down the hill and turn left, continuing north on Route 117 to **Sainte-Adèle** ⑦, which has the best of all worlds. Located halfway between Montréal and Mont-Tremblant, this busy town has the services and culture of a city, with the charm and relaxed atmosphere of the country. Visitors will enjoy theaters, galleries, fine restaurants, pedestrian walkways, and a host of festivals — all in amazingly fresh air.

Train lovers shouldn't miss the **Musée TrainOrama**, 1002 Rue Saint-Georges. This little museum illustrates the history of the railway line during the 1950s. A considerable electric model railroad delights visitors with light and sound, re-creating the former CP and CN railway lines through the Laurentians at a scale of 1:87. The set displays the types of trains used at the time as well as the typical architecture of the area. T:*(450) 229-2660. Open year-round, Fri.– Mon. 10–6. Admission $6 for adults, $4 for children under 14.*

PAVILLON des ARTS de SAINTE-ADÈLE ⑧, 1364 Chemin Pierre Péladeau, T:(450) 229-2586. *Open year-round, concerts are scheduled for every third Saturday 8pm. Admission $25 per person.*

This enchanting concert hall was originally an Anglican chapel, whose high ceilings, stone, wood, and glass make for a picturesque setting. With only 200 seats available, the pavilion is a beautiful and intimate venue to listen to fantastic concerts. The schedule offers a wide range of music programs, from chamber music to opera. Wine and cheese tasting (included in the price) follows each concert.

Turn right onto Route 370 and follow it to **Sainte-Marguerite-du-Lac-Masson** ⑨. Tucked away on the edge of **Lac Masson** is a delightful, quaint hamlet, whose small marina is surprisingly busy. Canoes, paddleboats, and kayaks are available for rental for a thoroughly enjoyable way to explore the lake. In the winter the lake is used for ice skating.

Turning right out of town, follow the narrow **scenic road** around Lac Masson for beautiful views in all seasons.

Trip 39

Sainte-Agathe-des-Monts to Saint-Donat-de-Montcalm

Such celebrities as Jacqueline Kennedy and Queen Elizabeth II have enjoyed this historic and cultured resort area. Founded in 1849, Sainte-Agathe-des-Monts became the region's first resort destination with the development of the Montréal and Occidental Railway. Known as the capital of the Laurentians, it is today as popular as ever for year-round sports enthusiasts and city dwellers seeking a peaceful retreat.

GETTING THERE:

By Car, Sainte-Agathe-des-Monts is 85 km (53 miles) north of Montréal. Take **Rte. 15** to Sainte-Agathe-des-Monts.

For the scenic lake drive, follow **Rue Principale** toward the lake. Just before the dock, turn right on **Rue Saint-Louis** and then turn left on **Chemin Tour du Lac**.

Follow **Rte. 117** north out of town and go right onto **Rte. 329** north. Take **Rte. 329** to Saint-Donat-de-Montcalm.

Take **Rte. 329** south, back to **Rte. 15** south, returning to Montréal.

PRACTICALITIES:

The scenery along this tour is particularly beautiful in fall, when the densely forested hills are a quilt of bright orange, red, and yellow. It is also well worth the trip in winter, to partake in the annual winter festival.

The **Bureau d'Information Touristique du Grand Sainte-Agathe** can be found at 24 Rue Saint-Paul, Sainte-Agathe, just off Route 117. **T**:(819) 326-0457 or 1-888-326-0457. Open year-round daily 9-5, until 8 in the summer.

FOOD AND DRINK:

Crêperie la Quimperlaise (11 Chemin Tour du Lac, Sainte-Agathe-des-Monts) Light meals, crêpes, pastas and fondues. **T**:(819) 326-1776. $$

Restaurant Del Popolo (1 Rue Principale, Sainte-Agathe-des-Monts) Casual and delicious Italian cuisine, including pasta, pizza, and veal. **T**:(819) 326-4422. $$

Chatel Vienna (6 Rue Sainte-Lucie, Sainte-Agathe-des-Monts) Situated in a beautiful house, built in 1900, overlooking Lac des Sables, and serving refined cuisine with local delicacies. Reservations are recommended. **T**:(819) 326-1485. $$$

LOCAL ATTRACTIONS:

Circled numbers correspond to numbers on the map.

Begin at **Sainte-Agathe-des-Monts** ①, a busy little town situated in an ideal spot resting on the edge of the Lac des Sables, encircled by hills and forests. Everywhere you look is beauty. The center of town bustles with activities. Cafés, restaurants, and shops invite visitors to stroll around town and enjoy all that is to be offered. Terraced pubs are ideal for conversation and people watching.

In 1849, the town formed around a sawmill. With the introduction of the railway in 1892, Sainte-Agathe became the first resort village to develop in the Laurentians. At the time when both the anglophone and francophone communities were beginning to settle in the area, Saint-Agatha was able to attract wealthy vacationers, drawn by the beauty of the lake and surrounding hills.

Each year, from mid-January through February, Sainte-Agathe-des-Monts hosts the **Hiver en Nord** — a grand and successful winter festival. Lac des Sables becomes a large groomed skating rink and the town proudly displays snow and ice sculptures around every corner. An ice palace and snow slides will please visitors of all ages. The festival also features a magnificent fireworks display. **T**:*(819) 326-2428.*

Le P'tit Train du Nord linear park can be accessed, for cycling and in-line skating, beside the tourist information office.

Sitting on the shores of the lake, **Lagny Park** ② is a popular spot with residents, and anyone looking for a place to relax and drink in the beauty of the area. Notice the impressive homes and estates along the lakefront.

The clear water of magnificent **Lac des Sables** ③ comes from natural springs. There are several sandy beaches along the lake for a quick dip or relaxing swim: Plage Major on Chemin du Tour-du-Lac, Plage Sainte-Lucie on Rue Larocque, and Plage Tessier on Rue Major. These have picnic tables, services, and play areas; while canoes, paddleboats, and kayaks are available for rent at Plage Major. **T**:*(819) 326-3330. Admission is $5 for adults, $3 for children.*

Scenic cruises ④ on the lake give visitors a chance to see the many spectacular estates along its shores. Entertaining, guided cruises depart from the dock at the end of Rue Principale. **T**:*(819) 326-3656,* **W**: *croisierealouette.com. Cruises run mid-May through Oct. daily at 10:30, 11:30, 1:30, 2:30, and 3:30; late June to late Aug. additional tours run at 5 and 7. Admission $12 for adults, $5 for children. Handicapped accessible.*

Chemin Tour du Lac ⑤ offers a spectacular look at Lac des Sables and the neighborhoods surrounding it. Shortly after crossing over a tributary of Rivière du Nord, you will come to a scenic viewpoint affording an extensive view of the lake. The drive along Route 329 passes by several scenic lakes and winds around lazy mountains. Note the sweeping views of Lac Archembault as you approach the town.

Saint-Donat-de-Montcalm ⑥ rests, snuggly, between the shores of Lac Archembault and Lac Ouareau. This little town is a popular resort destination in all seasons. The two large lakes, surrounding forests, and mountains provide activities and entertainment year-round.

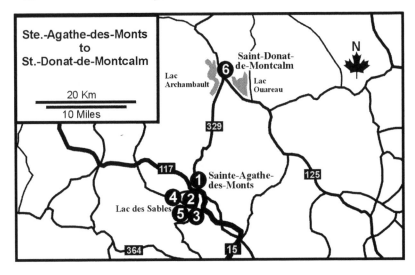

Lac des Sables

STE.-AGATHE-DES-MONTS 226

Mont-Tremblant and Lac Tremblant

The villages and parklands of Mont-Tremblant offer all of the best that is available in Québec — from internationally renowned skiing to gourmet dining, from pretty villages to breathtaking waterfalls, from deep glacier lakes to dense pristine forests.

Spend a day in the wilds, hiking, swimming, and canoeing in the Mont-Tremblant Park. When you've had your fill of nature and you're ready to relax, retreat to one of the area's world-class villages.

GETTING THERE:

By Car, Parc du Mont-Tremblant is about 140 km (87 miles) from Montréal. Take **Rte. 15** north from Montréal to the junction of **Rte. 117**. Follow **Rte. 117** to **Rte. 327** in Saint-Jovite.

Turn right onto **Rte. 327** and follow it north to Lac Tremblant. Turn right on **Chemin Duplessis** following signs for Lac Supérieur. At the intersection of the road from Saint-Faustin, turn left, following signs for the park.

Leave the park through the Saint-Faustin entrance. Go for nearly 3 miles, and then turn right, following signs for Lac Tremblant, returning along **Chemin Duplessis**.

Return along **Rte. 327** to Saint-Jovite. Turn left onto **Rte. 117** and continue to **Rte. 15**. Take **Rte. 15** south back to Montréal.

PRACTICALITIES:

In the summer, visitors may want to bring along swimsuits and towels to take advantage of one of the lake's beaches. Shoes suitable for hiking are also recommended for some of the trails within the park.

Tourism information about the villages and resorts of Tremblant can be found on the Internet at **W**: *tremblant.com*

The **Bureau Touristique Saint-Jovite**, 305 Chemin Brébeuf, Saint-Jovite, proudly expresses their goal "to satisfy our tourists and make them want to come back." **T**:(819) 425-3300, **W**: laurentides.com. Open summer daily 9–7, winter daily 9–5.

FOOD AND DRINK:

Grand Manitou (at the summit of Mont-Tremblant) Have a snack or coffee in this cafeteria with a heart-stopping view. **T**:(819) 681-3000. $

Microbrasserie Saint-Arnould (435 Rue Paquette, Saint Jovite) Micro-brew beer, authentic regional cuisine, specializing in beer-flavored dishes. **T**:(819) 425-1262. $$

Le Grappe à Vin (Vieux-Tremblant, Mont-Tremblant) Featuring gourmet European and Asiatic dishes. **T**:(819) 681-4727. $$ and $$$

Crêperie Catherine (Vieux-Tremblant, Mont-Tremblant) This crêpe house has one feature that's hard to come by in Québec — it's a non-smoking restaurant. **T**:(819) 681-4888. $$

SUGGESTED TOUR:

Circled numbers correspond to numbers on the map.

PARC du MONT-TREMBLANT ①, Chemin du Lac Supérieur, Lac Supérieur, **T**:(819) 688-2281 or 1-800-665-6527, **W**: sepaq.com. *Open year-round. Admission $3.50 for adults, $5 for family of 1 adult with children, $7 for family of 2 adults with children. Equipment rental is available.*

There are several legends surrounding the naming of this mountain — "Trembling Mountain." An Amerindian legend tells of a nature god who made the mountain tremble when man came. Another legend tells of the Algonquin naming the mountain "Manitonga Soutana" (Mountain of Spirits) because of the shaking caused by the many streams of water flowing down its sides.

This expanse of wilderness, stretching over more than 900 square miles of the Laurentides, is peppered with numerous lakes and scored by several rivers. A haven for nature lovers and outdoor enthusiasts, the park is home to moose, black bear, beaver, and wolves — the park's mascot. Visitors are treated to a wonderland for swimming, canoeing, hiking, and mountain biking during the summer and cross-country skiing and snowshoeing during the winter.

Shortly after entering the park, **Lac Monroe** ② appears on the left. This large, clear lake has a wide beach and aquatic activities. Across the street from the lake, a hiking trail leads to **Lac Femmes** and **Lac Lauzon**.

Road 1 follows the edge of Lac Monroe for a bit, offering beautiful views of the lake. The river winds along beside the **Rivière du Diable**, which snakes across the rugged terrain in tight twists and turns. The rocky river, sometimes swift, sometimes lazy, crosses the path of the road in several places.

Stop for a short hike, about a half-hour round trip, following the trail to the **Devil's Falls** ③. The path leads through the forest to a plank walkway and observation deck, overlooking the dark waters, which make a vertical drop to a deep pool before turning at a right angle and cascading farther down the hill.

The drive through the park offers many stunning views of forests, meadows, rivers, and lakes. The road criss-crosses with the river and is occasionally

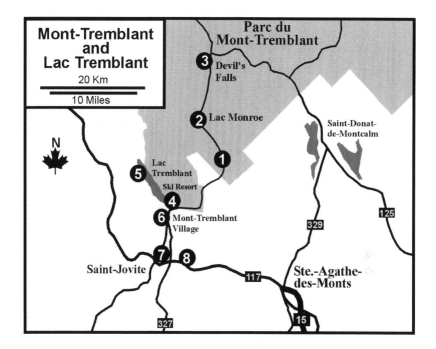

Mont-Tremblant and Lac Tremblant
20 Km
10 Miles

Parc du Mont-Tremblant

3 Devil's Falls

2 Lac Monroe

Saint-Donat-de-Montcalm

1

5 Lac Tremblant

Ski Resort

4

6 Mont-Tremblant Village

125

329

7 8

Saint-Jovite

117

Ste.-Agathe-des-Monts

327

15

flanked by lakes on either side.

Leave the park through the same gate. Return along Chemin Duplessis, following the signs for Lac Tremblant.

On the shore of Lac Tremblant, the **Mont-Tremblant Ski Resort** ④ comes into view like a fairytale village. The brightly-colored buildings, nestled at the foot of the ski slopes, invite visitors to get lost in the magical atmosphere. Note the quaint Roman Catholic **church**, with a bright red roof, sitting quietly at the edge of the resort.

The resort climbs up the slope of the mountain base, in full and inviting layers, packed with restaurants, activities, and shopping. A free gondola whisks visitors between the lower and higher levels of the resort, affording exciting views of the pools and mini-golf.

In the warmer months, the resort's pedestrian zones are alive with entertainment and artists. Strolling musicians, parades, concerts, and circus shows are a delight for everyone.

A **panoramic gondola** carries visitors and thrill-seekers up the slopes of Mont-Tremblant for a breath-taking view of the valley, resorts, and villages. An observation tower offers a 360° view of the area. Other activities at the summit include a labyrinth, outdoor adventure course, climbing wall, hiking, and wildlife observation. T:*(819) 681-3000. Running late May to mid-June, Sat.–Sun. 10:30–4:30; mid-June to mid-Sept., daily 10:30–5; mid-Sept. to mid-Oct., daily*

Mont Tremblant Resort

9:30–5. Admission starts at $13.65 for adults, $10.65 for children 6–17, children 5 and under are free.

Lac Tremblant ⑤, stretching out beside the forest like a long, narrow finger, is lined with impressive homes. Famous for its clean water and tasty fish, the lake also provides several beaches and a number of water sports. Guided **scenic cruises,** Quai Fédéral, of the lake provide glimpses of these luxurious estates, the neighboring forest, and Mont Tremblant. **T:***(819) 425-1045. Cruises depart July to mid-Oct., Tues.–Thurs. 11–7:30, Fri.–Mon. 11–4. Duration 1 hour and 15 minutes. Cost $15 for adults, $6 for children 15 and under, children 5 and under are free.*

Near the quai, note the **Décharge-du-Lac,** a tributary of the Diable River that twists away from the lake in a series of waterfalls and whirlpools.

Follow the road to the right, around the end of Lac Tremblant, into the **Ville de Mont-Tremblant,** which was formed in November 2000 by the merging of several municipalities.

Mont Tremblant Village ⑥ rests on the shore of Lac Tremblant and Lac Mercier. The picturesque mountain village is well known for its scenic main street and fine dining. Artist studios, galleries, and boutiques will delight art lovers and shoppers.

Regional artisans display their unique, fun and fancy wares at **Métiers d'Art en Nord,** 1982 Chemin Principal. **T:***(819) 681-7474. Open year-round, Sun.–Mon. and Wed.–Fri. 10–5:30, Sat. 10–6, closed on Tues.*

Mont-Tremblant Activities, 2001 Chemin Principal, arranges a wide variety of activities for outdoors and sports buffs. In the winter the friendly crew schedules trips for dogsledding, snowmobiling, and ice climbing. In the summer months, ask them about whitewater rafting, A.T.V. tours, and canoeing.

For a thrilling adventure, try an airborne tour with **Aviation Wheelair**, 399 Chemin Principale. Get a bird's-eye view of the area by seaplane. **T**:*(819) 425-5662. Tours run year-round, daily 9–8 by reservation. Guided tour lasts 20 minutes. Rates $52.50 per person, $157.50 for families with two adults and up to three children.*

After a day full of outdoor activity, pamper yourself at **Le Scandinave** Swedish-style spa, 555 Montée Ryan. The spa features a Finnish sauna, steam baths, waterfall and river bathing, and Swedish massage. **T**:*(819) 425-5524,* **W**: *scandinave.com. Open year-round, daily 12–9 by reservation. Admission to baths $38. Massages start at $97.50.*

Take Route 327 out of Mont-Tremblant Village. Note **Lac Ouimet** as you pass. Continue on Route 327 to the junction of Route 117 in **Saint-Jovite** ⑦. This charming little resort town has been incorporated into the Mont-Tremblant Village municipality.

LES JARDINS de MIREILLE ⑧, 495 Route 327 South, **T**:(819) 425-2544. *Open June–Oct. 9–5. Admission $7 for adults and children 12 and older, children under 12 are free.*

This stunning flower garden will delight visitors with the panoramic views, paths for strolling, and places to relax on the six-acre property. The aquatic garden features splendid waterfalls.

Section XI

DAYTRIPS IN THE
EASTERN TOWNSHIPS

Majestic mountain peaks, lavish valleys, and enticing lakes — the Eastern Townships offer a feast for your senses. Immerse yourself in the peace and beauty of Canada's Appalachian countryside.

This amazing region stretches across the southern part of the province. Located east of Montréal and southeast of Québec City, between the Chaudière River basin and the U.S. border, the region is home to orchards, vineyards, maple forests, rounded mountains and pristine lakes. This natural wonderland promises abundant outdoor recreational activities and relaxation year-round, making it a popular destination for harried city-dwellers.

The Abenaki Indians, the first to discover and understand the beauty and bounty of the area, left their mark in the foundation of many villages and the naming of local sites.

Owing to its location and natural wealth, the area has a rich blend of American, English, and French cultures. British Loyalists fleeing the American Revolution first settled the region. Gradually, French Canadians and Americans migrated into the area to work the railroads, mills, and lumber industry. These cultures combined to form villages and cities, rich in culture, spirit and community.

The tours in this section are easily accessible from Montréal and manageable as leisurely daytrips. Some could be combined for a longer day, or consider staying overnight and combining a couple of the trips for a fully relaxing country vacation.

Bromont, Route des Vins, Sutton

From a colorful, happy village, through the region's first township, past vineyards and rural crossroads, this driving tour will please your sense of history as well as your taste buds.

"Route des Vins" is the only area of Québec Province where the climate is ideal for the cultivation of grapes. The lush countryside — a patchwork of pastures, orchards, and vineyards — invites visitors to relax, picnic, and sample the local delicacies.

GETTING THERE:

By Car, Bromont, the first stop on the drive, is about 83 km (52 miles) east of Montréal. Take **Rte. 10** east from Montréal to **Exit 78**. At the traffic light, take a right onto **Rte. 241**, toward Bromont.

Continue on **Rte. 241** out of Bromont, then turn right onto **Rte. 104**, following signs to the industrial town of Cowansville.

Turn left onto **Rte. 202**, following signs to Dunham.

Continue on **Rte. 202** toward Stanbridge East. Turn right onto **Rte. 237**, following the signs for Stanbridge East and the Missisquoi Museum.

Go back on **Rte. 237** East, crossing over Rte. 202, and continuing to Frelighsburg.

In Frelighsburg, turn left onto **Rte. 213** (Rue Principale). Turn right onto **Rue Selby**. Continually following the signs for Sutton, turn right onto **Rue Dymond**. Note that parts of this road are gravel and dirt, so use caution.

Turn left onto **Rte. 139** to Sutton.

From Sutton, follow **Rte. 139** to **Rte. 10**. Take **Rte. 10** west back to Montréal.

PRACTICALITIES:

To take full advantage of the bounty offered along the Route de Vins, visit the area from late spring through fall. If you are planning your trip for winter, you can enjoy the winter sports available at Mont Bromont but some of the wineries will be closed.

The **Tourist Office of Bromont**, 15 Bromont Boulevard, is located on the right just off Autoroute 10. It's well stocked with maps and English-language guides. The people are very friendly and the office is open year-round. **T**:(450) 534-2006, **W**: granby-bromont.com

The **Tourist Office of Dunham**, 3638 Principale Street, is located in the library, before entering the town. Maps are available for Route de Vins with the location of the local vineyards. **T**:(450) 295-2621, **W**: ville.dunham.qc.ca

The **Sutton Tourism Office**, 11B Rue Principale, has self-guided historical tours of the town, as well as maps and brochures for the local attractions. **T**:(450) 538-8455, **W**: sutton-info.qc.ca. Open Mon.–Fri. 9–5, Sat.–Sun. 10–5.

FOOD AND DRINK:

Bromont has several places to have a snack after your drive from Montréal. Sit outside and enjoy fresh crêpes at **La Blanche Hermine** (632 Rue Shefford) **T**:(450) 534-5292, or have pastries and coffee at **Boulangerie l'Âme du pain** (702 Rue Shefford) **T**:(450) 534-4478. $ and $$

Aux Deux Clochers Bistro (Rue Principale and Rue l'Église, Frelighsburg) Enjoy a respite with classic cuisine in a pretty country setting. **T**:(450) 298-5086. $$

Bistro du Lapin Agile (4 Rue Maple, Sutton) Popular for regional Quebec cuisine in comfort. **T**:(450) 538-4355. $$ and $$$

The Beetle Resto Pub (19 rue Principale North, Sutton) Pizza, pasta, and light food promising "a friendly pub where good food and good company go hand-in-hand." **T**:(450) 538-3779. $$

SUGGESTED TOUR:

Circled numbers correspond to numbers on the map.

The happy town of **Bromont** ① greets visitors with brightly colored buildings, charming cafés, and shops boasting locally-made products. In 1792, Captain John Savage, being loyal to the king of England, fled the American Revolution. He and several of his compatriots settled this small village, which has grown to be a popular destination for tourists, sports enthusiasts, and industry. In 1976 the town hosted the Olympic equestrian competition.

Stop into the small **Musée du Chocolat**, 679 Rue Shefford, for an informative look at the history of chocolate and the chocolate-making process. End the tour with a sample of their delectable product or a homemade ice cream. The small shop also features regionally made jams, purées, sauces, and mustards. **T**:*(450) 534-3893. Open year-round, Mon.–Fri 10–6, weekends 9–5:30. Admission is $1.25 per person.*

For true chocolate lovers, visit Bromont in May for the **Fête du Chocolat**, where you can sample many chocolate delicacies, paint with cocoa, and attend the Chocolate Ball. **T**:*(450) 534-4078. Admission is $6 per person, children under 8 are free.*

May through October, Bromont is home to the largest **flea market**, 16 Rue Lafontaine, in the Eastern Townships. More than 350 vendors set up stalls to

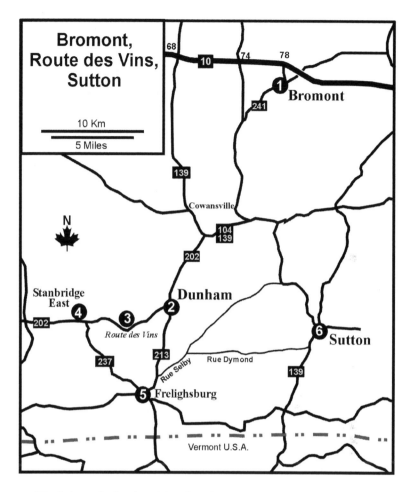

Bromont, Route des Vins, Sutton

10 Km

5 Miles

peddle their goods. *Sundays, May–Oct., 9–5.*

Nearby **Ski Bromont.com**, 115 Rue Champlain, provides family fun all year long, with a water park, mountain biking, hiking, mountain sleds, and world class skiing. **T**:*(450) 534-2200,* **W***: skibromont.com.* **Water Park***: Open June 10–4; July–Aug. 10–6:30; Admission $28 for adults, $23 for children, $13 for seniors and 3-5 year-olds.* **Chairlift** *rides: Open May, weekends 10–4; June daily 10–4; July and August daily 10–6:30; Sept.–Oct. weekends 10–4. Admission $8 for adults, $6 for children, seniors and children under five are free.* **Mountain sleds** *with chairlift ride: Open June 10–4; July–Aug 10–6:30. Admission $10, seniors and children under 5 are free.*

Dunham ②, brimming with stone-and-brick houses, typical of those built by the British Loyalists who fled the United States during the Revolutionary

War, has the distinction of being the first township in the area. The town's charm is also enhanced by its three church steeples: Sainte-Croix Catholic Church, the neo-classical United Church, and the Anglican All-Saints Church.

Dunham also boasts the area of Québec Province with a climate most suitable for growing grapes. The **Route des Vins** ③, along Autoroute 202, offers visitors picturesque vineyards and orchards for tasting wines and ciders in magnificent, distinctly French, country settings.

Les Trois Clochers, 341 Route 202, features red, white, and sparkling wine. Wine tasting and guided tours are available. Walking trails, which can be used for cross-country skiing in the winter, offer a beautiful look at the vineyard and countryside. **T**:*(450) 295-2034.*

Domaine Côtes d' Ardoise, 879 Route 202, makes red, white, and rosé, as well as aperitif and ice wine. Enjoy a guided tour and wine tasting, a casual country picnic or a hearty meal. A country store sells many local treats and gifts. **T**:*(450) 295-2020.*

Les Blancs Côteaux, 1046 Route 202, produces red and white wine, cider, ice cider, apple brandy aperitifs and cider vinegar. Guided tours and tasting is available. In season, visitors enjoy picking their own apples. Gourmet lunch baskets can be purchased for a fine country picnic. **T**:*(450) 295-3503. Open May 15 – October 15.*

Take a break from the wine tasting for a fun and informative visit to **Fleurs de Pommiers**, 1047 Route 202. Several varieties of ciders are produced here, as well as cider vinegar and other apple products. Guided tours and tasting is available. A country store allows you to purchase any of their apple-derived products. **T**:*(450) 295-2223.*

L'Orpailleur, 1086 Route 202, makes red, white, rosé, sparkling and ice wines. Along with guided tours and tasting, this vineyard features a wine museum and trails through the vineyards. There is a country-style restaurant with terrace for a relaxing and delicious meal. **T**:*(450) 295-2763.*

Also settled by British Loyalists, who fled the American Revolution, **Stanbridge East** is a quaint farming town, known mostly for its Loyalist architecture.

Les Jardins à Fleur d'Eau, 140 Route 202, Stanbridge East, is a peaceful oasis of ponds, waterfalls, and aquatic flowers. **T**:*(450) 248-7008,* **W**:*afleurdeau.qc.ca. Admission $8 for adults, $5 for seniors and children 12–18, children 11 and under are free.*

THE MISSISQUOI MUSEUM ④, 2 Rue River, Stanbridge East, **T**:(450) 248-3153. *Open daily, last Sun. in May to the second Sun. in Oct., 10–5. Admission $3.50 for adults, $3.50 for seniors, $1 for children and students.*

The museum comprises three historic buildings: the Cornell Mill, Hodge's General Store, and Bill's Barn. The three-story brick gristmill on the Pike River, built in 1830, is the heart of the museum. Here, the permanent exhibits illustrate the history and culture of the area from Indians to Loyalists, settlers and farmers.

Changing exhibits highlight specific aspects of the region's history. Near the mill, at 20 River Street, is Hodge's Store that stocks much of the same merchandise it did at the time of World War II. Continuing on River Street, near the intersection of Route 202, is the Annex, known locally as Bill's Barn. Originally a part of a creamery, the barn is now used as a museum of cars and farming machinery.

Cross over Route 202 and follow Route 237 east to **Frelighsburg** ⑤, a small crossroad village in the shadows of Pinnacle Mountain and home to artisans and apple orchards. Take a peek at the Gothic-Revival **Anglican Church**, built in 1884, sitting on top of the hill overlooking the village. The architecture of the church is unusual for Eastern Townships because of its oblong shape and the location of its steeple, at the side of the nave.

Turn left onto Rue Principale (Route 213), then right onto Rue Selby. Continually following the signs for Sutton, turn right onto Rue Dymond. The drive to Sutton will treat you with spectacular views of the countryside, valleys, and surrounding hills. Shutterbugs will be tempted to stop frequently along the rural roads to immortalize scenes of old-fashioned farms, lush valleys, winding rivers, and mountainsides blanketed by forests. Use caution on this drive, as some of the road is dirt and gravel.

A popular center for winter sports enthusiasts, located at the foot of Sutton Mountain, **Sutton** ⑥ has been nicknamed "Flat Sutton." British Loyalists fleeing the American Revolution, including expatriate Richard Shepard from New Hampshire, who was the first to clear land in 1799, settled the town. Around World War I and II, Europeans looking for a better life began to settle in Sutton, naming it "Little Switzerland in America."

Maple, Academy, and Pleasant Streets sport prime examples of Loyalist architecture. The town treats visitors to a host of elegant boutiques, fabulous restaurants, and unique galleries and artist studios. The **Tour des Arts**, in mid-July, enables art aficionados with the chance to visit artists and craftspeople in their studios. **T**:*1-800-565-8455,* **W**: *tourdesarts.com*

Visit **Le Musée des Communications et d'Histoire de Sutton**, 30A Rue Principale South, which documents local and railroad history, as well as giving visitors an interesting look at the arena of communications. **T**:*(450) 538-3222. Open Thurs.–Sun. 9–12 and 1–5.*

René Henquin's Chocolaterie, 8 Principale South, has an interesting museum illustrating the art of Belgian chocolate making. **T**:*(450) 538-0139.*

Sutton hosts three art galleries that are worth a peek, **Galerie d'Art Les Imagiers**, 10-3 Rue Principale North, **Galerie d'Art Tournesol**, 6 Rue Pine, and **Arts Sutton**, 7 Rue Academy.

Nearby **Mont Sutton**, 671 rue Maple, is heaven for those who enjoy winter sports, including 53 downhill runs, nine lifts, and four restaurants on the mountain. **T**:*(450) 538-2545,* **W**: *montsutton.com. Chairlifts are open Mon.–Fri. 9–4, Sat.–Sun. 8:30–4.*

Trip 42

Granby and Waterloo

Settled by British Loyalists in the early 19th century, Granby was named for the Marquis of Granby, John Manners. Sitting on the banks of the Yamaska River, the town developed quickly around the rubber and tobacco industries that grew here. Elegant Victorian homes give evidence to the wealth generated by the success of these industries.

Waterloo, settled by British Loyalists in 1796, sits side-by-side with Granby like a sibling — connected by their histories, as well as the bike trails that draw visitors from across Canada and beyond.

GETTING THERE:

By Car, Granby is 80 km (50 miles) east of Montréal. Take **Rte. 10** east to Exit 68, then **Rte. 139** north. Turn right onto **Rte. 112** for the town of Granby.

To reach the Granby Zoo, continue on **Rte. 139**, crossing over **Rte. 112**.

Continue on **Rte. 112**, out of Granby, to reach Waterloo.

Parc de Récréation de la Yamaska, turn left onto **Rte. 241** north.

To reach Safari Adventure Loowak and Route 10, follow **Rte. 112** through Waterloo and take a right onto **Rte. 241**. Pass the lake and turn left onto **Rue Western**, toward "Chambourg sur le Lac." Turn left onto **Rue Horizon**. Safari Adventure Loowak is on the left just before the junction of **Rte. 10**.

PRACTICALITIES:

If you're planning to go to Safari Adventure Loowak, you will need to make a reservation and you need a minimum of four people. They recommend reservations be made about 48 hours in advance. The adventures can be done year-round.

A **Tourist Office** for the Eastern Townships is located on Route 139, just off Route 10 at Exit 68.

Tourisme Granby, 650 Rue Principale, Granby, is open year-round. **T**:(450) 372-7273 or 1-800-567-7273, **W**: granby-bromont.com

Tourisme Waterloo, 5491 Rue Foster, Waterloo, is open seasonally. **T**:(450) 539-4650.

FOOD AND DRINK:

La Piazzetta (116 Rue Principale, Granby) Specializing in gourmet pizza that will excite the senses. **T**:(450) 777-5577. $$

Chez Trudeau (348 Rue Principale, Granby) Family restaurant with good, hearty meals. **T**:(450) 378-2874. $$

Faucheau (53-2 Rue Dufferin, Granby) Fine dining and gourmet French food in a comfortable atmosphere. **T**:(450) 777-2320. $$$

LOCAL ATTRACTIONS:

Circled numbers correspond to numbers on the map.

GRANBY ZOO ①, 525 Rue St. Hubert, **T**:(877) 472-6299, **W**: zoogranby.ca. *Open weekends in May 10–6; daily in June 10–8; daily July–Aug. 10–one hour before sunset; weekends Sept. to mid-Oct. 10–6. Admission $23.99 for over age 13; $17.99 for children 5–13, seniors and handicapped persons; $10.99 for children 2–4; $72.99 for families (2 adults and 2 children).*

This well-cared-for zoo is home to over 800 animals. Of the 163 species living here, more than a third are endangered. Watch families of gorillas in a tropical rainforest in the African Pavilion. Don't miss the nocturnal animals' cave that allows you to enjoy animals usually only seen at night. Other interesting sections of the zoo include Bear Mountain and Feline Pavilion. Not for the squeamish — check out the rattlesnakes and anacondas in the Reptile House.

Zoo admission also includes admission to **Amazoo**, a new water park by the zoo that has the largest heated wave pool in Québec province. *Open June–Aug.*

Granby ②, with a population over 44,000, is the second-largest city in the Eastern Townships. There are forty beautiful parks in the city, many with sculptured fountains. Pick up a pamphlet for the self-guided tour of the city at the Tourist Information Office.

Rue Elgin still has many beautiful Victorian homes, evidence to the successful industrial history of the town.

The city has a lot to offer visitors including a charming historic heart and many activities to keep visitors busy for days. There are also all of the trappings of our modern lifestyles.

The **Pavilion Faunique**, 270 Rue Denison East, boasts the largest collection of stuffed animals in Canada, with more than 700 animals displayed in their natural settings. Exhibits depict the birds, fish, and animals native to each of the Canadian provinces and territories. Interactive and entertaining games educate visitors on Québec fauna in a fun-and-friendly atmosphere. The site also has a miniature golf, indoors and outdoors. In the summer there are regularly scheduled shows at the Puppet Theater. **T**:*(450) 375-6525,* **W**: *pavillon-faunique-canada.qc.ca. Open June–Aug., weekdays 10–7, weekends 10–9; Sept.–May, Wed.–Fri. 1–5, Sat. 10–7, Sun. 10–5. Admission $9 for adults, $6 for children*

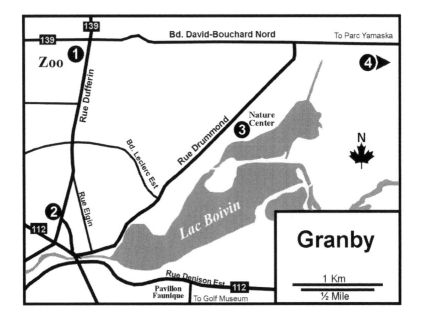

5-15, children 4 and under are free, $24 for families (2 adults and 2 children).

Parc Daniel Johnson, situated on the shores of Lake Boivin, has a lighted ice-skating rink in the winter, as well as snow sculptures.

Everyone will enjoy the **Musée du Golf**, 669 Rue Coupland — it's not just for golfers. The museum illustrates the history of golf. Games test visitors' knowledge of the game as well as their skills. **T**:*(450) 372-0167. Open daily during golf season, 8–8; off-season Wed.–Sun. 9–4.*

At **Hydromelerie les Saules**, located off Route 112 at Saxby Corner, you can taste and buy Mead (a sweet wine made from honey), fresh honey, and other bee products.

LAKE BOIVIN NATURE INTERPRETATION CENTER ③, 700 Rue Drummond, **T**:(450) 375-3861. *Open year-round, daily 8:30–4:30.*

Situated where the Yamaska River widens into Lake Boivin, this center is the perfect place to stroll along nature trails, amidst marshes and along the Yamaska River. If you're lucky you'll be able to catch sight of some of the local wildlife. Mont Brome and Mont Shafford can be seen from the observation tower.

Nearby, try your luck in the **Super Labyrinthe Jolibois**, **T**:(450) 777-8857. This circular maze, which looks like a wood fort, is challenging and fun. *Open May–June and Sept.–Oct., daily except Sun., 11 to 2 hours before sunset; late June to Aug., daily 11 to 2 hours before sunset. Admission over 13 years old $6.95, $4.95 for children 5–12. Handicap accessible.*

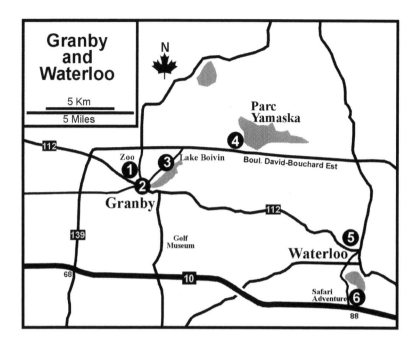

PARC de RÉCRÉATION de la YAMASKA ④, 1780 Rue David Bouchard, **T**:(450) 776-7182, **W**: sepaq.com. *Open Apr.–Nov. 8–sunset. Admission $3.50 for adults, $1.50 for children.*

This beautiful park, located along the banks of the Yamaska River, offers biking trails, nature walks, hiking, swimming at two beaches, water sports, and boat rentals. Its lake, the Choinère reservoir, which is bordered by forests and lush meadows, has long been a popular destination for aquatic sports enthusiasts.

Waterloo ⑤, a quaint town that was formerly the central point between the "Stanstead Shefford & Chambly Railroad" and the "South Eastern Railway" in the late-1800s, is now commonly known as the "cycling capital" of Canada.

Among the many architecturally interesting buildings in the town, the Gothic **St. Luke's Anglican Church**, Rue de la Cour, built in 1870, is worth a look for its beautiful leaded stained-glass windows.

Picturesque **Lac Waterloo** offers a full range of aquatic sports, including swimming and sailing. Stroll along the shores and take in the beauty of this small lake.

Miles of **cycling trails**, built on abandoned railroad tracks, weave through the countryside, between and among the cities of Granby and Waterloo. The trails can be used for biking, rollerblading, or walking. Information offices, rest and picnic areas are set up along the routes.

SAFARI ADVENTURE LOOWAK ⑥, 475 Boulevard Horizon, Waterloo, **T**:(450) 539-0510, **W**: safariloowak.qc.ca. *Open daily, year-round, 10–5, with reservations. Four-person minimum. Price varies based on which adventure you choose.*

This may very well be one of the coolest activities for your family. A safari guide will provide you with walkie-talkies, maps, compasses, and instructions. It's up to you to solve the mission at hand. Form a search party to find a missing plane that has crashed in the surrounding forest. Go on an "Indiana Jones" style expedition to uncover a precious treasure. More complicated and difficult missions are available for larger groups with a minimum of sixteen persons.

St.-Benoît-du-Lac Abbey, Trip 43

Knowlton, Saint-Benoît-du-Lac, and Mount Owl's Head

The picturesque Victorian village of Knowlton, with its white-trimmed red brick buildings, high-end boutiques and fabulous restaurants, is one of the most welcoming towns in the Eastern Townships. It makes a perfect small-town escape from the city.

Visitors will be treated to striking mountain views on the drive from Knowlton to the Saint-Benoît-du-Lac Abbey and Mount Owl's Head.

GETTING THERE:

By Car, Knowlton is about 112 km (70 miles) east of Montréal. Take **Rte. 10** east from Montréal to Exit 90. Follow **Rte. 243** south to Knowlton.

From Knowlton, continue on **Rte. 243** to South Bolton. Take **Rte. 245** north to Bolton Centre and then turn right toward Austin. Turn right onto **Fisher Road** and follow the signs for Saint-Benoît-du-Lac.

Return to South Bolton and continue on **Rte. 243** to Mansonville. Turn left and follow signs through Vale Perkins to Mt. Owl's Head.

Follow **Rte. 243** back to **Rte. 10** to return to Montréal.

PRACTICALITIES:

The Abbey is closed from 11:00 to 1:00 for lunch, so plan your arrival for either the morning or afternoon.

The **Tourist Information Office** is located at 696 Rue Lakeside, Lac-Brome. **T**:(450) 242-2870, **W**: knowltonquebec.ca

FOOD AND DRINK:

Bistro Knowlton Pub (267 Rue Knowlton, Knowlton) Offering hearty casual food in a comfortable environment. Open for lunch and dinner. **T**:(450) 242-6862. $$

Le Relais Restaurant-Bistro (303 Rue Knowlton, Knowlton) Serving gourmet country food and memories for over 150 years, including local delicacies like Brome Duck. **T**:(450) 242-2232. $$$

Auberge l'Aubergine (160 Chemin Cooledge, Mansonville) Regional cuisine with fresh, local ingredients, such as abbey cheese and local lamb. **T**:(450) 292-3246. $$

Restaurant La Vieille Bûche (241 Chemin Val Perkins, Mansonville) Exquisite restaurant featuring steak and local Brome Duck. **T**:(450) 292-0302. $$$+

SUGGESTED TOUR:

Circled numbers correspond to numbers on the map.

Knowlton ① was founded by settlers from New England in the early 19th century and named for Paul Knowlton, who built the community's gristmill and general store in 1834. Unlike typical French-Canadian villages that are built around the parish church, Knowlton grew up around the impressive public buildings. The first free public library in Québec Province was built here in 1894.

Many of the town's brick and stone buildings, common to the area, are now being used as antique shops, up-scale boutiques, and artist galleries. **Coldbrook Park** is great for a stroll or picnic by the tranquil waterfall.

This picturesque little village, on the southern end of Lake Brome, is so inviting and peaceful you may find it difficult to leave. Consider stopping here again at the end of your day, before heading back to the hectic city.

Nearby **Lake Brome** is popular for its windsurfing and duck, which is a popular item on local restaurant menus.

The **Brome County Historical Museum** ②, 130 Rue Lakeside (Route 243), Knowlton, has several interesting buildings that transport visitors back through time. There are military exhibits, including a German World War I fighter plane, in the Martin Annex. Feel the seriousness of the 19th-century legal system in the Courthouse and see a turn-of-the-century schoolroom in the "Academy," both built in 1854. There is also a period general store set up in the old "Fire Hall," built in 1904. **T**:*(450) 243-6782. Open mid-May to mid-Sept., Mon.–Sat. 10–4:30, Sun. 11–4:30. Admission $5.00 for adults, $3.00 for children.*

Parc du Mont Glen ③, 136 Chemin Glen, is a forest wonderland with fun for the entire family. Obstacle courses will challenge visitors in good shape — and a large labyrinth built into the forest will challenge everyone. In winter there's downhill and cross-country skiing and snowshoeing. Mountain biking trails criss-cross the mountain. **T**:*(450) 243-6142.*

SAINT-BENOÎT-du-LAC ABBEY ④, **T**:(819) 843-4080, **W**: st-benoit-du-lac.com. *Monastery is open daily 5–9. Store hours are Nov.–May, weekdays 9–10:45 and 1:30–4:30, Sat. 9–10:45 and 11:45–4:30; June-Oct., Mon.–Sat. 9–10:45 and 11:45–4:30. Women should call (819) 843-2340 or use the Internet for information.*

The Abbey, perched majestically on a hill surrounded by striking landscapes and breathtaking views, is inhabited by Benedictine Monks who have

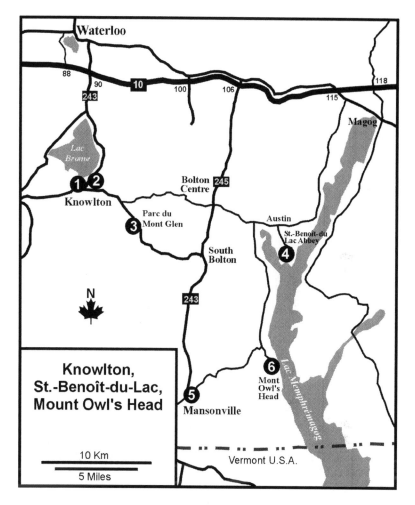

chosen to focus their lives on spirituality, prayer, study, physical work, and pastoral ministry. Part of the Abbey was designed by the French Benedictine architect Dom Paul Bellot, whose work is characterized by his search for harmony within the geometric patterns of nature. This is evidenced in the long hallways of brightly colored, geometric tiles. Bellot is buried in the Abbey's cemetery. A store sells products made by the monks, including cheeses and cider, as well as religious gifts. Respectable dress is required on the Abbey grounds and pets are not allowed.

Visitors to **Mansonville** ⑤, one of the small hamlets that make up Potton Township, may think they made a wrong turn, accidentally driving to New

KNOWLTON. ST.-BENOÎT-DU-LAC. MT. OWL'S HEAD   245

England. The quaint village has a small green park in the center of town, typical of small towns throughout that region. One of the last remaining **round barns** in Québec Province is located near Main Street, across from the Church of Cajétan. The Shakers who believed the circular form would prevent the devil from 'haunting any corner' designed the round barn. There is a **covered bridge** on Rue Bellevue.

MONT OWL'S HEAD ⑥, Chemin du Mont Owl's Head, **T**:(450) 292-3342 or (800) 363-3342, **W**: owlshead.com

According to legend, the profile of Abenaki Indian Chief Owl could be seen on the mountain after his death. This majestic mountain rises up from the shores of Lake Memphrémagog.

This is one of the most beautiful and most popular ski resorts in the Eastern Townships. There are more than 25 runs for skiers and snow-boarders of all levels. With two high-speed quads and five double chairlifts visitors spend their day skiing rather than waiting in lines.

In the warmer seasons there is hiking, mountain biking, tennis, golf, and a marina. Hike to top for stunning views of Lake Memphrémagog. The spectacular and challenging 18-hole golf course was designed by famous golf-course architect Graham Cooke.

Magog River Gorge
Sherbrooke
Trip 44

Trip 44

Sherbrooke

The Saint François and Magog rivers meet in a steeply sloping valley, surrounded by hills and mountain peaks. A village formed here, which the Abenaki Indians called "the great fork." Settlers from Vermont arrived at the beginning of the 19th century, then Gilbert Hyatt built a flourmill and the village became known as Hyatt's Mills. The name Sherbrooke was adopted in 1818 after the Governor-in-Chief of British North America, Sir John Coape Sherbrooke.

In the 19th century, mills sprang up along the banks of the rivers, helping to secure Sherbrooke's roll as the principal city of the Eastern Townships. With the opening of the university in 1954 the city also developed into a cultural and educational center for the region.

With a population of more than 78,000, Sherbrooke is by far the largest city in the Eastern Townships. The historical and cultural attractions, as well as the beauty of the city, help to make it one of the finest cities in the province.

GETTING THERE:

By Car, Sherbrooke is 149 km (93 miles) southeast of Montréal. Take **Rte. 10** East to **Rte. 112**. Follow **Rte. 112** into the town center.

Parc Blanchard is reached by turning right off Rue King onto **Boulevard Jacques Cartier** and crossing Pont Jacque Cartier. Turn right onto **Rue Roy** and then right onto **Rue Cabana**.

To reach the Magog River Gorge, turn left off Rue King onto **Rue Belvédère North**, just before the city center. At the light, turn right onto **Rue Montréal**. Take the first right onto **Island** and a left onto **Cliff**.

To reach Mont Bellevue Park, turn right off Rue King onto **Rue Belvédère South**. Bear right onto **Rue Dunant**.

To view Mena'Sen Rock turn left off Rue King onto **Rue Bowen**. Bear left onto **Boulevard St. François**.

For Parc Victoria turn left off Rue King onto **Rue Bowen**. Bear right onto **Boulevard St. François**. Turn right onto **Rue Terrill**.

To visit the Sanctuaire de Beauvoir, follow **Rue King West** (Route 112) across Pont Aylmer. Turn left onto **Rue Bowen** and then bear right onto **Boule-**

vard St. François. Turn right onto **Chemin de Beauvoir**, following the signs to the sanctuary.

Return back down **Chemin de Beauvoir**, turn right onto **Boulevard St. François**, and follow it to **Route 10**.

PRACTICALITIES:

Several of the city's main attractions are only available during the summer months. Sherbrooke is best visited from June to August to take full advantage of the outdoor cafés, the riverside parks, and all of the cultural attractions the city has to offer.

The **Tourist Information Office**, 2964 Rue King West (Route 112), west of the city center. **T**:(819) 821-1919, **W**: sdes.ca/en/index.html

FOOD AND DRINK:

Café Bla-Bla (2 Rue Wellington South) A bistro-terrace right in the heart of the city, perfect for good food and great people watching. **T**:(819) 565-1366. $$

Da Toni (15 Rue Belvédère North) With a reputation built over its 25 years of business for consistently serving excellent Italian and French cuisine. Free valet parking and a terrace are available. **T**:(819) 346-8441. $$$ and $$$+

Le Liverpool (28 Rue Wellington South) Inviting patrons to relax in a cozy living room and enjoy the fireplace, or play at one of the many pool and snooker tables. Choose from over 50 varieties of cigars to taste. **T**:(819) 822-3724. $$

Antiquarius Café (182 Wellington North) The perfect place to relax after peeking in the area's many shops and galleries. Enjoy a light meal or snack and coffee in a charming, eclectic atmosphere and browse through their antiques and gifts for sale. **T**:(819) 562-1800. $ and $$

LOCAL ATTRACTIONS:

Circled numbers correspond to numbers on the map.

Riverside Trail ① is a long series of walking/bicycling trails and parks that run beside the Magog River through the heart of Sherbrooke. **Parc Blanchard** invites visitors to enjoy a variety of outdoor and aquatic sports. Bicycles, scooters, canoes, kayaks, and paddleboats are available for rent. Or take a refreshing dip at the beach. **Parc de Pêche** challenges fisherman — pike, bass, and trout await. **Parc Jacque Cartier** is perfect for a picnic or relaxing stroll. The park hosts many events throughout the summer. **T**:(819) 821-5893, **W**: *sdes.ca/en/pleinair.html*

The **"Traces and Souvenances"** tour is an informative and entertaining theatrical bus tour. Guides dressed as historical figures relive regional history and bring to life some of the cities most interesting locales. **T**:(819) 821-1919. *Running July and August. Reservation required.*

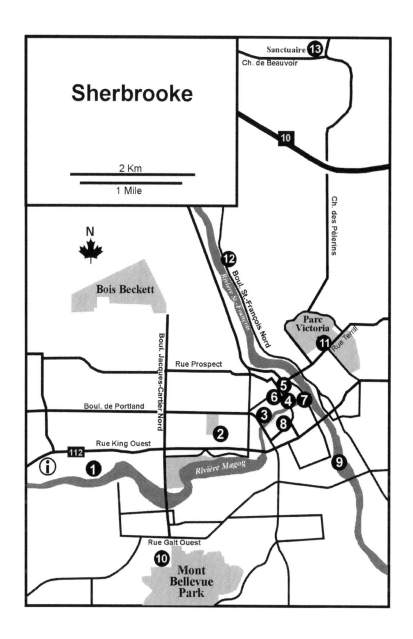

DOMAINE HOWARD PARK and the MUNICIPAL GREENHOUSES ②, 1350 Boulevard Portland. *The garden is open May–Oct. The greenhouses are open Mon.–Fri. all year 8–4, closed in Dec.*

Three Anglo-Normand buildings and a beautiful green garden make a unique and peaceful escape from the bustling city. The municipal greenhouses and outside gardens are wonderful for strolling and exploring the variety of plants and flowers.

MAGOG RIVER GORGE ③, **T**:(819) 821-5406. *Guided tours of the gorge are run late June to early Sept., Tues.–Thurs. at 10:30. The power plant is open late June to early Sept., Tues.–Sun. 9:30–4:30. Admission to the power station is $6 for adults, $3 for children 6–12, children under 6 are free.*

The powerful Magog River, coursing through the Sherbrooke city center, has formed a deep gorge. The Frontenac Power Plant and a damn were built across the gorge to harvest the river's power for electricity. Walkways along the river's edge and across the damn give visitors spectacular views of the river, waterfalls, and hydroelectric plant. The power plant, the oldest operational hydroelectric plant in Québec, has a nice terrace where you can sit in the middle of the gorge and enjoy a snack or lunch. An interactive exhibit inside the plant illustrates the history of Sherbrooke's power development.

MUSÉE des BEAUX-ARTS de SHERBROOKE ④, 241 Rue Dufferin, **T**:(819) 821-2115, **W**: mba.ville.sherbrooke.qc.ca. *Open late June to Labor Day, Tues.–Sun. 11–5, Wed. 11–9; Labor Day to late June, Tues.–Sun. 1–5, Wed. 1–9. Guided tours are available Wed. at 7:30 and upon reservations. Admission $6 for adults, $4 for children. Handicap accessible.*

Dedicated to the art and artists of the Eastern Townships, this museum building was originally a bank. The 19th-century building, designed by Montréal architect James Nelson, is considered the finest example of Second Empire architecture in the province, outside of Montréal and Québec. The three galleries host permanent and temporary exhibits, while temporary exhibits and educational activities help to involve visitors in the works of local artists.

CENTRE d'INTERPRÉTATION de l'HISTOIRE de SHERBROOKE ⑤, 275 Rue Dufferin, **T**:(819) 821-5406, **W**: shs.ville.sherbrooke.qc.ca. *Open Tues.–Fri. 9–5, Sat.–Sun. 10–5, off-season hours are 9–12 and 1–5. Admission $6 for adults, $2.50 for children. Handicap accessible.*

Visitors will experience Sherbrooke's 200-year history, from the start of colonization to modern times. Audiotapes can be rented for self-guided heritage tours of the city.

On the corner of Rue Dufferin and Rue Montréal, take a look at the two churches that stand, facing each other, on opposite sides of the street. **Plymouth Trinity United Church** is Sherbrooke's oldest standing church, built in 1855. **St. Peter's Anglican Church** was built in 1902.

MUSÉE du SÉMINAIRE de SHERBROOKE and MUSÉE de la NATURE et des SCIENCES ⑥, 222 Rue Frontenac. **T**:(819) 564-3200, **W**: mnes.qc.ca. *Open Tues.–Sun. 12:30–4:30, daily in summer, 10–5. Admission $7.50 for adults, $5 for children, children 3 and under are free. Handicap accessible.*

This museum, featuring interactive activities and exhibits is housed in two buildings:

Located behind the Sherbrooke Seminary, the **Centre d'Exposition Lèon Marcotte** is a science and nature museum with a variety of displays and interactive exhibits.

The **Musée de la Tour**, housed in the brick tower of the Sherbrooke Seminary, is the oldest natural history museum in Québec, established in 1879. It features a three-storied exhibition hall filled with thousands of animals, minerals, plants, and artifacts. The museum proudly displays religious items, weapons, furniture, art, and specimens of nature.

ST. MICHAEL'S CATHEDRAL ⑦, 130 Rue de la Cathédrale, **T**:(819) 563-9934. *Closed daily noon–2.*

Visible from some distance, towering protectively over the city, the cathedral is reminiscent of Europe's abbeys. This impressive church, consecrated in 1958 and long an important part of the culture and community of Sherbrooke, was built in the Gothic style. The cathedral has over one hundred impressive stained-glass windows, as well as paintings, sculptures, and mosaics. The carved oak statue of the Virgin Mary, to the left of the altar, is breathtaking.

The **City Center** ⑧ offers many boutiques, galleries, antique shops, and restaurants for visitors to browse and enjoy. Stroll along Rue Wellington north and south, and along Rue King. In the center of Rue King you will find a thin garden, stretching up to the **Monument des Soldats Disparus**, a war memorial depicting a group of soldiers with a winged angel guarding over them.

Place de la Cité, Rue King West and Rue Belvédère North, hosts shows and concerts during the summer at noon and sunset.

Head southeast to **Rocher Mena'Sen** ⑨. A lone pine tree *(mena'sen* in Abenaki) once stood on this islet in the Saint François River, but was destroyed in a storm in 1913. One legend has it that the tree commemorated the Abenaki victory over the Iroquois. Another legend tells of two young Amerindian lovers. Escaping capture in Massachusetts and fleeing north, they stopped and the girl died at this spot; her young lover then planted a tree in her memory. The tree was replaced by a lit cross.

To the southwest lies **Mont Bellevue Park** ⑩. This mountain park, located just south of the city center, provides outdoor activities year round. In the winter there is downhill and cross-country skiing, snow shoeing, and tubing. In the warmer seasons visitors enjoy hiking, mountain biking, and archery. There is a large cross, which is illuminated at night, and a spectacular view of Sherbrooke.

To the northeast is **Parc Victoria** ⑪. This park of wooded areas and peaceful clearings is great for a picnic or a little escape.

Strolling through the **St. François Marsh** ⑫, Boulevard St. François, in spring will treat you to a symphony of frogs.

SANCTUAIRE de BEAUVOIR ⑬, 169 Chemin Beauvoir, Bromptonville, **T**:(819) 569-2535, **W**: sanctuairedebeauvoir.qc.ca

A short drive north of Sherbrooke, resting high atop a mountain with breathtaking views of the surrounding countryside, this shrine is a place of peace, prayer, and pilgrimage. The charming stone chapel was built in 1920 by Father J. A. Laporte. There is also a large open-air chapel set in the woods. Stroll through the gardens to admire the statues depicting stories from the life of Jesus.

Lennoxville, Compton, Coaticook, and Georgeville

This is the rural heartland of Québec Province, where nature's bounty is plentiful. Your taste buds will be thrilled with the fresh produce, dairy, and honey products, while your eyes will feast on valleys alive with orchards and farms. The drive takes you through rolling green fields and twisting rivers.

GETTING THERE:

By Car, Lennoxville, the first stop, is 154 km (96 miles) east of Montréal. Take **Rte. 10** East to **Rte. 112**. In Sherbrooke, turn right onto **Boulevard Belvédère**. Turn left onto **Rue Galt West** (Route 112/143). After the railroad crossing turn right onto **Rte. 143** south.

Continue on **Rte. 143** for 2 miles and turn left onto **Rte. 147** south to Compton.

Continue on **Rte. 147** south to Coaticook.

Take **Rte. 141** west towards Magog, crossing the junction of **Rte. 143** to Ayer's Cliff.

Turn right onto **Rte. 208** to **Rte. 143** north

In Stanstead, turn north on **Rte. 247**.

Follow **Rte. 247** North, through Georgeville, to **Rte. 112** east to return to Sherbrooke.

PRACTICALITIES:

This area of the Eastern Townships is particularly fun to visit in the early fall, during harvest season, when there are many festivals.

There is a **Tourist Information Office** located at 635 Rue Child, Coaticook. **T**:(819) 849-6669, **W**: tourismecoaticook.qc.ca/

FOOD AND DRINK:

The Golden Lion Pub (2 College Street, Lennoxville) Québec's first microbrewery, established in 1986. T:(819) 565-1015. $$

Le Bistro-Bar Ailleurs (77 Rue Main West, Coaticook) Just as *ailleurs* means "elsewhere," diners will be transported with fine creative cuisine, local beer, and regional treats. **T**:(819) 849-9665, **W**: ailleurs.qc.ca. $$ and $$$

The Ripplecove Inn (700 Rue Ripplecove, Ayer's Cliff) An elegant Victorian country inn on the shore of Lake Massawippi with an award-winning gourmet restaurant. Enjoy a refreshing mid-day break with spectacular views or a mouth-watering intimate dinner. **T**:(819) 838-4296, **W**: ripplecove.com $$$ to $$$+

SUGGESTED TOUR:

Circled numbers correspond to numbers on the map.

One of the few towns left in Québec that is still predominately English-speaking, **Lennoxville** ① was settled by British loyalists in 1794 at the junction of Massawippi and Saint-François rivers. The town is commonly known as the educational and cultural center for the Eastern Townships anglophone community. It also features many quaint boutiques and antique shops.

The **Musée Uplands**, 9 Rue Spied, is in a beautiful Neo-Georgian home, built in 1862. The museum houses exhibits that depict the culture and history of the region, as well as works from local artists and craftspeople. Stroll the grounds and enjoy the beautiful woods and gardens. Savor a British-style afternoon tea and listen to stories about the Eastern Townships from guides in period costume. In the summer, tea is served on the veranda. Workshops, speakers, and concerts are scheduled throughout the year. **T**:*(819) 564-0409,* **W***: uplands.ca. Open late June to Labor Day, Tues.–Sun. 1–4:30; Sept.–June, Thurs.–Sun. 1–4:30. Admission $2. Reservations required for tea.*

The charming **Saint George's Anglican Church**, Rue Queen, is worth a look. Saint George's is the oldest of the three churches that rest in close proximity to each other along Rue Queen. The other two are the **United Church** and **Saint Antoine's Catholic Church**.

The medieval-style buildings at the **Bishop's University** are impressive. Founded in 1843, the university is one of only three English-speaking universities in Québec Province. A campus map and audio-guided tour are available. At the Gothic-Revival **Saint Mark Chapel**, built in 1857, the benches on each side face each other across the center. **T**:(819) 822-9600, **W**: ubishops.ca. *Open daily 8:30–5, Sun. 12–5.*

There are several **covered bridges** along Route 147 - look for signs on the side of the road. The span of 1873 that crosses Moe's River is on the left, just beside the road as you enter Milby.

Compton ② is the birthplace of Louis-Stephen Saint-Laurent, the twelfth Prime Minister of Canada (1948–57), and who had an important role in establishing NATO.

Lois-Stephen Saint-Laurent National Historic Site, 6 Rue Principale (route 147) has a replica of the J.B.M. Saint-Laurent general store that leaves you wondering what year it is. The shelves are stocked with the goods that were on

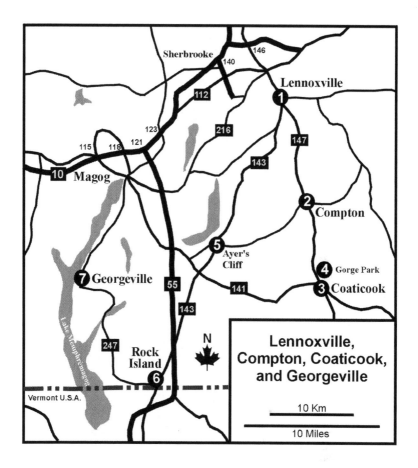

Lennoxville, Compton, Coaticook, and Georgeville

sale at the turn of the century. In its day, the store was the place to gather and exchange gossip. The Saint-Laurent family's home is also open to visitors. **T**:*(819) 835-5448,* **W***: parcscanada.gc.ca/stlaurent. Open daily mid-May to mid-Oct., 10–5; July–Aug. until 8 on Wed. Admission $4 for adults, $2 for children, children 6 and under are free.*

As you're driving, watch for the **Coaticook River** that snakes across the farmland, occasionally passing under the road and disappearing into a field before reappearing.

Continue south to **Coaticook** ③. Early Indians named this area *Koatikeku,* which means "river of the land of pines." The first settlers recognized the value of the nearby Coaticook River and waterfalls. As the town grew it became the center of Québec's thriving dairy industry. Every August the town celebrates its reputation as Québec's "Dairy Basin" with the **Festival du Lait**.

Several **historical buildings** in the town are worth a look: the old railway station built in 1900, the Sisco Memorial Church built in 1923 and now the home of the Pavillon des Arts et de la Culture, and Rivier College which dates back at least 125 years.

The breathtaking **Coaticook Gorge Park** ④, 400 Rue Saint Marc, off Route 147 at the Northern edge of town, is one of the highlights of the area. The river runs through a narrow gorge, with 165-foot sides, before turning and tumbling down several sets of waterfalls. A beautiful park lies beside the gorge, offering scenic paths for walking, hiking, or cross-country skiing. In winter, have a thrill tube-sliding down snow-covered slopes — a mechanical lift will bring you gently to the top. The park also features caves, a covered bridge, two observation towers, and a reproduction Abenaquis village. The suspension bridge, which made the Guinness Book of Records as the longest bridge of its type in the world, will astound you. **T**:*(819) 849-2331,* **W***: gorgedecoaticook.qc.ca. Open daily, July–Aug. 9–8; May–June and Sept.–Oct. 10–6; Dec.–Mar. 9–5. Admission $7 for adults, $4 for children.*

In the center of town is the **Centre d'Initiatives en Agriculture**, 129 Rue Morgan, an experimental farm that welcomes visitors to discover modern milk production, pet farm animals, and enjoy the gardens and games. **T**:*(819) 849-6669.*

Château Norton, 96 Rue de l'Union, a magnificent mansion built in 1912, is home to the **Beaulen Museum**. Several rooms of the mansion have been restored to their original splendor, complete with oak paneling and period furniture. The museum has an impressive collection of costumes and textiles from the area, as well as some of the tools used to make them. Take a leisurely stroll through the English gardens. **T**:*(819) 849-6560,* **W***: museebeaulne.qc.ca. Open daily, mid-May to mid-Sept., 11–5, July–Aug. until 8 on Tues.; mid-Sept. to mid-May, Wed.–Sun. 1–4. Admission $5 for adults, $2.50 for children, children under 6 are free.*

Perched above the southern tip of Lake Massawippi, **Ayer's Cliff** ⑤ was originally named Langmaid's Flat when the town was settled in the late 18th century by John Langmaid, who migrated to the location from New Hampshire. In 1799, Thomas Ayer bought the property to lay a railroad line and renamed it Ayer's Flat. In 1904, with an eye on the investment potential of the area brought in by the new rail lines, the town was renamed Ayer's Cliff. The County Fair Grounds and the citizens of Ayer's Cliff are host to one of the oldest county fairs in Québec.

Stanstead, a small granite-mining town, is in a unique position along the border to be culturally and economically shaped by two nations. The **Haskell Opera House**, 1 Church Street, built in 1904, is divided down the middle by the US-Canada border.

The Colby-Curtis Museum, 35 Dufferin Street, is located in the 19th-century Carrollcroft House. The neo-Renaissance house, built in 1859, was turned into a historical site complete with all of the original furniture, paintings and decorative art works. There is a gift shop, beautiful gardens, and a tearoom. **T**:*(819) 876-7322*, **W**: *colbycurtis.ca/. Open mid-June to mid-Sept., Tues.–Sun. 11–5; mid-Sept. to mid-June, Tues.–Fri. 10–12 and 1–5, Sat.–Sun. 12:30–4:30. Admission $5 for adults, $2 for children. Tea and a tour is $10.*

At the southern edge of Stanstead Plain, follow Route 143 to Route 247, through the tiny town of **Rock Island** ⑥, situated on a rocky island in the middle of the Tomifobia River which forms the border between Canada and the United States. For a cheap thrill, drive the "border road" where one side of the road is Canada and the other side of the road is the United States.

Leaving Beebe on Route 247, look for **Bernard Bee Bec**, 152 Rue Principale, **T**:(819) 876-2800, a friendly honey farm with a small museum and shop. See how honey is made with a clear view into a honeycomb and sample some of their delicious honey.

As you continue on Route 247 North, note the **covered bridge** on your left. Farther along, drive through the **Applecove** and **Griffin tree tunnels**.

Georgeville ⑦, established in 1855, is a charming New England-style hamlet on Lake Memphrémagog. Stop to enjoy the tranquility and views of Saint Benoît du Lac Abbey, Owl's Head and Jay Peak Mountain.

Trip 46

Magog, Parc du Mont Orford, and North Hatley

Beautiful villages and spectacular scenery, mountains and lakes, fabulous food and boutiques — this trip has it all. Offset a tour through the bustling town of Magog with a dip in the pristine Lac Stukely on Mont Orford and a relaxing stroll through the peaceful village of North Hatley. The scenery along the way is beautiful, and you will be tempted to stop for views of the many lakes and rivers in the region.

Wealthy Canadians and Americans have flocked here since the late 18th century for year-round vacations, taking full advantage of all the Appalachian Mountains have to offer.

GETTING THERE:

By Car. Magog is 118 km (74 miles) east of Montréal. Take **Rte. 10** East to **Rte. 112** South.

Parc du Mont Orford can be accessed via either **Rte. 112** or **Rte. 141**, north of Magog.

If you have time for a side trip to Saint-Benoît-du-Lac Abbey, it can be reached by following **Rte. 112** West to Saint-Benoît-du-Lac. In the village, turn left, following the signs to the Abbey.

To reach North Hatley, take **Rte. 108** east out of Magog. In the center of Sainte-Catherine-de-Hatley, bear left at the roadside cross, continuing on **Rte. 108**. Entering the village of North Hatley, turn left onto **Rue Capelton** (Rte. 108).

Return back along **Rte. 108**, through Magog, to **Rte. 10** West to Montréal.

PRACTICALITIES:

The region has a lot to offer for all seasons. Plan your trip according to your tastes. Late spring and summer are perfect for hiking, biking, swimming, or simply strolling. Fall is the time for foliage and harvesting of apples and grapes. The winter and early spring offer skiing, snow shoeing, and ice-skating. Take full advantage of the quaint towns, gourmet food, and artist boutiques all year long.

The **Tourist Office of Memphrémagog**, located at 55 Rue Cabana, off

Route 112, **T**:(819) 843-2744, is open year-round.

The **Tourist Office of North Hatley**, located at 300 Rue Mill, in the municipal parking lot behind the main street, is only open seasonally. Pick up a pamphlet for the self-guided walking tour of the village, with detailed histories for each of the town's historical buildings.

If time permits, consider the side trip to Saint-Benoît-du-Lac Abbey, which can also be easily visited from the Knowlton-Owl's Head tour (Trip 43).

Further information on the area can be found on the Internet **W**: tourisme-memphremagog.com or via e-mail at info@tourisme-memphremagog.com.

FOOD AND DRINK:

La Piazzetta (399 Rue Principale, Magog) Enjoy gourmet pizza and fine Italian cuisine. **T**:(819) 843-4044, **W**: resto-piazzetta.com $$$

Restaurant Le Villageois d'Orford (2355 Chime du Parc, Orford) Casual dining on hardy basic fare with a definite French flare. Burgers, pizza, pasta, fish, and chicken all reasonably priced. **T**:(819) 868-9142. $$

Resto-Bar Jessie (301 Rue Principale West, Magog) Removable windows give this rustic and comfortable restaurant an open-air effect. **T**:(819) 868-3857. $$

Pilsen (55 Rue Principale, North Hatley) Serving good, simple food, in a relaxed country atmosphere, on the shore of Lake Massawippi. **T**:(819) 842-2971. $$

SUGGESTED TOUR:

Circled numbers correspond to numbers on the map.

Magog ①, a beautiful and lively town situated between lakes and mountains, is a popular destination for anyone who loves to combine a taste of nature with culture, fine shopping, and terrific eating. Surrounded by lush forests, the town was built on the lumber industry, and was originally named Outlet for its location at the merge of lake and rivers. It's not clear where the new name for the city originated, either from the nearby Lake, or an Abenaki expression meaning "the place where salmon-trout can be found." The arrival of textile mills in 1884 transformed the village into an industrialized city. Today, with a population of 14,612, Magog is the fifth-largest city in the townships, well known for its quality of life and its dedication to the families who live here.

The main stretch of town is lined with boutiques featuring local artisans, restaurants and bars. Stroll the bustling streets or sit at one of the many outdoor cafés and people watch.

Lake Memphrémagog ② stretches, long and deep, from Magog to Newport, Vermont. If time permits, **Scenic Cruises**, for 1½ to 7 hours, introduce you to the intricacies of this beautiful lake, its shoreline and wildlife. **T**:*(819) 843-8068, **W**: croisiere-memphremagog.com.* Legend has it that a giant sea serpent, named Memphre, lives in the depths of the lake. Sightings date back to the 18th

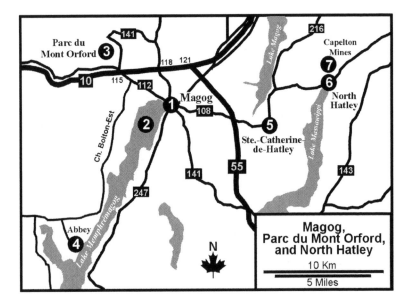

Magog,
Parc du Mont Orford,
and North Hatley

10 Km

5 Miles

century. As of 1997 there have been more than 200 well-documented sightings of the creature. In 1961, two fishermen reported seeing a creature they described as 40 feet long and black. In 1994, four people reported seeing a 30-foot-long creature that was black, with three humps.

Every year in July, Magog is host to the International Swimming Competition. Long-distance swimmers from around the world gather for this 24-mile race, from Magog to Newport, Vermont. The event also features cultural and sports activities for the entire family. **T**:*(819) 843-5000.*

Pointe-Merry Park and **Plage de Magog** offer relaxation with nature and amazing views of Mont Orford, Mont Owl's Head and Lake Memphrémagog. Located off Route 112 on the northernmost shores of the lake, there is a playground, beach, a grassy park, snack stand, and facilities. **Place Memphre**, a popular boardwalk stretching along the shore of the lake, is also great for a stroll, inline skating, and swimming.

Beside the park visitors will find **Labyrinthe Memphrémagog**, a large maze that can be explored on foot or roller blades. Spend an hour-and-a-half solving riddles, uncovering the secrets of the labyrinth, and laughing. **T**:*(819) 868-4188. Open May–October, daily 10–9; weekends out-of-season. Admission $7 for adults, $5 for children, $21 for families (2 adults and 2 children). Roller blade rentals available. Handicap accessible.*

There are a couple of spectacular wineries in the Magog area. **Vignoble Le Cep d'Argent**, 1257 Chemin de la Rivière, **T**:(819) 864-4441, **W**: cepdargent.com, is a wonderful stop to enjoy award-winning wine in a French country atmosphere. Guided tours are available. *Open daily May–Oct., 10–5:30,*

tours every 45 minutes; Nov.–Apr., 10–5, tours every hour. Admission, $5.
Vignoble Les Chants de Vignes, 459 Chemin de la Rivière, **T**:(819) 847-8467, greets visitors in a warm atmosphere, and offers bilingual tours and tastings of fine wines, apéritif and digestifs. *Open May–Oct., daily 9–5; Nov.–Apr., Wed.– Sun. 9–5, Mon. & Tues. by appointment. Admission $3.25.*

PARC du MONT ORFORD ③, **T**:(819) 843-9855, **W**: sepaq.com. *Park entrance fees, $3.50 for adults, $5 for families with 1 adult and 1 or more children, $7 for families with 2 adults and 1 or more children, $1.50 for children 6–18, children under 6 are free.*

Located just north of Magog and accessible via Route 112 or Route 141, this park is a natural wonderland with cultural flair, covering 23 square miles of Appalachian Mountain territory.

The mountain is thick with old-growth forests, perfect for hiking and mountain biking. Visitors are powerless over the enticing pull of the clean and scenic Lake Stukely. A small beach is perfect for family fun, a picnic, and relaxation, while the lake is ideal for canoes and paddleboats. Nautical equipment and mountain bikes are available for rent.

The 18-hole Golf Mont Orford is a Scottish-style course with several beautiful mountain views.

The **Orford Arts Center**, 3165 Park Road, Orford Township, is internationally renowned for the development of gifted young musicians, and has been providing advanced musical training for nearly 50 years. In summer the center also hosts the **Festival Orford**, which puts on more than 30 concerts. The grounds, with sculptures tucked in among the maple and birch trees, are perfect for a quiet stroll. **T**:*(819) 843-9871, 1-800-567-6155,* **W**: *arts-orford.org*

In winter the park offers downhill and cross-country skiing as well as ice-skating. There are more than 25 miles of ski trails on Mont Orford, which comprises three peaks, Orford, Giroux, and Alfred Desrochers, and from which visitors can see miles of mountains, valleys, and lakes. The **Mont Orford Tourist Station** has one of the highest vertical drops in Eastern Canada. **T**:*(819) 843-6548, 1-800-567-2772.*

SAINT-BENOÎT-du-LAC ABBEY ④, **T**:(819) 843-4080, **W**: st-benoit-du-lac.com. *Monastery is open daily 5–9. Store hours are Nov.–May, weekdays 9–10:45 and 1:30–4:30, Sat. 9–10:45 and 11:45–4:30; June–Oct., Mon.–Sat., 9–10:45 and 11:45–4:30. Women should call (819) 843-2340 or use the Internet for information.*

The Abbey, perched majestically on a hill surrounded by striking landscapes and breathtaking views, is inhabited by Benedictine Monks who have chosen to focus their lives on spirituality, prayer, study, physical work, and pastoral ministry. Part of the Abbey was designed by the French Benedictine architect Dom Paul Bellot, whose work is characterized by his search for harmony within the geometric patterns of nature. This is evidenced in the long hallways of brightly colored, geometric tiles. Bellot is buried in the Abbey's cemetery. A store sells products made by the monks, including cheeses and cider, as well as religious gifts. Respectable dress is required on the Abbey grounds and pets are not allowed.

Sainte-Catherine-de-Hatley ⑤, known by its English name Kateville, is a small village on top of a hill along Route 108. Stop to admire the beautiful **Sanctuary of Saint Christopher**, in the center of the village and the roadside cross. The church offers spectacular views of Lake Magog and Mont Orford.

The **Kateville Marsh** is home to over 226 species of birds and offers many beautiful walking trails.

North Hatley ⑥, nestled snuggly around the northern end of Lake Massawippi, offers large doses of regional history in a peaceful, picturesque setting. This little village originally developed around the agriculture and wood industries. However, word of the beauty of the location quickly spread and it wasn't long before the town became a prime vacation destination.

Several gazebos are perched around the lakefront providing shelter from the summer sun and encouraging visitors to sit and watch the activity on the lake. The town beach is the perfect place for a quick dip or leisurely swim in the lake, or a great starting place for snorkeling. Grassy **Dreamland Park**, lying lazily along the shore of the lake, has concerts in the summer.

The village has many magnificent homes, built by wealthy plantation owners who chose to flee the American South in 1860-65, after the Civil War. Pick up a guide at the Tourist Office for a walking tour of the town's historical buildings. Of particular note is: **Connaught Home**, 77 Main, which was built in 1904 by the town's first mayor, Dr. C. J. Edgar and served as his residence and hospital; **Town Hall**, 210 Main, built in 1892–93, was originally the railway station; **The Baptist Church**, at the corner of Capelton and Magog, was North Hatley's first school house and now rests on land that native Indians used in spring and fall to trade with settlers; **St. Barnabas' Church**, 640 Sherbrooke, built in 1894, has stunning tinted cathedral glass; **The Hatley Inn**, 325 Virgin Hill, was built by the Holt family of Montréal as a summer home, with dormer windows for the children's rooms so that they each had a view of the lake.

A delightful **market** is held Saturdays on School Street. Local farmers sell fruits and vegetables in the morning and artisans sell their works in the afternoon.

Excavated in 1863 with picks and shovels by candlelight, the **Capelton Mines** ⑦, 800 Route 108, were the oldest copper mines in Québec. Tour the underground caverns and travel back in time to uncover some of the riches of the area, and experience the hardships of the miners. Visitor will delight in the rainbow of colors on the mine walls, stalactites and stalagmites. A visit to the mines takes about 2 hours. **T**:*(819) 346-9545,* **W**: *minescapelton.com. Open*

April–June and Sept.–Oct., weekends; July–Aug. daily (reservations recommended). Admission, $17.75 for adults, $3.50–$15 for children. Bring a sweater or jacket, as the mines are cold all year-round, reaching only about 48° in the summer.

Section XII

DAYTRIPS
WEST OF MONTRÉAL

The Outaouais Region covers a vast expanse of land west and northwest of Montréal. An Algonquin tribe, the Outaouais, inhabited the region before the first settlers began migrating here. Samuel de Champlain traveled through in 1613 in his continued search for the Northwest Passage to the Orient. It wasn't until the beginning of the 19th century, when Philemon Wright founded Hull, that the area began to develop.

Sculpted during the Ice Age, the area is graced with a bounty of natural resources. Taking full advantage of the dense forests of red and white pines, the forest industry grew in the area, forming its economic backbone.

While this immense area has a lot to offer, only the "Urban Region" is reachable in a daytrip from Montréal. Comprising the two main cities of the region, Hull and Gatineau, and several smaller towns, the "Urban Region" is the cultural and economic center of the Outaouais.

Trip 47

Hull

Located directly across the river from Ottawa, Ontario, Hull is an annex for the federal government of Canada. The city faces Ottawa across the wide Rivière Outaouais, providing impressive views from many locations throughout town.

Hull is renowned for its art of living well, with one of the province's premiere museums and gourmet international cuisine. Although an American, Philemon Wright, founded the city, there is a decidedly French atmosphere today. The city has retained much greenery, with parks and gardens encircling it. The main attractions are located around the edges of the city, on the shores and waterways of the Rivière Outaouais.

GETTING THERE:

By Car, Hull is 195 km (122 miles) from Montréal. Take **Rte. 40** or **Rte. 20** west to **Rte. 13**. Take **Rte. 13** north to **exit 15**. Follow **Rte. 148** west all the way to Hull.

Follow **Rte. 148** east to Gatineau.

Get back on **Rte. 148** east, returning to Montréal.

PRACTICALITIES:

Consider staying overnight in the area to take advantage of the sites in Trip 48 as well. Hull has a wide selection of accommodations at every price level. The brand new **Hilton Lac Leamy**, 3 Boulevard du Casino, is a beautiful hotel, central to all sites. **T**:1-866-488-7888. The **Best Western Hôtel Jacques-Cartier**, 131 Rue Laurier, is smaller and more affordable. **T**:1-800-265-8550.

Association Touristique de l'Outaouais, 103 Rue Laurier, Hull, **T**:(819) 778-2222 or 1-800-265-7822, **W**: western-quebec-tourism.org. Open mid-June through Aug., Mon.–Fri. 8:30–8, Sat.–Sun. 9–6; Sept. to mid-June, Mon.–Fri. 8:30–5, Sat.–Sun. 9-4.

FOOD AND DRINK:

Brasserie Le Vieux Hull (50 Rue Victoria) Delicious and fresh regional cuisine for breakfast and lunch. **T**:(819) 771-5462. $

Le Twist (88 Rue Montcalm) Casual Canadian cuisine, featuring mussels and the "best hamburgers in town." **T**:(819) 777-8886. $$

Le Pied de Cochon (242 Rue Montcalm) Traditional French cuisine in an authentic atmosphere. In warm weather, enjoy the terrace. **T**:(819) 777-5808. $$$

La Marina (at Casino de Hull) Featuring fresh seafood and local delicacies. **T**:(819) 772-2100. $$$

LOCAL ATTRACTIONS:
Circled numbers correspond to numbers on the map.

*CANADIAN MUSEUM of CIVILIZATION ①, 100 Rue Laurier, **T**:(819) 776-7000 or 1-800-555-5621, **W**: civilization.ca. *Open May–Sept., daily 9–6, Thurs. 9–9; Oct.–Apr., Tues.–Sun. 9–5, Thurs. 9–9. Admission $10 for adults, $6 for students, $4 for children 3–12, children under 3 are free. Additional fees, varying, for IMAX and OMNIMAX presentations. Handicap accessible.*

This amazing museum, made up of a number of individual and specific museums, is situated in one of the most striking buildings of the 20th century. Stand and gaze at the curved corners of the building, looking remotely like an ancient statue. With widely diverse exhibits, a beautiful setting, and a great view of Ottawa's Parliament Building across the river, the museum has much to offer everyone.

The **Museum of Civilization** has several permanent exhibits in the Grand Hall and the First People's Hall. Exhibits focus on the native peoples of Canada, displaying more than forty impressive authentic totem poles, and Canadian history.

The **Canadian Children's Museum** is an extremely popular family destination for locals and visitors. Interactive exhibits entertain and educate as children explore nations and cultures from around the world.

The **Canadian Postal Museum** explores postal communication and displays an array of stamps through history.

A combined **IMAX/OMNIMAX** theater offers amazing shows.

The museum also hosts more than fifteen **temporary exhibits** each year, as well as films, lectures, and festivals.

Beside the museum is the pleasant **Parc Jacques-Cartier** ②, a beautiful green space, with gardens and fountains.

Also enjoyable is **Parc Lac Leamy** ③, Boulevard Fournier. This beautiful green space on the small Lac Leamy is a busy spot for windsurfing, swimming, picnicking, hiking, and snowshoeing. **T**:*(613) 239-5000,* **W**: *capcan.ca*

Maison du Citoyen ④, 25 Rue Laurier, **T**:(819) 595-7175, is the seat of the city's municipal and regional government, as well as cultural center. In addition to offices and the public library, the building is home to a Concert Hall and Art Gallery. **Le Galerie Montcalm** exhibits a range of contemporary art styles from local artists and historical masters.

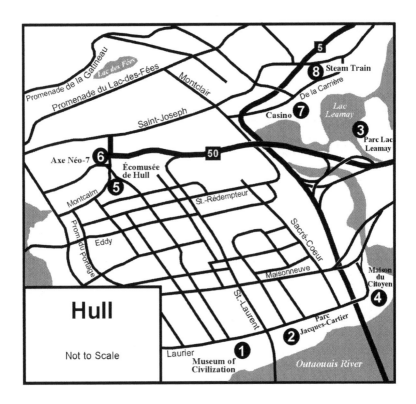

ÉCOMUSÉE de HULL ⑤, at the corner of Rue Montcalm and Rue Papineau, T:(819) 595-7790. *Open May–Aug., daily 10–5; Sept.–Apr., daily 10–4. Admission $7 for adults, $5 for children 6-15, children under 6 are free.*

This quaint museum is situated in a beautiful historic building. Exhibits trace the origins of life on Earth, up to modern man. The Insectarium displays more than 5,000 species of insects from around the world. A simulator enables visitors to experience the earth move beneath their feet in an artificial earthquake.

AXE NÉO-7 ⑥, 205 Rue Montcalm, T:(819) 771-2122, W: axeneo7.qc.ca. *Open Sept.–June, Wed.–Sun. 12–5.*

Fun and funky! The center is devoted to contemporary art and local artists, with a variety of activities, including exhibits and presentations, supporting contemporary art in Québec.

CASINO de Lac-Leamy ⑦, 1 Boulevard Casino, T:(819) 772-2100 or 1-800-665-2274. *Open year-round, daily 11-3. Admission and parking are free. Visitors must by 18 years or older. Proper attire is required.*

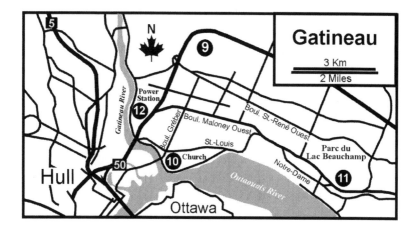

With more than 1,400 slot machines, 55 game tables, two restaurants, two bars, and a fabulous view of Lac Leamy, the casino is a world-class destination. The Promenade du Roi, on the third floor, exhibits artwork by local and regional artists.

HULL-CHELSEA-WAKEFIELD STEAM TRAIN ⑧, 165 Rue Deveault, **T**:(819) 778-7246 or 1-800-871-7246, **W**: steamtrain.ca. *Scenic tours scheduled mid-May through Oct. Sunset dinner tours run mid-May to mid-Sept. Admission mid-May to mid-Sept. $39 for adults, $35 for students, $19 for children; mid-Sept. to mid-Oct. $45 for adults, $40 for students, $23 for children; children under 2 are free; dinner train is $89 per person.*

Travel through time while you tour the picturesque Gatineau Hills on one of the last authentic steam-powered trains still operating in Canada. The train, built in 1907, runs along the scenic route from Hull to Wakefield. In Wakefield, watch as attendants turn the train around manually for the return trip to Hull. Try the dinner train for a gourmet French meal, in an interesting setting, with beautiful mountains, rivers and forests out the window.

Head south to **Gatineau** ⑨. Located at the junction of the Ottawa and Gatineau Rivers, the area originally served as an assembly point for the large lumber rafts built by Philemon Wright for transport to Montréal and Québec in the 19th century.

The city was created in 1975, with the merging of seven separate municipalities. With a population of more than 100,000 people, Gatineau is the most populous city in the Outaouais Region and the fifth-largest in Québec Province. Many **historical homes** still stand along the shores of the Ottawa River.

Every year, on Labor Day weekend, the skies above Gatineau burst into color and the city is flooded with visitors for the annual **Gatineau Hot Air**

Balloon Festival.

Église Saint-François-de-Sales ⑩, on the corner of Route 148 and Rue Jacques-Cartier, is the oldest church in the Outaouais.

Parc du Lac Beauchamp ⑪ is a beautiful spot to relax, walk, canoe, or swim. In the winter, ice skate on the lake, cross-country ski, or sled. Located in the city center, the park is a natural respite enjoyed by families throughout the area. **T**:*(819) 669-2548.*

RAPIDES-FARMERS POWER STATION ⑫, Route 307, **T**: 1-800-365-5229. *Open, by tour only, mid-May through June, Mon.–Fri. 9, 10:30, 12, 1:30 and 3; July–Aug., Wed.–Sun. 9:30, 11, 12:30, 2 and 3:30. Admission is free.*

The interesting tour enables visitors to see the workings of the power station, up close.

Gatineau Park

This splendid park sits snuggly between the valleys of Rivière de Outaouais and Rivière Gatineau on 137 square miles of rolling hills. The park was named after Nicolas Gatineau, a fur trader from Trois-Rivières, who disappeared in 1683 on the river that is now named for him. William Lyon Mackenzie King, the tenth prime minister of Canada, helped to create this protected park in 1938.

Several Federal Government buildings lie within the boundaries of the park. The Prime Minister's summer estate sits on Lac Mousseau. The official government meeting house, the Willson House, is located on the shore of Lac Meech. The controversial Lake Meech Accord of 1987, which attempts to recognize Québec as a "distinct society," was written at the Willson House.

GETTING THERE:

By Car, Hull is 195 km (122 miles) from Montréal. Take **Rte. 40** or **Rte. 20** west to **Rte. 13**. Take **Rte. 13** north to **exit 15**. Follow **Rte. 148** west all the way to Hull.

Turn right onto **Promenade de la Gatineau** to reach the south gate into the park. Follow the scenic route to the Champlain lookout.

Leaving the lookout, bear right and follow the scenic drive to the **Chelsea Gate**.

From Chelsea, turn left onto **Rte. 5** to Wakefield.

Turn right onto **Rte. 307** to Val-des-Monts.

Follow **Rte. 366** south to **Rte. 50** east. At the end of Rte. 50, turn right onto **Rte. 315** south. At the junction of **Rte. 148**, turn left, heading east, returning to Montréal.

PRACTICALITIES:

Consider staying overnight in the area to take advantage of the sites in Trip 47 as well. Hull has a wide selection of accommodations at every price level. The brand new **Hilton Lac Leamy**, 3 Boulevard du Casino, is a beautiful hotel, central to all sites. **T**:1-866-488-7888. The **Best Western Hôtel Jacques-Cartier**, 131 Rue Laurier, is smaller and more affordable. **T**:1-800-265-8550.

Tourist information, as well as facilities and maps of the park, are available at the **Gatineau Park Visitor Center**, 33 Rue Scott, Chelsea, for facilities, maps and information about the park. **T**:(819) 827-2020. Open mid-May through Aug., daily 9–6; Sept. to mid-May, daily 9–5.

FOOD AND DRINK:

Moorside Tearoom (at the Mackenzie King Estate) Enjoy a light meal or scrumptious afternoon tea. **T**:(819) 827-2020. $$

Resto Péché Mignon-Chocolaterie (205 Chemin Vieux Chelsea) Fresh gourmet Italian cuisine in a comfortable atmosphere. **T**:(819) 827-3405. $$$

Les Fougères (783 Route 105) French cuisine, featuring local Outaousis dishes. **T**:(819) 827-8942. $$$

LOCAL ATTRACTIONS:

Circled numbers correspond to numbers on the map.

GATINEAU PARK ①, south entrance on Boulevard Teché, Hull. **T**:(819) 827-2020 or 1-800-465-1867, **W**: canadascapital.gc.ca/gatineau/index_e.asp. *Open year-round, daily.*

This vast natural wonderland of steep hills and dense forests, dark lakes, and meandering streams offers a wide variety of outdoor recreational activities for all seasons. Visitors enjoy hiking and mountain biking, or swimming at one of the six supervised beaches. Canoes are available for rental at **Lake la Pêche**. Explore **Lusk Cave** at Philippe Lake. In the winter, the extensive circuit of trails is available for cross-country skiing and snowshoeing.

Every autumn the park celebrates the bounty and color of the season with the annual **Fall Rhapsody Festival**.

Follow Promenade de la Gatineau for a **scenic drive** ② through the park. The road passes high pink granite cliffs and cuts through dense forests affording awe-inspiring views of the Outaouais River Valley, shimmering lakes, and working farms.

The rolling rounded hills of the park come to an abrupt cliff known as the Eardley Escarpment, which defines the edge of the Canadian Shield. Impressive views of the escarpment can be seen from along the scenic drive.

Continue from the scenic road to the **Belvédère Champlain** ③ for a full appreciation of this gorgeous area. A path descends below the lookout leading to eight observation stations where interpretive panels identify local vegetation.

Stop to enjoy **Domaine Mackenzie-King** ④, the summer home of William Lyon Mackenzie King. An avid naturalist and outdoorsman, King made this estate his summer home for nearly 50 years. Networks of paths criss-cross the wooded landscape and gardens past re-created ruins and restored cottages. Exhibits and interpretive panels inform visitors about the Canada of the past. *Open mid-May to mid-Oct., Mon.–Fri. 11–5, Sat.–Sun. 10–6. Admission $9 per car.*

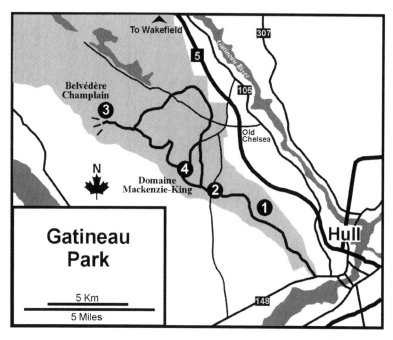

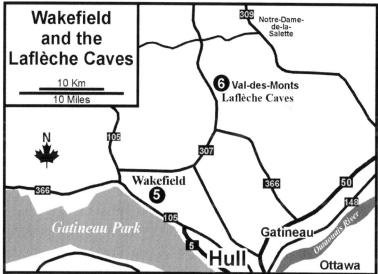

Stroll around the quaint and historical village of **Wakefield** ⑤. Enjoy the many boutiques, galleries and cafés.

THE LAFLÈCHE CAVES ⑤, **T**: (819) 457-4033 or 1-877-457-4033. *Open year-round by reservation. Admission $12 for adults, $8 for children 13–17, $6 for children under 13. The caves are cold year round — warm clothing and good shoes are recommended.*

These large caves of white marble were carved into the hill of Lac Armida by water and ice during the Ice Age. The caves are home to small brown bats.

A trained guide leads visitors into the mysterious underground world of the largest caves in the Canadian Shield. The massive main chamber is quite impressive. Guides explain the geological, biological, and historical evolution of the area amidst rock walls, dark caverns, and huge ice stalactites and stalagmites. Visitors also have access to an array of beautiful nature trails and two lookout towers, providing views of the surrounding area.

Spelunking, or wild caving, with an experienced guide is also available. The adventure brings visitors through narrow passageways and large caverns that are not open to the general public. Coveralls, a caving helmet with headlamp, and insurance are included in the price. The thrilling tour lasts approximately three hours. *By reservation only. Children under 12 are not permitted. Admission $45 per person.*

Section XIII

APPENDIX

MENU TRANSLATOR

Abricot apricot
Achigan black bass
Agneau lamb
Ail garlic
Aloyau porterhouse or T-bone steak
Amande almond
Ananas pineapple
Anchois anchovies
Aneth dill
Arachide peanut
Artichaut artichoke
Asperges asparagus
Ataca cranberry
Aubergine eggplant
Avocat avocado
Baguette long loaf of French bread
Bajoue pork jowl
Banane banana
Barbotte catfish
Basilic basil
Béarnaise sauce with egg yolks, butter, white wine and seasonings
Béchamel white sauce
Beignet doughnut
Bette beet
Beurre butter
Beurre d'érable maple butter
Bière beer
Bière froide cold beer
Binnes pork and beans
Blé d'Inde corn
Bluet blueberry
Boeuf beef
Bouquet shrimp
Breuvage beverage
Brioche yeasty, sometimes sweet, bread
Brochette shishcabob

Cachou cashew
Caille quail
Calvabec apple liqueur
Canard duck
Canneberge cranberry
Cannages preserves
Caribou wine and pure alcohol
Cerises cherries
Carotte carrot
Cassis blackcurrant
Céleri celery
Cerises cherries
Cervelles brains
Champignons mushrooms
Chapon capon
Chèvre goat cheese
Chiard ground meat
Chou cabbage
Choufleur caulifower
Ciboulettes chives
Cipaille type of meat pie
Cipâte type of meat pie
Citron lemon
Citron vent lime
Clamme clam
Clémentine tangerine
Cochon pig
Concombre cucumber
Confit de conard duck preserved in its own fat
Confiture preserves, jam
Consommé clear broth
Coq cock, hen
Coq au vin chicken stewed in red wine
Coquetel cocktail
Cornet cone (ice cream)
Côte Veal rib
Côtelette cutlet
Côtes levées spareribs
Courgette zucchini
Crémage icing
Crème cream
Crème caramel custard
Crème de blé cream of wheat
Crème glacée ice cream
Crème glacée molle soft ice cream
Crêpes pancakes
Cresson watercress
Cretons pork fat, minced

Crevette shrimp
Croissant buttery, flaky crescent-shaped roll
Croquignola homemade French-Candian doughnut
Carotte carrot
Cassis blackcurrant
Céleri celery
Cerises cherries
Cervelles brains
Champignons mushrooms
Chapon capon
Chèvre goat cheese
Chiard ground meat
Chou cabbage
Choufleur caulifower
Ciboulettes chives
Cipaille type of meat pie
Cipâte type of meat pie
Citron lemon
Citron vent lime
Clamme clam
Clémentine tangerine
Cochon pig
Concombre cucumber
Confit de conard duck preserved in its own fat
Confiture preserves, jam
Consommé clear broth
Coq cock, hen
Coq au vin chicken stewed in red wine
Coquetel cocktail
Cornet cone (ice cream)
Côte Veal rib
Côtelette cutlet
Côtes levées spareribs
Courgette zucchini
Crémage icing
Crème cream
Crème caramel custard
Crème de blé cream of wheat
Crème glacée ice cream
Crème glacée molle soft ice cream
Crêpes pancakes
Cresson watercress
Cretons pork fat, minced
Crevette shrimp
Croissant buttery, flaky crescent-shaped roll
Croquignola homemade French-Candian doughnut
Crosse de fougère fiddlehead
Croupe beef rump

Croustilles chips (potato)
Cru raw
Crudités raw vegetables
Déjeuner breakfast
Dinde turkey
Dîner lunch, dinner
Doigt-de-dame ladyfinger
Draffe draft beer
Écaillé sturgeon
Échalotte green onion
Épaule beef shoulder
Épices spices
Épinards spinach
Escargots snails
Estragon terragon
Facture bill
Faisan pheasant
Farine flour
Faux-filet rib eye
Fenouil fennel
Fesse d'agneau leg of lamb
Fève bean
Fèves jaunes wax beans
Fèves rouges kidney beans
Fèves vertes green beans
Flan custard tart
Flanc flank (beef, ham, veal)
Foie liver
Foie gras goose liver
Fondue melted cheese dish
Fondue chinoise hot oil for self-cooking meat and vegetables
Forçure liver
Fraîche chilled
Frais fresh
Fraises strawberries
Framboises raspberries
Fricassée stewed
Fricot feast
Frit fried
Fromage cheese
Fromage cottage cottage cheese
Fruitages wild berries
Fruits de mer seafood
Gadelle rouge redcurrant
Gadelle noire blackcurrant
Gambas large prawns
Garnotte small potato
Gâteau cake

Gâteau aux fruits   fruit cake
Gâteau des anges   angel food cake
Gibelotte   fish and vegetable stew
Glacée   iced
Gomme   chewing gum
Gorlot   small potato
Gratin   topped with cheese and bread crumbs
Grenouilles   frog legs
Grillade   grilled meat
Grillée   grilled
Gros filet   porterhouse
Goudille   hot dog bun with coleslaw
Gourgane   type of bean; smoked pork chop
Grand-père   dumpling
Grévé   gravy
Grillade   fried salt pork
Gruau   porridge
Guernaille   gristle
Hambourgeois   hamburger
Hareng   herring
Homard   lobster
Huile   oil
Huîtres   oysters
Instantané   instant (coffee, etc.)
Jambon   ham
Janbonneau   pork shank
Jarret   shank (beef or pork)
Julienne   shoestring potato
Jus   juice
Lait   milk
Lait deux pour cent   2% milk
Lait écrémé   skim milk
Lait homogénéisé   homogenized milk
Lapereau   young rabbit
Lapin   rabbit
Lard salé   salt pork
Légumes   vegetables
Longe   loin (pork or lamb)
Mâchemâlo   marshmellow
Maïs   corn
Maquereau   mackerel
Marinades   sweet mixed pickles
Marrons   chestnuts
Menthe   mint
Miel   honey
Moules   mussels
Moutarde   mustard
Nanane   candy/goodies

Navet turnip
Noisette hazelnut
Noix walnuts, nuts
Nombril de pâte doughnut hole
Oeuf egg
Oeuf frit fried egg
Oignons onions
Oreille de christ fried larding bacon served during maple syrup time
Ouananiche land-locked salmon
Pain bread
Pain blanc white bread
Pain de blé concassé cracked wheat bread
Pain de blé entier brown bread
Pain doré French toast
Palette stick of gum
Pamplemousse grapefruit
Paparmane peppermint
Pastèque watermelon
Patate potato
Patates au gratin scalloped potatoes
Patates bouillies boiled potatoes
Patates frites French fries
Patates jaunes potatoes cooked in pork fat
Patates pilées mashed potatoes
Patates rôties fried potatoes
Patates sucrées sweet potatoes
Pâté cold minced meat or fish spread
Pâte chinois shepherd's pie
Pâtes pasta
Pâtisseries pastries
Pécane pecan
Pêche peach
Persil parsley
Petits pois green peas
Pignons pine nuts
Piments pimentos
Pinotte peanut
Piquante spicy
Pistache pistachio
Pistou pesto
Plorine type of pork pie
Poché poached
Pointe de Poitrine beef brisket
Pointe de surlonge sirloin tips
Poire pear
Poireau leek
Pois verts green peas
Poisson fish

Poitrine beef plate
Poivre pepper
Poivron sweet red pepper
Pomme apple
Ponce toddy
Poularde capon
Poulet chicken
Poulpe Octopus
Poutine pudding; French fries with cheese and gravy
Prune plum
Pruneau prune
Quiche pie of egg, cream and cheese
Racinette root beer
Radis radish
Ragoût stew
Ragoût de boulettes meatball stew
Ragoût de pattes French Canadian pigs feet stew
Raisins grapes
Ratatouille vegetable casserole
Réduit thin maple syrup
Reliche relish
Riz rice
Ronde round steak
Rôti roast
Rôtie piece of toast
Roulade rolled and stuffed
Safran saffron
Safre glutton
Salade lettuce
Salade de chou coleslaw
Salade verts green salad
Salé salted
Saucisse sausages
Sauge sage
Sel salt
Sorbet sherbet
Soupane hot cereal
Soupe soup
Souper supper
Steak haché ground steak
Steak tartare minced and seasoned raw beef
Stimé steamed
Suçon lollipop
Sucrages candies, goodies
Sucre sugar
Sucre à la crème toffee, homemade candy
Sucre du pays maple syrup
Surette sour candy, lemon drop

Surlonge sirloin
Talon de ronde heel of round (beef)
Tarte pie
Tarte à la mode pie with ice cream
Tarte au sucre French Canadian sugar pie

A GLOSSARY OF DINING TERMS

Meal repas
Breakfast petit déjeuner
Lunch dîner
Dinner dîner
Supper souper

The menu, please le menu, s'il vous plaît
Set meal menu table d'hôte
Ordering items individually à la carte
Today's special spécial du jour
Terrine cold baked minced meat or fish
Tête fromagée headcheese
Tête de violon fiddlehead
Thon tuna
Thym thyme
Tiraille gristle
Tirasse gristle
Tomate tomato
Tournedos center cut beef fillet
Tourtière French Canadian meat or game pie
Trempette piece of bread soaked in maple syrup
Une patate an order of French fries
Vapeur steamed
Veau Veal
Viande meat
Viande fumée smoked meat
Vichyssoise cold potato and leek soup
Vinaigre vinegar
Vinaigrette oil and vinegar dressing
Vinaigrette au fromage bleu blue cheese salad dressing
Vinaigrette française French dressing
Yaourt yogurt

The wine list le menu des vins, la carte des vins
Another serving of ..., please encore un ..., s'il vous plaît
The check, please la facture, s'il vous plaît
Cover charge couvert
Tip included service compris
Tip not included service non compris

Plate assiette
Knife couteau
Fork fourchette
Spoon cuillère
Teaspoon cuillère à thé
Glass verre
Cup tasse
Napkin napquine, serviette

Drink boisson
Cocktail coquetel
Before dinner drink apértif
After dinner drink digestif
White wine vin blanc
Red wine vin rouge
Rosé wine vin rosé
Half-bottle demi-bouteille
Beer bière
Cold beer bière froide
Mineral water eau minérale
Carbonated gazeuse

Hot chaud
Cold froid
Rare saignant
Medium à point
Well done bien cuit
Sweet doux
Dry sec
Bread pain
Butter beurre
Salt sel
Pepper poivre
Mustard moutarde
Oil huile
Vinaigre vinegar

Coffee café
Coffee with cream café crème
Coffee with milk café au lait
Tea thé
Lemon citron
Chocolate chocolat
Milk lait
Sugar sucre
Jus juice

A DRIVER'S GLOSSARY

Accotement non stabilisé soft shoulder
Allumez vos phares turn on head lights
Arrêt stop
Arrêt interdit no stopping
Attention danger, be careful
Au pas slow
Autres directions through traffic
Billet ticket
Bifurcation junction
C'est pas allable You can't go through
Cahot bump in road
Cahoteux rough road
Carrefour crossroads
Carte grise car registration papers
Centre Ville town center
Chemin road
Chute de pierres falling rocks
Circulation interdite no through traffic
Croche turn
De gravier gravel road
Demi-tour U-turn
Descente dangereuse steep hill
Détour detour
Déviation detour
Eau water
École school
Entrée interdite no entrance
Est east
Fermé closed
Fin d'interdiction end of restriction
Fin de limitation de vitesse end of speed restrictions
Fourche fork in road
Gaz gasoline
Gravillons gravel surface
Halte stop
Halte routière rest area
Hauteur limitée low clearance
Impasse dead-end road
Interdiction de doubler no passing
Interdiction de stationner no parking
Itinéraire bis alternative route
Jetée causeway
Lave-auto car wash
Limitation de vitesse speed restriction
Nids de poule pot holes

Nord north
Ouest West
Ouvert open
Passage interdit entry prohibited
Pente dangereuse steep incline
Piétons pedestrians
Pont bridge
Ponté log-paved road or bridge
Privé private
Raccroc sharp curve
Ralentir reduce speed
Rappel previous sign still applies
Réservée aux piétons pedestrians only
Rond point traffic circle
Route barrée road closed
Route de gravelle gravel road
Route étroite narrow road
Route glissante slippery road
Sens interdit wrong direction
Sens unique one-way street
Serrez à droite keep to the right
Serrez à gauche keep to the left
Sortie exit
Stationnement parking
Stationnement interdit no parking allowed
Sud south
Toutes directions all directions
Travaux road work
Traverse crossing
Traverse d'animaux cattle/deer crossing
Verglas slippery road
Virages curves ahead
Voie unique single-lane traffic

DAYS AND MONTHS

Lundi Monday
Mardi Tuesday
Mercredi Wednesday
Jeudi Thursday
Vendredi Friday
Samedi Saturday
Dimanche Sunday
Aujourd'hui today
Demain tomorrow
Hier yesterday
Semaine week

Mois month
Janvier January
Février February
Mars March
Avril April
Mai May
Juin June
Juillet July
Août August
Septembre September
Octobre October
Novembre November
Décembre December

ABOUT THE AUTHOR

Karen Desrosiers is a writer living in New Hampshire with her young son. Growing up in a military family Karen developed the travel bug from a young age. She has spent most of her life traveling across the United States, Canada, and Europe. She now travels with her son, spending many weekends exploring. A direct descendant of Louis Hébert, one of the first settlers of Québec, Canada is like going home for Karen. Her connection to and love for the country are evident. In addition to travel articles and guides, Karen writes essays on single parenting, other non-fiction books, and novels.

Index

• OTHER AMERICAN TITLES •

NEW YORK
By Earl Steinbicker. Completely rewritten and sporting many new maps for its eighth edition, Daytrips New York now features 10 walking tours of the Big Apple itself. Beyond that, the book describes some 40 one-day adventures in nearby New York State, Connecticut, New Jersey, and Pennsylvania. 338 pages, 68 maps, and 27 B&W photos. ISBN: 0-8038-2021-6.

WASHINGTON, D.C.
By Earl Steinbicker. 50 one-day adventures in the Nation's Capital, and to nearby Virginia, Maryland, Delaware, and Pennsylvania. Both walking and driving tours are featured. 368 pages, 60 maps. Revised 2nd edition. ISBN: 0-8038-9429-5.

PENNSYLVANIA DUTCH COUNTRY & PHILADELPHIA
By Earl Steinbicker. Completely covers the City of Brotherly Love, then goes on to probe southeastern Pennsylvania, southern New Jersey, and Delaware before moving west to Lancaster, the "Dutch" country, and Gettysburg. There are 50 daytrips in all. 288 pages, 54 maps. ISBN: 0-8038-9394-9.

SAN FRANCISCO & NORTHERN CALIFORNIA
By David Cheever. 50 enjoyable one-day adventures from the sea to the mountains; from north of the wine country to south of Monterey. Includes 16 self-guided discovery tours of San Francisco itself. 336 pages, 64 maps. ISBN: 0-8038-9441-4.

NEW ENGLAND
By Earl Steinbicker. Discover the 50 most delightful excursions within a day's drive of Boston or Central New England, from Maine to Connecticut. Includes Boston walking tours. Revised 2nd edition, 320 pages, 60 maps. ISBN: 0-8038-2008-9.

• PACIFIC TITLES •

HAWAII
By David Cheever. Thoroughly explores all the major islands — by car, by bus, on foot, and by bicycle, boat, and air. Includes many offbeat discoveries you won't find elsewhere, plus all the big attractions in detail. 2nd edition, 288 pages, 55 maps. ISBN: 0-8038-2019-4.

EASTERN AUSTRALIA
By James Postell. Discover the 60 most exciting excursions from Sydney, Melbourne, Brisbane, Rockhampton, the Outback, and Cairns. Enjoy encounters with Australia that tourists usually miss. 400 pages, 48 maps, 24 B&W photos, appendix, glossary, index. ISBN: 0-8038-2501-8.

• EUROPEAN TITLES •

LONDON
By Earl Steinbicker. This long-time favorite guide explores the metropolis in 10 one-day walking tours, then describes 45 daytrips to destinations throughout southern England — all by either rail or car. 7th edition, 352 pages, 61 maps, 32 B&W photos, glossaries and a menu translator. ISBN: 0-8038-2056-9.

SCOTLAND & WALES

By Judith Frances Duddle. From Neo-Classical cities and historic towns to the beautiful, untouched countryside and tranquil villages, both Scotland and Wales offer something for everyone. The book includes 37 one-day adventures throughout both lands. 206 pages, 43 maps, 24 B&W photos, appendix, index. ISBN: 0-8038-2055-0.

IRELAND

By Patricia Tunison Preston. Covers the entire Emerald Isle with 55 one-day self-guided tours both within and from the major tourist areas, plus sections on shopping. Expanded 2nd edition, 400 pages, 57 maps. ISBN: 0-8038-2003-8.

FRANCE

By Earl Steinbicker. Describes 48 daytrips—including 5 walking tours of Paris, 24 excursions from the city, 5 in Provence, and 14 along the Riviera. 6th edition, 332 pages, 60 maps, photos, glossaries and a menu translator. ISBN: 0-8038-2061-5.

HOLLAND, BEGIUM & LUXEMBOURG

By Earl Steinbicker. Many unusual places are covered on these 40 daytrips, along with all the favorites plus the 3 major cities. 4th edition, 288 pages, 45 maps, photos, plus Dutch and French glossaries and a menu translator. ISBN: 0-8038-2062-3.

ITALY

By Earl Steinbicker. Features 40 one-day adventures in and around Rome, Florence, Milan, Venice, and Naples. 5th edition, 314 pages, 45 maps, 40 B&W photos, glossaries and a menu translator. ISBN: 0-8038-2058-5.

GERMANY

By Earl Steinbicker. 60 of Germany's most enticing destinations can be savored on daytrips from Munich, Frankfurt, Hamburg, and Berlin. Walking tours of the big cities are included. 6th edition, 352 pages, 68 maps, 36 B&W photos, glossaries and a menu translator. ISBN: 0-8038-2033-X.

SPAIN & PORTUGAL

By Norman P.T. Renouf. 50 one-day adventures by rail, bus, or car — including many walking tours, as well as side trips to Gibraltar and Morocco. All the major tourist sights are covered, plus several excursions to little-known, off-the-beaten-track destinations. Revised 2nd edition, 382 pages, 51 maps. ISBN: 0-8038-2012-7.

SWITZERLAND

By Norman P.T. Renouf. 45 one-day adventures in and from convenient bases including Zurich and Geneva, with forays into nearby Germany, Austria and Italy. 320 pages, 38 maps. ISBN: 0-8038-9417-7.

HASTINGS HOUSE/DAYTRIPS
Book Publishers

P.O. Box 908, Winter Park, FL 32790-0908
Phone orders toll-free 1-800-206-7822
Internet: www.DaytripsBooks.com
Internet Blog: www.HastingsHouseAndUs.com
E-mail: Hastings_Daytrips@earthlink.net